D

SCREEN METHODS
comparative readings in film studies

SCREEN METHODS
comparative readings in film studies

edited by Jacqueline Furby & Karen Randell

 WALLFLOWER PRESS LONDON & NEW YORK

First published in Great Britain in 2005 by
Wallflower Press
6a Middleton Place, Langham Street, London W1W 7TE
www.wallflowerpress.co.uk

A catalogue for this book is available from the British Library.

ISBN 1-904764-34-7 (pbk)
ISBN 1-904764-35-5 (hbk)

Book design by Elsa Mathern

Printed at Replika Press Pvt Ltd., India

contents

scape film form and method

views theory and method

scenes new technology and method

acknowledgements

The idea for this collection came out of a year-long seminar series that we ran and that was held and financed by the University of Southampton, to whom we are indebted. We would like to thank the speakers at those seminars, many of whose work is included here, and also the students and academics who made up the audience and who contributed their enthusiasm and intellectual generosity. In particular we would like to thank Tim Bergfelder, Pam Cook, Cathy Fowler, Mike Hammond, David Lusted, John McGavin, Peter Middleton and Michael Williams. Our thanks also go to Linda Ruth Williams for initially suggesting the project and for her continued support and inspiration. We also thank Yoram Allon at Wallflower Press for his patience and guidance.

We are extremely grateful to our families for putting up with absences and hysteria: thank you Jason Lucas, Vicky, William and Alex Brant, Neil, Matthew and Katie Furby.

Thank you to Edinburgh University Press for kind permission to reproduce Robynn J. Stilwell's essay 'Sound and Empathy: Subjectivity, Gender and the Cinematic Soundscape' from Kevin Donnelly (ed.) (2001) *Film Music: Critical Approaches*. Monica B. Pearl's essay appeared in an alternative version in the e.journal *EnteText*, vol. 2, no. 3 (2003). John Phillips' essay 'Masochism, Fetishism and the Castrating Gaze: Female Perversions in Catherine Breillat's *Romance*' appears published in a similar form as 'Catherine Breillat's *Romance*: Hard Core and the Female Gaze' in *Studies in French Cinema* (2000), vol. 1, no. 3, 133–40. Jacqueline Furby's essay, 'Rhizomatic Time and Temporal Poetics in American Beauty', appears in a similar form in *Film Studies*, no. 7 (2006).

This book is dedicated to Pat Lawson and Stella Cousins.

notes on contributors

Melenia Arouh is Lecturer in Film Theory and Production at the American College of Greece (Deree). Her recent publications include 'Aesthetics of the Film Biography: Painters and Paintings' in *Experience and Understanding: an Anthology on Biography and Biography-Theory* (Unipub, 2005) and 'Schindler's List Revisited' in *Cultural Forum*, published by the Jewish Community of Thessaloniki (forthcoming 2006).

Christine Cornea is Lecturer in Film and Television Studies at the University of East Anglia, UK. She is the author of *Science Fiction Cinema* (Edinburgh University Press, forthcoming 2006); other recent publications include articles in *Velvet Light Trap*, *Understanding Film Genres* (McGraw-Hill, 2004), *Blackwell's Companion to Science Fiction* (Blackwell, 2005), *The Blade Runner Experience: The Legacy of a Science Fiction Classic* (Wallflower Press, 2005) and *American Cinema Since 1960* (Open University Press/McGraw-Hill Education, forthcoming 2006).

Michael Chopra-Gant is Lecturer at the London Metropolitan University, UK. He is currently working on publications on *The Waltons* and the relationship between cinema and history. Recent published work includes *Hollywood Genres and Postwar America: Masculinity, Family and Nation in Popular Movies and Film Noir* (I. B. Tauris, 2005) and articles and chapters in the *Journal of Comparative American Studies*, *Genre Matters: Essays in Theory and Criticism* (Intellect, 2005) and *Hollywood Motherhood* (Wayne State University Press, forthcoming 2006).

Jacqueline Furby is Lecturer in Film Studies at Southampton Solent University, UK. She is currently working on a full-length study on the temporality of film, and two edited collections: *Thresholds of Identity* and *A Queer Feeling*. Other publications include a forthcoming article in *Film Studies*.

Deborah Jermyn is Lecturer in Film and TV at Roehampton University, UK. She is author of *Crimewatching: Investigating Real Crime TV* (I. B. Tauris, forthcoming 2006). Other recent publications include articles in the *International Journal of Cultural Studies*, *Feminist Media Studies* and *Screen*. Her co-edited collections include *The Audience Studies Reader* (Routledge, 2002), *The Cinema of Kathryn Bigelow: Hollywood Transgressor* (Wallflower Press, 2003) and *Understanding Reality Television* (Routledge, 2004).

Darren Kerr is Lecturer in Film and Television Studies at Southampton Solent University, UK. He has published chapters and articles in edited collections and journals, including in *Perspectives on Evil and Human Wickedness* (Rodopi, 2004) and *Early Modern Literary Studies*.

Peter Krämer is Senior Lecturer in Film Studies at the University of East Anglia, UK. He is the author of *The New Hollywood: From Bonnie and Clyde to Star Wars* (Wallflower Press, 2005) and has published essays on American film and media history in *Screen, Velvet Light Trap, Theatre History Studies, Historical Journal of Film, Radio and Television, History Today, Film Studies, Scope* and numerous edited collections. He is co-editor of *Screen Acting* (Routledge, 1999) and *The Silent Cinema Reader* (Routledge, 2003). He also co-authored a children's book entitled *American Film: An A–Z Guide* (Franklin Watts, 2003).

Martin Lister is Professor of Visual Culture in the School of Cultural Studies, the University of the West of England, Bristol, UK. He has written widely on photography, visual culture and new media technologies. His numerous publications include articles in *The Handbook of Visual Analysis* (Sage, 2000) and *Photography: A Critical Introduction* (Routledge, 2000). He is editor *of The Photographic Image in Digital Culture* (Routledge, 1995) and co-author of *New Media: A Critical Introduction* (Routledge 2003). He also co-authored and produced the interactive CD-Rom *From Silver to Silicon: Photography, Culture and New Technologies* (ARTEC, 1996).

David Lusted was an Education Officer at the British Film Institute and for the last 15 years has worked in higher education. He is author of *The Western* (Pearson/ Longman, 2003). He is also co-editor of *The Television Studies Book* (Edward Arnold, 1997) and editor of *The Media Studies Book* (Routledge, 1992) and *Raymond Williams: Film TV Culture* (BFI/NFT, 1989). He has contributed chapters to *A Necessary Fantasy?: The Heroic Figure in Children's Popular Literature* (Garland, 2000), *The Family Way: The Boulting Brothers and British Film Culture* (Flicks Books, 1999), *Writing and the Cinema* (Longman, 1999) and *The Movie Book of the Western* (Studio Vista, 1996).

William Merrin is Lecturer in Media Studies at the University of Wales, Swansea, UK. He is author of *Baudrillard and the Media: A Critical Introduction* (Polity Press, 2005). He is also co-author of *New Media: Key Thinkers* (Berg, forthcoming 2006), and has published numerous articles in collected works and journals including *Visual Delights II* (John Libby Press, 2005), *Cultural Theory* (Sage, 2005), the *International Journal of Baudrillard Studies* and *Fifty Key Sociologists: The Contemporary Thinkers* (Routledge, forthcoming 2006).

Monica B. Pearl is a Lecturer in the Department of English and American Studies at the University of Manchester, UK. Her publications include articles in *The Body's Perilous Pleasures: Dangerous Desires and Contemporary Culture* (Edinburgh University Press, 1999) and *GLQ: A Journal of Lesbian and Gay Studies* (Duke University Press, 2005). Her current research is on autobiography, life-writing, and visual and written self-representation.

John Phillips is Professor of French Literature and Culture at London Metropolitan University, UK. He has published widely on aspects of both eighteenth- and twentieth-century French literature and film. His books include *Nathalie Sarraute: Metaphor, Fairy-Tale and the Feminine of the Text* (Peter Lang, 1994), *Forbidden Fictions: Pornography and Censorship in Twentieth-Century French Literature* (University of Michigan Press, 1999), *Sade: The Libertine Novels* (Pluto Press, 2001), *How To Read Sade* (Granta, 2005) and *The Marquis de Sade: A Very Short Introduction* (Oxford University Press, 2005).

Karen Randell is Principal Lecturer in Film Studies at Southampton Solent University, UK, and Associate Lecturer for the Open University, UK, on Film and History. Her research interests include trauma and war film, the films of Lon Chaney, and trauma in early and contemporary American cinema. Recent publications include an article in *Screen*, and a chapter in *Art in the Age of Terrorism* (Paul Holberton Press, 2005).

John Sedgwick is Lecturer in economics at London Metropolitan University, UK. He is author of *Filmgoing in 1930s Britain: A Choice of Pleasures* (Exeter University Press, 2000) and co-editor of *An Economic History of Film* (Routledge, 2005). Recent chapters and articles appear in the following edited collections and journals: *Hollywood and the Social Experience of Movie-going* (Exeter University Press/California University Press, 2005), *Americanisation in Twentieth-Century Europe: Business, Culture, Politics, Vol. 2* (Centre de Recherche sur l'Histoire de l'Europe du Nord-Quest, University, 2002), *The Unknown 1930s: An Alternative History of the British Cinema, 1929–39* (I. B. Tauris, 1999), *Economic History Review*, *Journal of Economic History* and *Homo Oeconomicus*.

Robynn Stilwell is Assistant Professor (Music-Film) in Performing Arts, Georgetown University, US. Her research and teaching interests include music for film, dance and theatre; Russian, French and American art music; popular music; and music and identity formation. She is co-editor of a number of collections including *The Musical: Hollywood and Beyond* (Intellect, 2000), *Changing Tunes: Issues in Music and Film* (Ashgate Press, 2005) and *Composing for the Screen in the USSR and Germany* (Indiana University Press, 2005).

Damian Sutton is Lecturer in Historical and Critical Studies at the Glasgow School of Art, UK. He is the author of *Photography, Cinema, Time* (University of Minnesota Press, forthcoming 2006). He has published chapters and articles in edited collections and journals including *The Visual-Narrative Matrix: Interdisciplinary Collisions and Collusions* (Southampton Institute of Higher Education, 2000), *Screen, Source* and *Scope*, and is a co-editor of the online salon *Film-Philosophy*. He is also co-editor of *The State of the Real: Aesthetics in the Digital Age* (I. B. Tauris, forthcoming 2006).

Michael Williams is Lecturer in Film Studies at the University of Southampton, UK. He is author of *Ivor Novello: Screen Idol* (BFI, 2003). He has also published chapters and articles in a number of journals and edited collections including the *Journal of Romance Studies, Pimple Pranks and Pratfalls: British Film Comedy Before 1930* (Flicks Books, 2000), *British Stars and Stardom: From Alma Taylor to Sean Connery* (University of Manchester Press, 2002), *Young and Innocent?: Cinema and Britain 1896–1930* (University of Exeter Press, 2002) and *British Queer Cinema* (Routledge, 2005).

Introduction

Jacqueline Furby and Karen Randell

'There can be a madness in methods. Methodologies cannot be allowed to become ends. They are means, tools to help construct models of how things work.'
  – Bill Nichols (1976: 1)

Thirty years on from Bill Nichols' introduction to his first *Movies and Methods* anthology, it is still the case that clear methodology is the key to a successful academic piece of writing. But where do you start? How do you decide which is the best methodological course for your idea? This book has been put together with these questions in mind. It is designed to provide students and academics with examples of current work in Film Studies to carry them into future research and writing. In recent years a new mood of interdisciplinarity has meant that film's theoretical catchment has spread rapidly (and perhaps confusingly) beyond existing limits. As teachers of undergraduates we are aware that these factors have led to a proliferation of approaches, models and tools for film analysis which, although exciting and stimulating, also have the potential to confuse or disorientate those coming new to studying film and its associated technologies and industries. The case studies in this book, then, are designed to be 'how to' research aids as well as complete pieces of research in their own right. They represent exemplars of recent and on-going theoretical work on film and point the way to how Film Studies may develop in the future.

The essays in this collection developed from 'work in progress' research papers presented at a University of Southampton seminar series called 'The Present in Cinema'. The purpose of the series was to discover what academics were doing to analyse the film text and film industry in the twenty-first century. It was open to research students and established academics alike and this mix is reflected here. What we found was that there was a vast array of interdisciplinary – or can we say *extra*-disciplinary? – methodologies being applied to the study of film. This is not a new discovery; Film Studies has been borrowing from other disciplines for much of its academic life. However, what is pertinent to reveal is that of the twenty-five papers given there was not once a duplication of methodology. The contributors to this book come from an array of academic disciplines: Philosophy, Economics,

Television Studies, Cultural Studies, French Studies, Art History, Photography and Film Studies. Their papers reflect these backgrounds and provide a rich dipping pot of twenty-first-century research into film and related media.

So, there are now more ways to think through and write your ideas about film than ever before. Where should you start? Since Bill Nichols' formative anthology there have been many other collections of essays published, including *Movies and Methods*, Vol. II (1985), which now give us a historical overview of the last thirty years of Film Studies. One key text is *Film Theory and Criticism: Introductory Readings* (1999), edited by Leo Brady and Marshall Cohen; a book so useful that it is now in its fifth edition. More recent collections have combined this historical approach with newer diversions in Film Studies. For instance, Jane Hollows, Peter Hutchings and Mark Jancovich's edited collection *Film Studies Reader* (2000) juxtaposes Theodor W. Adorno and Max Horkheimer's 1947 work, 'The Cultural Industry: Enlightenment as Mass Deception' with Eileen R. Meehan's contemporary work on Batman fandom and commodification, 'Holy Commodity Fetish, Batman: The Political Economy of Commercial Intertext'. Other collections and Readers move beyond the text itself into analysis of production, exhibition and distribution to create a film history model that seeks to research the surrounding discourse of the film text. Annette Kuhn and Jackie Stacey's *Screen Histories: A Screen Reader* (1998) is a useful starting point for students who wish to think through the implications of the reception of film. *Screen Methods: Comparative Readings in Film Studies*, then, can be seen as complementary to these existing collections in that the essays contained within it point to the future of Film Studies whilst often revisiting the past in terms of appropriating existing academic discourses. In another recent anthology, Christine Gledhill and Linda Williams asked, 'where is Film Studies now?' (2000: 3). The answer lies, in part, with the essays here.

This book is divided into three sections which each contain five to six case-study chapters that seek to explain their methodology to the reader, so that you can know 'how to' exercise similar methodological approaches or appropriations in your own work. The book has been structured according to the types of methodologies that are being applied; however, this is always an arbitrary process when interdisciplinarity is at play. Therefore the sections are arranged thematically. Section One, 'Scape: film form and method', contains case-study essays that explore film's formal properties: those of frame, space, time and sound. The methods adopted range from philosophy to fine art criticism to art history to musicology.

Thus, in chapter one, Melenia Arouh uses a philosophical approach to frame space to argue that film's 'unique' form needs to be understood within a wider context of our relationship to other spaces, both performative and everyday. Jacqueline Furby (chapter two) then develops an argument from philosophy to consider a fourth dimension in film – time. Damian Sutton (chapter three) takes us on a visual journey from the paintings of Jacques-Louis David to the CGI construction of the arena in *Gladiator* (Ridley Scott, 2000) and asks how far we have really come, whilst in chapter four Martin Lister interrogates the sensory space of virtual media environments to discuss the usefulness of thinking about such immersion as 'stepping through a window'. In chapter five musicologist Robynn Stilwell develops the notion of 'soundscape' in popular cinema and discusses the way in which music can be understood as creating yet another dimension.

Section Two, 'Views: theory and method' contains case-study essays that explore existing theoretical positions concerned with subjectivity. These methods include spectatorship and psychoanalysis, queer theory, post-modernity and post-colonialism, gender studies and cultural studies. The questions here must be those of how does one interrogate a film text using existing academic dialogues differently?; how might you appropriate a grand *meta*-theory to your own work? Darren Kerr (chapter eight), for instance, shows how theories of adaptation are used as a framework within which to discuss the portrayal of sexual deviance in the fictional character, Mr Hyde. John Phillips (chapter six) uses a psychoanalytic model to explore the possibility of a female gaze in Catherine Breillat's *Romance* (1999) and Michael Williams' essay asks if queer theory necessarily precludes other readings of a text (chapter nine). Such contributions illustrate that theoretical engagement and textual analysis are still vibrant and useful ways to understand the address of a film. However, essays such as Michael Williams' discussion of *A Room with a View* (James Ivory, 1985), and Monica B. Pearl's essay in chapter ten on the representation of AIDS and race in *Philadelphia* (Jonathan Demme, 1994) demonstrate that this theoretical approach combined with a discussion of the cultural surround of a film produces an intertextual reading. Such debates with the discourses 'outside' of the text are taken up in the essays in Section Three.

Gill Branston has said that 'Film Studies is in a state of reconfiguration as the boundaries of what we call "film" shift from celluloid, cameras and photochemistry into video, television, digital and computer technologies and screens' (quoted in Gledhill & Williams 2000: 18). The third section of this volume, 'Scenes: new technology and method', illustrates how this shift is developing. In chapters twelve to fifteen various audience research methodologies are utilised or developed to understand the appeal or distaste of new 'film' technological forms. For example, anxieties and moral panics about the Internet are discussed in the essay by David Lusted alongside textual analysis of Hollywood 'spectacles' within a framework of film and television history scholarship (chapter fifteen). Deborah Jermyn's essay on BBC TV's *Crimewatch* (chapter fourteen) combines a Film Studies model of textual analysis with empirical research and theoretical perspective to explore the constructed 'reality' of this television crime programme. Peter Krämer (chapter twelve) and John Sedgwick (chapter thirteen) apply an economics model to utilise audience figures for analysis of film's success and failure at the box office. The final essay, by William Merrin, asks us to consider the future of film itself in the light of emerging Virtual Reality technology.

This book, then, celebrates the diversity of methodologies that are being deployed to investigate the power of the visual, aural and spatial on the screen. It is intended to inspire and assist you in your own research and writing and to aid you in developing your own ideas about screen media: for that moment when you are watching and wonder, how could I write about that?

Bibliography

Brady, L. and M. Cohen (eds) (1999) *Film Theory and Criticism: Introductory Readings*. Oxford: Oxford University Press.
Gledhill, C. and L. Williams (eds) (2000) *Reinventing Film Studies*. London: Arnold.

Hollows, J., P. Hutchings and M. Jancovich (eds) (2000) *Film Studies Reader*. London: Arnold.
Kuhn, A. and J. Stacey (eds) (1998) *Screen Histories: A Screen Reader*. Oxford: Clarendon Press.
Nichols, B. (ed.) (1976) *Movies and Methods*, Vol. I. Berkeley: University of California Press.
_____ (1985) *Movies and Methods*, Vol. II. Berkeley: University of California Press.

scape
film form and method

Introduction

Jacqueline Furby

This section groups together a selection of essays that deal with film's formal context. These discussions appear together under the banner of 'Scape' because in some sense they are all concerned with the environment of film and to greater and lesser degrees with the impact that environment might have on the reader of film. I do not use the term 'spectator' here, nor 'viewer', because these terms privilege the visual sense over other senses that we also take to the cinema. We do not simply watch a film; we listen to, understand, and respond to complex and variable sounds; we feel movement and fluctuating rhythms of light, colour, image, shape, music, dialogue and other aural clues which all appeal to our time sense. We read space and perspective and position ourselves geometrically to the film frame and its content, which is, after all, a two-dimensional representation of a three-dimensional image (four-dimensional event if we include time). And a film's environment, its 'scape', includes its relationship to the history of visual art, aural art, and to the history of film art and technology, which we read and interpret, depending upon our knowledge and interest, with our cognitive sense. So, in the scapes presented here we move from a discussion of the nature of film space, through to a discourse on the cinematic soundscape, via time, the image's cultural and artistic legacy, and how new immersive technologies might change our understanding of the nature of perspective.

Melenia Arouh's approach to film is that of a philosopher. This is a welcome and refreshing look at film space from within a discipline that traditionally might be said, following the Greek philosopher Plato (c. 429–347 BC), to be prejudiced against the visual image. Plato's *The Republic* offers the myth of the cave in which he describes the philosophically unenlightened as prisoners able to see only shadows, and who perceive these shadows to be reality. Philosophical enlightenment is only achieved on release from the cave into the sunlight where we find the real objects. Plato's message, therefore, is that the senses mislead us and we must rely on reason alone in the construction of a world view. The parallels are clear between Plato's cave and cinema. We can use this positively, though, as a cautionary tale about being so seduced by the power of cinema, the stories that it tells us, and the marvellous effects that it is able to show us, that we forget to look at it in a detached and critical way. A central irony to Plato's cave story, is that it is exactly that, a *story* used to illustrate his vision of philosophical thinking. We can, in turn, use cinema, and its stories, as a mirror through which to view and understand ourselves and the nature of our cultures, and in a reciprocal gesture, use a variety of disciplines as optical glasses through which to view and better understand the phenomenon of film.

Among other things, Philosophy may be described as the study of the nature of things, and a number of philosophers work towards achieving a comprehensive definition and precise delineation of terms and ideas. Here Arouh applies philosophical argument to the question of cinematic space. Space is all around us in the everyday world and therefore it is perhaps understandable that we may take it for granted. Space is likewise an essential condition of cinema because the visual element of film, the image, always requires space in order to be visible, and will always exist in at least two dimensions. But this can also be said of other visual arts. So, how do we define cinematic space, and how and in what ways, then, if at all, is cinematic space unique? Arouh draws on the work of philosophers of film, and film theorists, in order to reach a definition of and to elaborate upon cinematic space's four main characteristics, and to debate philosophical aspects of realism, spatial orientation and audience expectations.

She identifies an essential duality of cinema space: the 'screen-space' and the 'action-space' and discusses how this dualistic cinematic space might, or might not, be seen to differ from space encountered in other media or by us in our everyday world. In the process she elaborates on the ways that screen space is implicated in the particular relationship that the cinematic image has with reality. Arouh's conclusion is that cinema space may not in itself differ sufficiently from the spatial features of other art forms to justify a claim for uniqueness, and to arrive at a more thorough definition of cinema's formal properties and how they may be distinguished from other media it is necessary to consider space alongside such cinematic characteristics as time, colour and sound.

With Jacqueline Furby's essay we do move on to consider film time, although not from the philosophical viewpoint adopted by Arouh. Furby's methodological approach is that of close textual analysis in order to illustrate what she describes in terms of the internal temporal poetics within individual shots that can add to our understanding of how films make and communicate meaning. Furby suggests that the kind of variable rhythms found in film is one of film's pleasures as it appeals to the 'human aesthetic rhythmic sensibilities' and provides an antidote to the regularity of clock time by which we must regulate much of our waking lives. Although Furby is thinking in terms of a timescape, she has not strayed far from the idea of space because she regards the rhythm inherent in the image contained within the space of the frame as a kind of *mise-en-abîme* representative of a more general trend in the nature of film's temporality.

Damian Sutton and Martin Lister both deal with contemporary film's relationship to the pictorial art of a previous epoch, but in different ways. Sutton sees the relationship across time and space between eighteenth- and nineteenth-century French painters Jacques-Louis David and Jean-Léon Gérôme and Ridley Scott's film *Gladiator* (2000) a twenty-first-century, classically epic take on the Roman Empire. What links Scott to David and Gérôme, says Sutton, is a tradition of realism, and in Scott and David particularly is found a way of representing a blend of past and present in such as way as to set up a convincing dialogue of heroism and verisimilitude. Sutton's analysis borrows from fine art criticism in that his style is evocative of Sister Wendy, the charming bewimpled nun who graced British television screens in the 1990s. This essay, however, does not stop at the boundary of art criticism, but strays into the territory of philosophy, historical hermeneutics, cultural theory, and of course film theory and criticism, to discuss a wide range of ambiguous resonances that can be found operating in Scott's film.

With Martin Lister we are still located in media space, and we continue to think about the relationship between twenty-first-century visual art and much earlier representational art forms. Lister examines ways of thinking about, and the validity of metaphors to describe, the experience of immersion in virtual reality environments. One of the metaphors used to describe this experience is that of 'stepping through a window'. The window in question is that conceived of by Leon Battista Alberti, fifteenth-century theorist of perspective. Lister's essay examines the position of the spectator within an immersive environment, what happens when the frame – and therefore traditional ideas of perspective – is no longer part of the pictorial space, and what kind of relationship is formed between the spectator and the image.

The final essay in this section is by musicologist Robynn Stilwell. Not unexpectedly for someone so concerned with the aural, Stilwell calls for more attention to be paid to what we hear when we go to the cinema. Her essay begins by usefully placing the 'soundscape', her term for the combination of music, speech and sound effects, within a context of existing film theory. It then argues that the subject position of the listener is taken to be feminine in contrast to the masculine subject position with which the spectator is aligned (following Laura Mulvey's work on the male gaze). The case study that Stilwell offers builds on this by offering a close analysis of narrative, images and soundscape of *Closet Land* (Radha Bharadwaj, 1991), a film which follows the interaction between a male interrogator/torturer and a female prisoner. Stilwell demonstrates how the 'female audit' operates in the film to align the spectator/listener with the female character and therefore the victim subject position (although the film complicates this by not allowing the male character total domination of the female victim).

The introduction of gender and subjectivity in this final essay points towards the concerns of Section Two in which theoretical approaches to subjectivity are explored.

Bibliography

Mulvey, L. (1975) 'Visual Pleasure and Narrative Cinema', *Screen*, 6, 3, 6–18.
Plato (1966) *Plato's Republic*. Cambridge: Cambridge University Press.

CHAPTER ONE

Mapping Cinema Space

Melenia Arouh

In this essay, I shall give an account of 'cinema space',[1] which draws on ideas that have been advanced by philosophers of film (most notably by Alexander Sesonske, Haig Khatchadourian and F. E. Sparshott), and attempts to synthesise and elaborate on those ideas, in a way that I hope will illuminate the subject further.[2] Primarily, this account will explore cinema space as a formal category of cinema and elaborate on its four main characteristics. Furthermore, I shall discuss some philosophical aspects of cinema space, in particular, matters of realism, spatial orientation and audience expectations. I will also try to assess the claim, often made by philosophers of film, that by examining cinematic form we will be able to establish the uniqueness of cinema as an art kind. In doing so, I shall be considering whether the essential characteristics of cinema space are peculiar to *cinema*, or also true for other art kinds.

The first essential characteristic of cinema space, which is examined in some detail in Sesonske's work, is that it has a certain logical, although not phenomenological, duality (1973: 402). On the one hand, there is the actual space of the screen, 'screen-space', which consists of shadows and light on the surface of the screen. On the other hand, we have the apparently three-dimensional 'action-space', the space of the recorded performance. Why is this characteristic essential? When an image is projected on a screen, or any surface for that matter, a duality is created: of the space of the surface and of the space within the image. In this respect, the existence of cinema space is part and parcel with this kind of duality.

Sesonske, discussing this distinction, claims that the duality of cinema space is a characteristic peculiar to cinema, and, specifically, what distinguishes it from stage space (1973: 408–9). In the theatre, according to Sesonske, there is no such duality: the space of the stage just *is* the space of the action; consequently, theatre space is much more limited. Erwin Panofsky raises a similar point, arguing that cinema space – action-space – is wider than stage space, since the camera can shift from one place to the other (1999: 282). But Haig Khatchadourian, in his criticism of Sesonske's analysis, argues that the space of the stage has a similar kind of duality to cinema space. According to Khatchadourian, the duality of theatre space is between the actual stage space where the drama takes place (the equivalent of cinematic screen-space), and the space that is represented in the world of the narrative (the equivalent of cinematic action-space) (1987: 175–6). In this respect, I cannot step from my seat in the theatre to Never-Never Land, as the one is in real space and the other in represented space. This sort of duality of space seems to be present in paintings and comics as well, since in these cases we can distinguish between the space of the drawing or the painting, that is, their location in real space, and the space that is created, represented in the drawing or painting. I conclude, then, that although the duality of cinematic space is in fact an essential characteristic of it, it is not one that is unique to cinematic space, and hence does not in itself do anything to establish the uniqueness of cinema as a medium.

The second characteristic of cinema space concerns the two-dimensionality of the cinematic image. Because action-space, that is, the recorded three-dimensional space, is presented on a two-dimensional surface, it will, by necessity, be two-dimensional, although it will appear as three-dimensional. Because of this lack of a third dimension, it sometimes appears quite peculiar or distinctive, as for example when we try to look 'in the picture', trying to see what is behind, say, an object by stretching our heads either to the left or right. Or when in the opening credits of many films, the two-dimensional titles are projected on the same plane with action-space, which appears three-dimensional.

Because action-space is only apparently three dimensional, some film theorists, for example Ralph Stephenson and J. R. Debrix, and Rudolph Arnheim,[3] have considered it as a counter-example to the claim that cinema is an essentially realistic medium. The realists main claim was that what is unique and peculiar to cinema as an art form is its capacity to reproduce realistic images. For example, Siegfried Kracauer argued that films can claim aesthetic validity only if 'they build from their basic properties … that is, they must record and reveal physical reality' (1997: 37). For Kracauer, films that ignore the basic principle behind cinema – its photographic nature – are not truly cinematic. The filmmaker's 'formative tendencies', his/her artistic imagination, must comply to 'the medium's substantive concern with our visible world' (1997: 39). So, the affinity with reality that cinematic images have, becomes cinema's principal consideration.[4] But it seems that the two-dimensional nature of cinematic images in general and of action-space in particular puts into question the degree of resemblance that cinematic images have to the real world. We become aware that although the images may resemble reality, important differences, such as shape or depth distortions, cannot be ignored. Although these distortions can almost be 'corrected' in post-production, certain films, such as, *The Cabinet of Dr. Caligari* (Robert Wiene, 1920), and some of Orson Welles' films, especially *The Trial* (1963) deliberately put two-dimensional distortions of action-space to artistic use, and as a result heighten our awareness of them. Although cinema has the potential to 'copy' reality to some extent, differences such as the two-dimensionality of action-space, suggest that 'cinematic reality' is not completely reducible to reality. Of course, the same principle applies to slides, comics and paintings, where three-dimensionality is represented two-dimensionally. In this respect, although the two-dimensionality of the cinematic images is a necessary characteristic of action-space, it seems that it is not peculiar to it, and therefore not sufficient to establish the uniqueness of cinema as an art kind.

The third essential characteristic of cinema space that I wish to discuss is discontinuity. Sesonske distinguishes between two kinds of discontinuity: on the one hand, action-space is discontinuous from our normal world; on the other, it is discontinuous in itself – that is, the spatial locations between scenes and shots can be as far apart (both spatially and temporally) as the narrative demands (1973: 403). Of these two, the former is an essential characteristic as it is a necessary consequence of the nature of action-space, while the latter is essential only as a potential. This I hope will become more explicit in what follows.

Concerning the first kind of discontinuity, we are, for better or worse, physically outside the action-space. Noël Carroll in his ontological analyses of the moving image makes a similar observation. Carroll argues that film spectatorship involves 'disembodied viewpoints': although in real life, one can direct his or her body towards what one is looking at, in cinema, action-space is phenomenologically disconnected from the space we exist in and is only visually available (1995: 70–1). In other words, there is no continuity between the space I occupy as a human being and action-space. If I attempt to step into the world of the narrative, namely, action-space, I will probably collide with a wall.

But, is this phenomenological discontinuity a unique characteristic of cinema? If we consider Khatchadourian's claim mentioned before, it seems that it is not. For, in the same manner that cinematic action-space is different from screen-space, stage-space is different from represented drama-space. As mentioned earlier, I cannot step from my seat to Never-Never Land. But there seems to be a difference in the way these two kinds of space are discontinuous from our real one; the discontinuity, on the one hand, is between the recorded representation and us, and on the other, between what is represented and us. That is, the photographic nature of cinema becomes an extra barrier between the action of a film and us. More specifically, whereas the discontinuity in cinema is between three-dimensionality and two-dimensionality, in theatre, where this difference in dimensions is lacking, what separates us from the world of the narrative is more in terms of common sense, imagination and convention. Thus, this kind of discontinuity differentiates cinematic action-space from theatre drama-space, although, again, cinema shares it with painting, photography and comics.

But apart from being phenomenologically discontinuous from our normal space, action-space is discontinuous in itself. From one scene to the other spatial or temporal relations can change and these changes do not need to follow the laws of our ordinary world. Of course, the nature of these relations and how they evolve is a matter of narrative structures and stylistic choices. We may become vividly aware of the potential of discontinuity when filmmakers such as Bernardo Bertolucci or Jean-Luc Godard play with the spatio-temporal expectations some of us have developed from watching too many Hollywood movies.

How is spatial discontinuity within action-space articulated? Usually, as Arnheim and Burch have elaborated, there are two kinds of discontinuity. The first is by showing places with no spatial proximity, for example from Earth to where no one else has gone before. In general, we have no problem following these changes when watching films, since filmmakers find ways of hinting what and where these places are – with titles, or voice-over, or lines in the dialogue, or by showing places already established. These devices might not even be needed if the narrative is constructed so as to explain everything to the viewer.

The second kind of discontinuity, as Burch especially argues, is between places where there is some spatial proximity as, for example, the kitchen and bedroom of the same house, or, when there is a change of camera view but within, say, the same room. This mode of discontinuity brings to the surface matters of spatial orientation. For realistic purposes, filmmakers will maintain sufficient spatial orientation with the use of eye-line matching, same use of props, and so on (see Burch 1981: 9).

But it might be wondered, is spatial orientation really that important when watching a film? For example, in many battle scenes, the shifts from one spatial position to another are very fast. In such cases spatial orientation becomes minimal, if non-existent. A good illustration is *Pearl Harbor* (Micheal Bay, 2001), where each shot, during the air-fighting sequences, lasts an average of two-and-a-half seconds. There, spatial orientation is almost completely lost; where the characters are and the spatial relations to one another remains significantly vague. This line of thinking makes explicit our peculiar relation to action-space. Whereas in real life spatial orientation is of immense importance and loss of it may require medical attention or even be fatal, somehow, when watching a film we do not have such strict expectations.

The last characteristic of cinema space I shall consider is off-screen space. Off-screen space is a necessary characteristic because of the presence of the frame.[5] As Noël Burch has elaborated, the presence of the frame amplifies action-space, forming 'off-screen space'. We have six more imaginary spatial segments, 'the immediate confines of the first four of these areas are determined by the four borders of the frame, and correspond to the four faces of an imaginary truncated pyramid projected into the surrounding space' (1981: 17). The fifth segment is the space 'behind' the camera, and the sixth where the actors 'go' after, say, exiting from a door. For Burch this segment is the 'space behind the set', 'beyond the horizon' (ibid.). So, action-space has a duality as well, what we perceive on the screen and what we do not perceive, but affects our viewing and understanding of the film narrative.

Typically, on screen we see what the filmmaker wants us to see, which is usually relevant to the story at a given time. In this respect, we seem to disregard what is off-screen as of secondary interest to the action. There is an underlying assumption that filmmakers will show us only what is somehow relevant to what we have already seen, or will see in the film, and even more, that it will somehow make sense. Of course this is not always the case. But I think the expectation we have as cinema viewers that what we see (and hear) will make sense, is true for most art forms. For this reason, audiences examine Pieter Bruegel's painting *The Fall of Icarus* until the title makes sense, or watch David Lynch's *Lost Highway* (1997) again and again to try to find something *in* the film that will explain the narrative's ending.

It is interesting to note here that our attitude towards cinematic off-screen space is a defining difference with the nature of videogames' off-screen space. In videogames, such as *Tomb Rider*, we have the potential to explore what is off-screen by taking Lara Croft where we want, or moving her head up or down. It seems that whereas in films we tend to ignore what is off-screen as irrelevant to the action, in videogames we strive to explore off-screen space, because ultimately it is there that all the action waits (Vermillion 2001: 2).

How is the existence of cinematic off-screen space determined? According to Burch, the most usual ways are either by actors entering and exiting, or from camera movements, or by actors looking or pointing off-screen, or by seeing only part of an actor's body (1981: 21–5). More explicitly, when an actor enters, say, from the door, the space behind the door takes some sort of shape in the viewers' imagination, although a precise delineation of how this off-screen space might be does not occur. It is only when the action-space becomes empty of any action or movement that we become more aware of off-screen space. Crudely put, there might be something more interesting happening there. When the frame is left empty of action two things may occur: the first is when we know that the action we are interested in is carried on off-screen, like in the infamous ear-cutting scene in Quentin Tarantino's *Reservoir Dogs* (1992). In such cases, our attention is diverted to off-screen space (often aided by off-screen sound), because the camera is not where the action is. The second possibility is when the frame is left empty of any action and we may become uncertain as from where the next segment of action will occur. Here, all off-screen space becomes important and potential for action. This is a common feature of some of Yasujiro Ozu and Takeshi Kitano's films, where we become intensely aware of off-screen space, since in certain shots there is nothing happening on-screen. For Burch, there is one more possibility of off-screen space awareness, when camera or actor movement is continuous (1981: 18–19). In these cases, as for example in *Reservoir Dogs*, there is no sharp distinction between on- and off-screen space, as the one constantly converts into the other.

The assumption we form as audiences, that what we need to know is on-screen, along with the use of off-screen space, can become a unique cinematic tool. The play with our conventional expectations and our lack of knowledge of off-screen space, can be used either as an element of shock or surprise or for comic effect. To use a classic example, in a scene of Charlie Chaplin's *The Immigrant* (1917), we see Chaplin leaning over the railing of the boat with the rest of the passengers and we assume that he, like them, is seasick. In fact he is simply trying to fish. The assumption we have that what we need to know is on-screen and the revealing of what is off-screen, produce a comic effect. The use of off-screen space to produce shock or suspense is also an interesting case. Frequently, in thrillers or horror films, while the desperate heroine is trying to save her life, the camera will follow her movements from a very close distance, so we are unable to see where the killer/demon/psychopath is in relation to her. Characteristically, horror filmmakers will lead us to form an assumption as to where the attacker is, and then, bring him/her/it in from a completely different off-screen place that catches us off-guard. Another classic use of off-screen space is when what is threatening to the heroes of the narrative is kept off-screen, as for example, the shark in *Jaws* (Steven Spielberg, 1975), or the alien hunter in *Predator* (John McTiernan, 1987). There, what is off-screen and (almost) never seen becomes more frightening.

Is off-screen space a unique characteristic of cinema? It is definitely different from painting and photography, since there we do not have the option of *seeing* what is beyond the frame. There seems to be a similarity with comics, since we can see what is outside the frame on the next frame. Also, the use of off-screen space in cinema seems to be different from that of the stage, but interestingly enough, not too much. If we consider the use of lighting in the theatre, then the same characterisations with cinema off-screen space can be applied. What we see under, say, the spotlight can be considered similar to what we see on-screen, and what remains in the dark is analogous to the off-screen space. Again, we make the assumption in stage plays that what remains in the dark is not as important as to what is illuminated. What can be concluded is that off-screen space is an essential characteristic whenever a segment of space is framed, as in comics or paintings. Therefore, it is not a characteristic that is unique to cinema.

F. E. Sparshott makes an interesting observation regarding the differences between cinema and theatre off-screen space. He argues that when in the theatre an actor/actress exits, he or she loses his or her 'existence' in the mind of the viewer, since theatre off-screen space is not acknowledged. In film, however, we attribute 'infinite continuity', we feel like we 'glimpse only part of the world' (1985: 295). So, when a character exits from on-screen, his or her fictional existence is just transferred off-screen. Sparshott when discussing 'infinite continuity' seems to be making the same mistake that Panofsky and Sesonske do, namely, failing to recognise the duality of stage space. They assume that what we see on stage ends where the wing curtains begin. But as already mentioned, this is mistaken. The place that is represented in theatre is as infinitely continuous as the cinematic one. Furthermore, there seems to be something misleading in the suggestion that when characters exit from the stage, they cease to exist for the audience. Does that mean that we are surprised whenever they re-enter? Do we assume them to be the ghosts of characters past? Since nothing of the sort happens, I assume that Sparshott is wrong. Actors that are out of sight are *not* out of mind, either in the theatre or the cinema.

In this essay I have ventured to analyse the four essential characteristics of cinema space so as to provide a map of cinema space. Throughout this discussion, I have examined aspects that have some philosophical interest, such as the extent of photographic realism in cinema, or matters of spectatorship and in particular the expectations we develop as viewers. I have focused more, however, on whether these four essential features of cinema space are peculiar to cinema. By comparing and contrasting them with spatial features of other art forms, especially theatre, I hope to have shown that they are not unique to cinema either individually or collectively, although they might differ in some of their modes, as for example the manner in which drama space in the theatre is different from action-space. To argue, as philosophers of film such as Sesonske, Sparshott, or Pierre Rouve, have done, that cinema is a distinct kind of art because of uniqueness in terms of form, seems unjustified if one examines cinema space alone. What may be true is that, if cinematic uniqueness in terms of form is to be pursued as a claim, then the other essential formal characteristics of cinema, such as time, colour or sound, should be examined in a similar manner.[6]

Notes

1   For the purposes of keeping the analysis simple, this account will be separated from 'cinema time'. Ralph Stephenson and J. R. Debrix in their book, *The Cinema as Art* (1976), provide a good analysis of 'cinema space-time' as a unity.

2   Film scholars have also discussed cinema space. Most significantly, David Bordwell, Kristin Thompson and Janet Staiger in their book *The Classical Hollywood Cinema* (1999); Stephen Heath in his essay 'Narrative Space' (1986); Mary Ann Doane in her essay 'The Voice in the Cinema: The Articulation of Body and Space' (1999); Ralph Stephenson, especially in his book with J. R. Debrix, *The Cinema as Art*; Barbara Bowman in her book *Master Space: Film Images of Capra, Lubitsch, Sternberg and Wyler* (1992); last and most importantly, Noël Burch in his book *Theory of Film Practice* (1981). Because my focus is more on the philosophical aspects of cinema space, I choose not to elaborate on their views. Some of their insights and comments, however, are considered in what follows.

3   Stephenson and Debrix in chapters two and three of their book *The Cinema as Art*, and Arnheim in part two of his book *Film* (1993).

4   André Bazin was of a similar opinion, especially concerning spatial realism and constant re-framing of action. For an excellent analysis of Bazin's position, see chapter two of Noël Carroll's book *Philosophical Problems of Classical Film Theory* (1988).

5   A brief note should be made on the functionality of the frame: the frame, as Sesonske argued, has a dual role, on the one hand it is a constant reminder of screen-space, and on the other a container for the visual action (1973: 405). As a result, spatial relations on the screen are seen in relation to the frame, and in this sense, the frame becomes a criterion of symmetry and composition.

6   I would like to thank Alex Neill and Albert Arouh for their helpful comments and corrections during the preparation of this essay.

Bibliography

Arnheim, R. (1993) *Film*. Trans. L. M Sieveking and I. F. D. Morrow. London: Faber & Faber.

Bordwell, D., J. Staiger and K. Thompson (1999) *Classical Hollywood Cinema: Film Style and Mode of Production to 1960*. London: Routledge.

Bowman, B. (1992) *Master Space: Film Images of Capra, Lubitsch, Sternberg and Wyler*. New York: Greenwood Press.

Burch, N. (1981) *Theory of Film Practice*. Princeton: Princeton University Press.

Carroll, N. (1995) 'Towards an Ontology of the Moving Image', in C. A. Freeland and T. E. Wartenberg (eds) *Philosophy and Film*. New York and London: Routledge, 68–85.

Doane, M. A. (1999 [1980]) 'The Voice in the Cinema: The Articulation of Body and Space', in L. Braudy and M. Cohen (eds) *Film Theory and Criticism: Introductory Readings*. Oxford: Oxford University Press, 363–75.

Heath, S. (1986) 'Narrative Space', in P. Rosen (ed.) *Film Theory Reader: Narrative, Apparatus, Ideology*. New York: Columbia University Press, 379–420.

Khatchadourian, H. (1987) 'Space and Time in Film', *The British Journal of Aesthetics*, 27, 2, 169–77.

Kracauer, S. (1997) *Theory of Film: The Redemption of Physical Reality*. Princeton: Princeton University Press.

Panofsky, E. (1999) 'Style and Medium in the Motion Pictures', in L. Braudy and M. Cohen (eds) *Film Theory and Criticism: Introductory Readings*. Oxford: Oxford University Press, 279–92.

Rouve, P. (1972) 'Aesthetics of the Cinema', *British Journal of Aesthetics*, 12, 148–57.

Sesonske, A. (1973) 'Cinema Space', in D. Carr, E. S. Casey and M. Nijhhoff (eds) *Explorations in Phenomenology*. The Hague: Martinus Nijhhoff, 399–409.

Sparshott, F. E. (1985) 'Basic Film Aesthetics', in L. Braudy, M. Cohen and G. Mast (eds) *Film*

Theory and Criticism. Oxford: Oxford University Press, 284–304.

Stephenson, R. and J. R. Debrix (1976) *The Cinema as Art*. London: Penguin.

Vermillion, B. (2001) *Bringing it to the Screen: Off-screen Space in Film and Video Games*, http://www.english.uiuc.edu/newmedia/verillion.htm.

Rhizomatic Time and Temporal Poetics in *American Beauty*

Jacqueline Furby

This essay deals with the temporality of film through an examination of narrative, structure and image in Sam Mendes' film *American Beauty* (2000). Beyond Film Studies, temporality invites an interdisciplinary approach in that the study of time has traditionally been conducted within both the science and humanity faculties, being a focus of attention of both physical scientists and philosophers. Within Film Studies ideas around time and temporality have tended to emerge from discussions of narrative structure. Exceptions to this often purely narratological focus include Gilles Deleuze's full-length philosophically-based studies of time in cinema – *Cinema 1: The Movement-Image* (1983) and *Cinema 2: The Time-Image* (1989) – and subsequent commentaries that these texts have provoked. What follows takes something from the narratological approach, and at the same time refers to Deleuze's work and also that of Henri Bergson on whom Deleuze draws in his discussion of time.

At the simplest level a film's temporality lies in its very nature; film unfolds in time. More complex temporalities are transmitted through the narrative layer – through presentation of plot order, duration and frequency, and the relationship between story, plot and screen time, which can be orchestrated to impart a variety of rhythms – in the editing, framing and relationship between components at every level, from individual photograms, to shots, sequences, scenes and whole films. The presence, absence and deployment of actors, cameras, settings, props, lighting, sound, dialogue, colour and other aspects of *mise-en-scène* all contribute to a film's sense of time. And most obviously time can be a film's subject or theme, either overtly or covertly. Examples of films that feature time as a manifest theme include *Groundhog Day* (Harold Ramis, 1993), *Sliding Doors* (Peter Howitt, 1997) and *Memento* (Christopher Nolan, 2000), or the many varieties of time-travel narratives such as *Timescape* (David Twohy, 1991), *Timecop* (Peter Hyams, 1994), *Twelve Monkeys* (Terry Gilliam, 1995) and *Frequency* (Gregory Hoblit, 2000). More frequently the manipulation of plot time provides the structural basis for economical and effective storytelling, through a wide repertoire of narratorial and technical devices, such as flashback, flashforward, elliptical editing, montage sequence, freeze-frame, slow-motion, fast-motion, rewind, dissolves and wipes.

American Beauty employs few of these time manipulation techniques, nor does time feature obviously as a manifest theme, but as I seek to show, it does provide an interesting platform for the discussion of certain kinds of embedded filmic temporality. It presents its story sequentially with no transgression of natural temporal order apart from the short pre-title scene that shows Jane being filmed by Ricky. The entire film takes place in the present tense, although chronologically it is the past, being a memory partially narrated, at the point of death, by the principle character, and although screen time is approximately two hours, and story time around a year, plot time occupies apparently no time (or, alternatively, all time), situated in the interstices between life and death. We learn this from the narrator, Lester, who tells us towards the end that he had 'always heard your entire life flashes before your eyes the second before you die. First of all, that one second is not a second at all, it stretches on forever like an ocean of time.'

Apart from this relatively rare trope of point of death, or post-death narration or action (other films of this type include *Sunset Blvd.* (Billy Wilder, 1950) and *Jacob's Ladder* (Adrian Lyne, 1990)), the interesting moments of slow motion and repetitive motion episodes (that emphasise the fantasy sequences, and the various reactions to the sound of gunfire that signals Lester's death), the film includes several scenes that invite speculation about their temporal layering. These scenes are those cinematically self-reflexive scenes that involve on-screen video recordings. The first scene shows Ricky playing Jane a videotape he has recorded of a paper bag tossing and falling in the wind. He narrates a story about this moment and how significant it was for him and how he recorded the event to remind him. This is a simple image of two people using film, the embodiment of memory, to look into the past. We are in the present of the two characters and we are watching an image of the past (this is all contained within the contextual envelope of the past being remembered and narrated during a 'single' elastic present moment).

We can regard this scene's temporality in two ways: either time is layered, or thickened. In the first model the present moment exists alongside the past moment, represented by the video recording, and any future moments that Ricky will have recourse to the recording to refresh his memory, and past, present and future remain discrete yet stacked together, an atomistic view of time. In the second model the present moment is enriched, or fattened, to contain the past moment and future moments, without any division between the temporal zones. This is a view of time as durational flow that suggests the work of French philosopher Henri Bergson.

Bergson was, ironically, contemptuous of the new medium of film. Nevertheless, Bergson's accounts of memory, motion and time invite filmic comparison and are hard to read without seeing the connection between his ideas and the way that they are dealt with in film. This connection is the basis of Deleuze's work in his extended meditation on time and film in his two cinema books, for which he draws on Bergson. One definition of Deleuze's time-image, explicated in the second of his two cinema books, is that it is located where 'two images are constantly chasing one another round a point where real and imaginary become indistinguishable. The actual image and its virtual image crystallise' (1995: 52). In this image one can see layers of time, and the image 'is able to catch the mechanisms of thought' (ibid.).

This scene then, and, more particularly, two later scenes where the characters film one another, can be used to explicate Deleuze's ideas about time and film.

The temporal organisation of both later scenes, which feature Ricky filming Jane, and then Jane filming Ricky, is the same, so after a brief description of both scenes, I shall concentrate my discussion on the latter. In the first of these scenes Ricky stands at his bedroom window filming Jane who is at her bedroom window in the house opposite. From each character's point of view we see the other framed by their window, and this image resonates with the framing effect of the cinema screen. Beside Ricky, in his frame, is his television monitor in a separate window frame, on which is shown the image of Jane as he films her.

Jane's image as it appears on Ricky's monitor is caught in frame on the left, whilst Ricky is on the right, looking, not directly at Jane, but at her tiny image on the screen of the digital video camera he holds in his hands. Jane, who is aware that Ricky is filming her, is slowly taking off her clothes. This scene foregrounds film's scopophilic economy in a style resonant of Alfred Hitchcock's *Rear Window* (1954), and includes an active, exhibitionist dynamic that underlines film's purpose and desire to be looked at and an awareness of the viewing spectator. A later scene with an equally voyeuristic and exhibitionist economy is the reciprocal scene in which Jane films the naked Ricky while he relates, without apparent discomfort, a potentially difficult and traumatic passage in his own recent history (below).

Ricky is to the left of frame (backed by the window-like sections of his bookcase on which are housed his collection of books, music and videotapes). Jane is centred in the frame. The film's spectator, represented by the camera position over her left shoulder, sees Ricky's image on the small video camera screen (centre), which Jane also watches. Ricky's image also appears on the large television monitor to the right of frame.

This scene therefore gives us an image of the present time (Ricky talking to Jane); an image of the present growing and becoming the recent past (the act of recording); an aural image of the more remote past (Ricky's history); and in Ricky's television image a complex amalgam of the present moment which when accessed

Figure 1   Present time: Jane filming Ricky, in *American Beauty* (2000)

at any point in the future will be a piece of the past (watching a movie is like look-ing into the past) brought into the present (film's tense is the continuous present) of that future time. The previously formed past is represented by Ricky's video and music archive, and his books. So this one scene can be thought of as a thickened 'moment' of the present, which contains memory of the past and anticipation of the future, or as layers of space-time, past, present and future coexisting, or as the present moment sending out rhizomatic shoots connecting it to other, past and future, moments in time.[1] This last metaphor allows us to imagine that Jane and Ricky are actively constructing time (and their own lives, rather than their lives being something that happens to them). Time – past, present, future and the relationship between them – is 'growing' outwards from the kernel formed by the dynamic of their interconnection. The temporal cultivation is assisted by their honesty about the past. Recollection has a therapeutic value. Ricky has not buried or repressed his potentially traumatic history, but actively keeps the pathways (roots) into the past alive (during an earlier scene he says that he makes recordings because of his need to remember). His carefully archived recordings of past moments are testament to his active anamnesis.[2]

With its dynamic interplay between temporally embedded elements, this scene illustrates Deleuze's notion of the 'crystal-image' where the actual and the virtual form an internal circuit (1989: 68–97). In the preface to Cinema 2: The Time-Image, Deleuze writes of the time-image that 'the image itself is the system of relationships between its elements, that is, a set of relationships of time from which the variable present only flows ... What is specific to the image ... is to make perceptible, to make visible, relationships of time which cannot be seen in the represented object and do not allow themselves to be reduced to the present' (1989: xii). I suggest that this scene is an example of such 'visible ... relationships of time', that form part of Deleuze's definition of a cinematic time-image.

The order of time represented in this scene clearly shares few characteristics with our commonsense view of time that advances at the rate of a second every second in a single direction. Ricky and Jane's version of temporality is both rhizo-matic, in that it reaches into other moments of the past and future, and crystalline, in that it is multi-faceted. These models of time may be used to describe the tem-porality of human subjectivity. The rhizomatic quality expresses the way in which the present moment is infiltrated by the past through memory and accretions of the unconscious, and by the future through anticipation of what is to come, whilst there is always the desire that present action can redeem (change) the past and protect the future. The crystalline quality expresses the multiple nature of time that we confront in everyday life, which is summed up by social theorist Barbara Adam when she says that 'it is not either winter or December, or hibernation time for the tortoise, or one o'clock, or time for Christmas dinner. It is planetary time, biologi-cal time, clock and calendar time, natural and social time all at once' (1990: 16). Furthermore, time as we experience it passing is also multi-faceted because, for example, the time of individual consciousness runs at varying speeds depending on context. We notice temporal change in the world by witnessing the change reg-istered on clocks and calendars, the changing seasons, nature's cycles of growth and decay, and the biological and physiological rhythms and changes. Yet the speed of change – the speed of time – of our inner experience alters according to the fluctuations of the condition of our subjective experience (that is, our journey through time may seem rapid during sleep, when we are enjoying ourselves, or as we age, and slow during a period of anticipation, when we are bored, or when we are very young).

Our variable experience of living in time was at the heart of Bergson's philosophy. He said that 'the duration lived by our consciousness is a duration with its own determined rhythm, a duration very different from the time of the physicist' (1988: 205) which he dismissed as homogenous clock time. Bergson wrote this, in the late nineteenth century, during a period still dominated by the legacy of Isaac Newton's views of an absolute and atomistic clockwork universe, and Bergson was therefore innocent of the revolution in ideas about space and time that was to be initiated by Albert Einstein's work on relativity in 1905. One of the consequences of relativity physics is that we now know that the speed of time is relative to the position and velocity of the observer. The time of the physicist, in theory at least, now resembles subjective Bergsonian time in that it also possesses 'its own determined rhythm'. Yet how we live within time in our ordinary everyday lives in modern Western society still feels Newtonian because we must by necessity organise our lives according to the clock. I shall now go on to suggest, again using *American Beauty* as a model, that although film shares characteristics with both Newtonian and Einsteinian/Bergsonian time, film, as an art of time, has more in common with the latter, and this accounts for one of the pleasures that film has to offer.

The film charts the progress of Lester Burnham's life in one direction from his so-called mid-life crisis from a middle-aged man who feels 'sedated' to a youth who feels 'great', and at the same time the film follows his rapid transition through time in the other direction from life to death. This bi-directional journey unfolds within the regular repetitive structure of the daily cycle wherein occur variable day-to-day events. Such patterns (biological cycles implicated in day-to-day rhythms, life-cycles initiated at birth and arrested at death, oscillations of regret, nostalgia, anticipation, regret, desire and fulfilment) constitute a human rhythmic design. Harvey Gross asserts that 'it is rhythm that gives time a meaningful definition, a "form"' (1965: 11). The rhythm of which Gross speaks is not the invariable periodic rhythm of homogenous machine time, but the aperiodic heterogenic rhythm of poetry and prose where there is repetition with variation.

Change occurs in time, and time can only be registered through the recognition of change. The antithesis of homogenous time therefore is a rhythmic, changing pattern constituted through presence and absence, action and rest. This natural, human timing can be summarised as repetition with variation. A rhythm of repetition with variation lies at the heart of *American Beauty*'s formal structure and sense of time. The image of Lester crouching on the path (opposite) can be used as a starting point for a discussion to clarify this statement.

Lester is framed within the front area of garden. He is slightly off centre and to the right. The diminishing perspective of the path draws us in towards Lester in the foreground and beyond, towards the bright red colour of the front door in the background. The red front door is the central axis of the background around which plants and columns are symmetrically arranged. This symmetrical framing implies that the viewer should be alert to other balanced arrangements within the image. Yet the shot as a whole is strictly asymmetrical because there are three windows

Figure 2 Repetition with variation: Lester Burnham, in *American Beauty*

to the left of the door, and only one to the right. The added 'weight' of the extra window, however, is compensated for by Lester, whose presence in front of the missing window provides the necessary balance. Reading the image from left to right, and taking the central door as a kind of pause, we find that the elements to the left of the central door are repeated on the right, but with variation. This style of near symmetry is repeated extensively throughout the film, and examples can be see in the two dinner table scenes, notable for the combination of head-on tableau composition and depth of field. In both shots shown here (overleaf) Jane occupies the central position, and the frame achieves balance from Carolyn on the left and Lester on the right. The shots differ slightly, so I shall deal with them in turn, starting with one that takes place first.

In the centre of the table in this shot is a bowl of red roses. The red roses, and the pool of light from the lit candles, direct our attention to the central axis of the frame, in which Jane is positioned, after which the eye scans to either side to collect information about the other characters and their surroundings. The image is only nearly symmetrical because the windows are not equally balanced either side of Jane's central position, and there is a lamp behind Carolyn, but no corresponding item of equal 'weight' behind Lester. The tableau composition, and the symmetrically arranged people, invite us to expect symmetry in all planes, but this is not offered: the background to the left of centre is repeated in the background to the right, but with variation.

The second dinner table scene has obvious elements in common with the first. The characters are similarly deployed. There are also obvious differences. The table is laid this time not with red roses but with a white bowl on white linen.

There is also a marked difference in the characters' body language. In the first scene Lester crouches, diminishing his height, and this reveals his low self-esteem at this point in the film. Carolyn and Jane appear relaxed. In the second scene Lester asserts himself (he has just thrown a plate of asparagus at the wall), and his new attitude is displayed in his upright posture, whilst Carolyn's shock is evidenced by her drawing her body away from the table, placing distance between him and her. Jane looks at her father from beneath her brows, avoiding confrontational eye con-

Figure 3 First dinner table scene, in *American Beauty*

tact. The lack of red roses, the introduction of the white cloth, and the unlit windows, add an austere note to the second scene which is lacking in the first.

This, again, is repetition with variance. Apart from the visible differences already mentioned, there is greater weight, rhythmically speaking, in the second scene. This, I suggest, is because the scene is given extra emphasis through repetition, just as a word or phrase gains significance when repeated (or referred back to, in poetry, for example, by a close rhyme). It is recognised as significant because it is a repetition and this significance is supported by the heightened emotion surrounding Lester's character's development. The repeated scene thus reinforces the film's theme of change by forcing comparison between the two. It also involves a moment of 'thickened' time, where the present refers back to an earlier event, and sets up expectations of future repetitions.

This scene takes place near to the beginning of the first act, and the second scene near to the end of the second act. Between these two lies the shot of Ricky and his mother and father watching television (opposite).

Colonel Fitz is centrally placed, with his son and wife either side of him. The lamps, tables, windows, chairs, wife and son are all deployed symmetrically around his reference point, a visual pointer to the dynamics of their relationship. As a triadic family grouping it forms a set with the other two already discussed, which are placed either side of it in the film's chronological order, and once joined by the second dinner table scene, serves to suggest the near symmetrical pattern that the film appears to seek to point at. Other clues are in the deployment of the three households linked together. On one side of the Lester household is the homosexual couple, the two Jims, and providing balance on the other side is the homophobic colonel.

The near symmetry (where something on one side of a plane is repeated or balanced on the other side, but with variation) has an affinity with rhyme, in that it is the significant arrangement of similar, but not identical, elements in the same way as a poem will use two or more words whose initial consonants differ, but whose main vowel and succeeding consonants agree (might/fight). A number of different 'rhyming' elements can be found in *American Beauty,* many of which come to form

Figure 4 Second dinner table scene, in *American Beauty*

patterns of expectation and fulfilment. For example, the scene before the opening titles is a section of a later scene of Jane being filmed by Ricky, and is the first of nine occasions where we see Ricky filming her. A number of car journeys punctuate the film. Lester's voice-over accompanied by an aerial shot appears in the opening scene and is repeated at the beginning and at the end of the third act. And perhaps the most visually striking rhyming element are the eponymous red roses that are seen throughout as Lester's companion in his home and fantasy lives. The red of the rose, echoed elsewhere in red lipstick, door, clothes, lamp and, notably, blood, is the most eye-catching colour in an otherwise restrained, generally monochrome palette. In the shooting scene we see the rose shape in the splatter of Lester's blood on the kitchen wall. This final variation in the rose's image sends a shock-wave back through the preceding film, rewriting what was originally a colourful accessory, and accompaniment of sexual reverie into a *memento mori*.

These rhymes provide the film with a rhythmic structure that echoes the rhythm of the daily life portrayed, while the changes that occur with each repetition speak

Figure 5 Ricky and his parents, in *American Beauty*

of the variable nature of each day and the linear progression that constitutes both story and life. Harvey Gross writes that 'in the arts of time ... rhythmic forms transmit certain kinds of information about the nature of our inner life. This is the life of feeling which includes physiological response as well as what psychologists term affect' (1965: 11). The simplest example of a rhythmic pattern found in film is probably the action and rest inherent in the ignition of curiosity about story events that is (usually) satisfied after an intervening delay.

Film production is a mechanical process reliant on clockwork technology. This process suggests one particular kind of regulated, machine-like, Newtonian time. Time of a different order is also inherent in the story-telling process; and in the rhythms, durations and tempos of visual, audio and kinetic representation of images and sounds. Time is also, as already mentioned, embedded in film's subject matter: in the stories told, and in the iconography of the objects and forms used to tell these stories. To the narrative film adds the audio and kinetic dimensions of other time-based arts such as music, dance and theatre, and the rhythms of colour and form from static visual arts such as painting and sculpture. These audio and kinetic dimensions contribute to the spectator's sense of immersion in a temporal environment that is sympathetic to human time and addresses the needs of the desiring subject.

The repetition of formal elements (for example, images, settings, colours, shapes and textures) create a kind of internal rhyme that appeals to human aesthetic rhythmic sensibilities and further invites the spectator's imaginative interplay. Too much repetition can dull the senses, however, and suggests machinic, context-free regularity, so the filmic metre is relieved by a continuous variety of modulation. When elements are repeated with variations, that grow out of meaning and context, I suggest that this temporal pattern speaks of a particularly human rhythmic design, and provides an escape from the 'standardised, context free, homogeneous' clock time 'that structures and times our daily lives' (Adam 1995: 11).

Notes

1 The Oxford English Dictionary definition of 'rhizome' is that it is 'a continuously growing ... underground stem, which puts out lateral roots at intervals'. I have therefore borrowed the word to suggest a kind of temporality that actively reaches out in any direction.
2 'Anamnesis: the recalling of things past; reminiscence' (Oxford English Dictionary).

Bibliography

Adam, B. (1990) *Time and Social Theory*. Cambridge: Polity Press.
_____ (1995) *Timewatch: The Social Analysis of Time*. Cambridge: Polity Press.
Bergson, H. (1988 [1896]) *Matter and Memory*. Trans. N. M. Paul and W. S. Palmer. New York: Zone Books.
Deleuze, G. (1983) *Cinema 1: The Movement-Image*. London: Athlone Press.
_____ (1989) *Cinema 2: The Time-Image*. London: Athlone Press.
_____ (1995) *Negotiations: 1972–1990*. New York: Columbia University Press.
Gross, H. (1965) *Sound and Form in Modern Poetry: A Study of Prosody from Thomas Hardy to Robert Lowell*. Ann Arbor: University of Michigan Press.

CHAPTER THREE

Inside the 'Black Box': From Jacques-Louis David to Ridley Scott

Damian Sutton

The title of this essay presents a problem: how do we get from Jacques-Louis David to Ridley Scott? Grand conceptual genealogies, connecting Revolutionary France with the present day, may seem unlikely at first, yet at stake in both is the manipulation of image technologies and the precarious relationship that this has with political ideology. In particular, the essay looks at Scott's film, *Gladiator* (2000), in the light of an essentially populist narrative that taps into contemporary themes of individualism, compassion, social responsibility and even intellectualism, and that has resonance in the political rhetoric of the pamphleteers of the 1780s.

Gladiator is an example of a high earning and critically acclaimed industrial product whose reliance on an excessive visual style and integration with marketing demonstrates a masking of the film's ideological significance behind the twin 'alibis' of mass entertainment and high cultural pedigree. As an example of the epic genre, *Gladiator*'s pedigree stretches back through to Cecil B. DeMille and D. W. Griffith, and even back to classical and Republican painting. Indeed, the highly charged and melodramatic content of Jacques-Louis David's *The Oath of the Horatii* from 1784 (overleaf), matched with its apparently classical-realist depiction of time and space, can be seen as a direct ancestor to Scott's tale of honour and revenge set against a Roman world delivered onscreen with uncanny accuracy. Images of Republican Rome, with its connotations of prosperous Empire, honour, democracy and power of the popular identity, have been attractive as propaganda for a long time. The question that remains, then, is just how exactly do we get from David to Scott? Perhaps the best way to answer this question is to begin as many academic essays do – with a hunch – and develop a picture of the film's cultural and material determinants along the way. We would thus be writing the essay backwards…

Conclusions

The principle connection between Scott and David, *Gladiator* and *The Oath of the Horatii*, is the ambiguous image of antiquity that they share as cultural products.

Figure 6 *The Oath of the Horatii*, Jacques-Louis David (1784)

This is an ambiguity borne of their seamlessness in presenting the heroic senti-ments of the present in the guise of the past, and an ambiguity in which the novel gives authority to the antique. It was David's radical style of painting in *The Oath of the Horatii* that set it apart from academic painting of its time, his use of expressive pose and off-centre framing jarring the contemporary viewer's eye. Both create a historically-known world that appears with veridical realism – as essentially and unquestionably lifelike – and into which is inserted a contemporary narrative of populism, romantic love, honour and destiny: 'true nobility and grace … in the imaginary form' (Crow 1985: 220). In both cases, a novel technique attracting comment on its own gives authority to those ideological intentions for which it is imagined.

The difference between the two is subtle. *The Oath of the Horatii* presents an image of mythology to provide commentary on a society changing under the tot-tering *ancien régime* of eighteenth-century France, a commentary that would have been noticed by all who saw the painting. *Gladiator* elides its politics by deflecting its audience towards its visual deceit: the ability of computer-generated imagery (CGI) to present a diligent depiction of history that brooks no question, and which attempts to make its artifice disappear. Already headline news for the publicity of films such as *Titanic* (James Cameron, 1999), CGI such as is used in *Gladiator* inherits the historian's reputation, simultaneously fetishised by DVD features, by trying to convince its audience that it is an innocent tool in the recovery of the past.

In this event, there is renewed emphasis on the *trust* we can place in the image, its provenance, or its fidelity to an otherwise unquestionable source such as the weight of ancient history. However, the use of CGI in *Gladiator* guarantees a fidelity, if not to a classically accurate depiction of the Roman Empire, then at least to a late twentieth-century interpretation of it: one that is in turn a re-interpretation of the Roman-esque, orientalist, or 'Empire' movements of nineteenth- and twentieth-century culture. This attachment of CGI to 'fidelity' as a representational ideal has replaced a former trust in the photochemical image as a direct and causal representation of reality. In the past we might have theoretically 'guaranteed' the photochemical image by saying that the object was actually there to be photographed. Where we once might have questioned the *mise-en-scène* or production design of Universal Pictures' earlier *Spartacus* (Stanley Kubrick, 1960), we did so because the photographic image that conveyed it was *beyond* question. Now, in *Gladiator*, the transition from digital to chemical image is seamless, and conventions of representation are hidden by a perceived historical accuracy that is supported by the digital code used to turn the film's piecemeal set into a fully-rounded diegetic space.

The code

The key here is the code itself, or at least the intentions of the programmer. CGI responds to directions given it by its program. This makes it contiguous with, rather than separate from, chemical photography. If we understand that every intervention with the technology of image-making is a coded act as part of a system of meaning, then that leads us to the inevitable conclusion that photography in every form responds to a series of codes, from the chemical or digital/industrial, to the economic/industrial, to the socio-economic, to the social/ideological and so on. This is what the philosopher Vilém Flusser described as a hierarchy of programs, a chain of information in which each program that informs the image, from the optical program up to the ideological and beyond, responds to a wider metaprogram, to the extent that such a hierarchy is open at the top. All images, made using whatever apparatus, always replicate certain elements of meaning passed down through the technology: 'The structure of the cultural condition is captured in the act of photography rather than in the object being photographed ... choice is limited to the categories of the camera, and the freedom of the photographer remains a programmed freedom' (2000: 30–4). Each possible decision to be made is an element of a hierarchy of programs that no one person can grasp in its entirety. It is a 'black box' because the workings are hidden from us, and because we know merely 'how to feed the camera ... and how to get it to spit out photo-graphs' (2000: 27).

This idea clearly follows Louis Althusser's concept of Ideological State Apparatuses, institutions of state and culture that 'inform' an individual's ideological view of the world. Any image created is ultimately a snapshot of the ideology informed by these apparatuses: 'All ideological State apparatuses, whatever they are, contribute to the same result: the reproduction of the relations of production ... The communications apparatus [does so] by cramming every "citizen" with daily doses of nationalism, chauvinism, liberalism, moralism etc' (1971: 146). As photography has developed it has adopted the characteristics of representation desired by its users. The aesthetic desires of earlier photographers have formed the very shape and technical specifications of the camera and the photographic image. Flusser therefore formed a desperate vision of photographic culture in which the technical or guaranteed image hides our reliance on the ideological concepts behind image-making: we still believe in our own autonomy. Whilst all this might seem far removed from the apparently benign new capabilities given to representation by the onset of CGI, Flusser treats the difference between the chemical and digital image as inconsequential to his overall view of photography as an apparatus responding to a hierarchy of programs. Whilst the technology of the image changes, the tenets of representation remain the same. Behind *Gladiator*'s 'fidelity' lies a program to which it is being faithful.

Gladiator's fidelity is a veridical depiction of ancient Rome, as if it were photographed. *Gladiator* therefore uses the arbitrary nature of the photochemical image to reinforce its digital one. Scott McQuire has suggested that the seamlessness of CGI puts the fidelity of the photographic image under pressure, since it can be seen to alter its very nature (1999: 385). On the other hand, as the CGI image is revealed as more abstract a representation (that is, created more or less entirely through simulation), so it elevates the status of the chemical image as a faithful record of a state of things. This in turn validates the strenuous efforts in CGI to mimic it. Complex shots of grand spectacle, such as when we 'hover' over the Coliseum, demonstrate this from two perspectives. The independent movement of animated figures raising the velarium (the canvas awning) gives a sense of veridical realism by presenting what appears to be the randomness of life. At the same time, the high angle mimics the often-seen 'blimp' shot that is a staple of major sports events. One element emphasises the attention to historical detail and the triumph of the animator, whilst the other 'camera reality' puts the gladiatorial games into twentieth-century context (as if to say 'it's as big as the Super-Bowl or the FA Cup Final'). Both are validated by the appearance of 'having been filmed' (McQuire 1999: 387).

The look of *Gladiator*

Gladiator's visual style is in fact based upon sources in classical painting after David, and in the Romantic or Academic style. Sir Lawrence Alma-Tadema's exacting standards in the depiction of classical architecture were a touchstone for production designer Arthur Max, who described his desaturated rendering of the Roman cityscapes as 'Black-Tedema' (sic) (see Magid 2000: 55). Similarly, the original pitch for *Gladiator* by executive producer Walter Parkes to Ridley Scott simply involved showing the director Jean-Léon Gérôme's *Pollice Verso* of 1872 (opposite).[1]

There is no Republican message explicit in *Pollice Verso*, and if his politics are discernible, they are so in Gérôme's many paintings of Napoleon Bonaparte throughout the 1860s (see Ackerman 1986: 78–101) – a passion for the Emperor that he shared with David. Gérôme executed Roman paintings throughout his career, mostly as excursions from his usual subject matter, the Middle East. What all his paintings share, however, is a deep ambiguity in his representations of the exotic. Even in his lifetime, Gérôme was criticised over the accuracy of his ethnography, and indeed it is difficult not to see his work as orientalist, in both the nineteenth-century and our own conceptions of the term. *Pollice Verso* exemplifies this ambiguity by combining a sharp attention to archaeological detail with an essentialisation of the Roman world into easily identifiable and characteristic moments. It acts as a 'mental snapshot' of Rome: encompassing all those things that appear as quintessentially

Figure 7 *Pollice Verso*, Jean-Léon Gérôme (1872)

Roman. This is no less a cultural interpretation than was David's. However, instead of painting a characteristic moment combining politics and mythology – as David connected patriotism with Republicanism – Gérôme simply paints something close to a Roman 'genre painting'. Ridley Scott picks up on the peculiar lighting of *Pollice Verso*, created by the canvas awning, for scenes in the African gladiator school. With cinematographer John Mathieson describing them eloquently as 'long knives of light', this visual reference allows Scott to demonstrate his trademark chiaroscuro lighting through dusty or smoky air (see Bankston 2000a: 44). An Empire aesthetic has remained in this sequence, but as in Alma-Tadema and Gérôme, the ideology appears to have gone; or at least gone under the surface.

However, if we can suggest that David's paintings might employ ideological tactics, then should we not suggest the same of the Scott's appropriation of Empire? In fact, this is something that is tacitly acknowledged by both Scott and Arthur Max. As Max admits: 'We copied them copying the Romans, which added an extra layer and another cultural interpretation' (quoted in Magid 2000: 55). This is most evident in the scene of Commodus' triumphant entry into Rome. The influence in this sequence of Leni Riefenstahl's film of the Nuremburg rally, *Triumph des Willens* (*Triumph of the Will*, 1935), is acknowledged by Scott and Max, and Mathieson used a desaturated image to mimic 1930s newsreel footage (see Bankston 2000a: 44). Partly made in an effort to incorporate a vocabulary of 'big' that was demanded by Scott, the sequence also serves as an audience shorthand for the development of the character of Commodus' regime – and of Commodus himself – as one of totalitarianism or even fascism.

Figure 8 Russell Crowe in *Gladiator* (2000)

The above examples demonstrate the two different lives that an apparently arbitrary or veridical image can have: the photographic image is employed on a stage set to create an atmospheric but otherwise realistic impression of heroic death, and the same seductive image, albeit a CGI composite, to make a metonymic point about despotism. Beauty and ideology merge seamlessly, creating an ideological ambiguity that mirrors a technical one: that of the creative use of the realistic image.

A matter of economics

Grossing over $450 million and boasting over 4 million DVD sales,[2] *Gladiator*'s economic success owes a certain amount to the ways in which its CGI technology was employed to seduce an audience that had shown little recent interest in the Roman genre. The period of time since the last major studio production, *The Fall of the Roman Empire* (Anthony Mann, 1964), might also have suggested that interest in the genre had all but disappeared. Even after *Gladiator*'s appearance, reviewers still struggled to contextualise a film that appears to have come from the graveyard of film genres, with *Variety* describing *Gladiator* as a sort of 'ancient Roman [WWF] "smackdown"' (Gray 2001).

All of this suggests a gamble for DreamWorks SKG, the film's principle production company, to take on a genre that had not seen its heyday since the 1960s. DreamWorks has been forging a reputation for standard fare, exploiting its expertise in special-effects, including science fiction (*Galaxy Quest*, Dean Parisot, 1999), horror (*The Haunting*, Jan De Bont, 1999), and animation (*Shrek*, Andrew Adamson and Vicky Jenson, 2001). However, the same expertise has also been instrumental in the recreation of 1930s Chicago in *Road to Perdition* (Sam Mendes, 2002), and helped turned an English backlot into a World War Two-ravaged Europe in the company's highly successful joint television venture with the BBC and HBO, *Band of Brothers* (2001). It is possible to assume then, that DreamWorks' interest in the Roman epic was assured by more than the narrative: if the generic attraction of the epic did not hold up in the theatres, then the attraction of CGI itself would help the film recoup its financial outlay.

The classic picture we have of Hollywood economics is of big-budget mass-appeal films that combine a number of derivative (and therefore 'safe bet') audience-pleasing elements such as major stars, a spectacular or highly-finished visual style, and obvious and desirable merchandising opportunities. Justin Wyatt suggests that this view of Hollywood investment in high economic returns achieved from a combination of 'an emphasis on style and an integration with marketing and merchandising' – dubbed "high concept" – is both a critical *and* industrial principle (1994: 7). Albeit a crude distinction, 'high concept' refers to films with essentialised or transparent narratives which can be pitched to both financial backer and audience in a few words, which exploit collective audience knowledge of 'pre-sold' elements such as stars and genres, and which have a high potential for economic return through distributive industries. In opposition we might offer here the notion of 'low concept' films, appealing mostly to niche audiences and having less potential for marketing integration. Such products might be perceived as having a higher intellectual content, or with production values that engage a discerning or educated viewer.

Given its excessive visual style, home entertainment sales and its Oscar success, *Gladiator* would appear at the outset to fall mid-way between high and low concept. For example, whilst *Gladiator* garnered an Oscar for costume designer Janty Yates – a sign of its perceived critical worth – the film undoubtedly develops its characters through visual style as well as through its acting. Commodus' appearance is highly stylised, with his oversized armour and darkly shadowed eyes often making him appear like silent-screen villain. Similarly, *Gladiator* is a test case for the development of distributive markets beyond the basic video and soundtrack sales areas. The *Gladiator* DVD was one of the first to feature a significant amount of extra-textual information on a second disc. Features including directorial and production commentaries appeal to the cine-literate, whilst features on the history of gladiatorial games reinforce the film's quest for historical fidelity. Whilst the home entertainment release is a staple of high concept market integration, *Gladiator* was also released as a 35mm print suitable for screening in upmarket IMAX cinemas. This paralleled by the commercial release of two soundtrack albums, the second of which includes remixes of the film's score that clearly nod to the dance-floor as well as the study.

The best example of this economic and critical ambiguity lies in *Gladiator*'s use of CGI 'restoration' as a pre-sold property. With veteran actors Richard Harris and Oliver Reed in only lesser roles, the film lacks the star quality that mainstream vehicles often rely upon. Instead, the CGI reconstruction of Rome, after the manner of the previous year's *Titanic*, provided the film with both a 'star' performer and a high concept byline that simplifies narrative appeal: What Hollywood did for the Titanic (and old Titanic movies), it does for Ancient Rome (and old Roman epics).

The original pitch to director Ridley Scott, which used Gérôme's *Pollice Verso* so effectively, easily fits the high concept paradigm. It was followed with the development of a look that could be easily 'read' by the both high and low concept 'audiences', and which could be summed up in a production concept (Black-Tadema) to ensure a coherent overall style. Finally, added to this is a further pre-sold element of action cinema as developed by DreamWorks' own *Saving Private Ryan* (Steven Spielberg, 1998). *Saving Private Ryan* had pioneered the use of specially adapted shutters with high-frame rates and hand-held cameras to heighten the immediacy of battle on screen. For Scott, the central aim in filming the early battle sequence in *Gladiator* was to follow the example of *Saving Private Ryan* by replicating its 'interpretation of what the experience would be like'. Describing the opening sequence of *Saving Private Ryan* as feeling 'absolutely real and documentary', Scott proposes that Spielberg 'raised the stakes … So now *we* have to go and raise the level' (quoted in Bankston 2000b: 52). This added a gritty appearance of realism to *Gladiator* complementing the opulent spectacle of other scenes. *Gladiator*, it appears, is a film that has it all.

Whilst *Gladiator* certainly had the action and spectacle elements suitable for attracting young, 'Saturday night' audiences, the style of the film and its subject certainly appeals to an older audience who remember the epics of the 1960s. For this latter audience is added the twin critical values of historical diligence and adherence to the nostalgia for the epic genre. The antiquarian and art historian Amelia Arenas, for example, praised the film's 'spectacular historical constructions' and compared it with her own experience of being taken as a child to see *Cleopatra* (Joseph L. Mankiewicz, 1963) as 'a lesson in ancient history' (2001: 1). These apparently academic roots appear to counteract the film's mass appeal to a young, multiplex audience (an assumption of its low intellectual value). *Gladiator* was seen by many as ideologically safe and even as educative, even though this did not challenge the spectacular attraction of Rome as developed in the 1960s epics. As Arthur Max admits, for most people, epics are 'what they know of Rome, they don't know what's down in the basement of the British Museum or the archives of Pompeii. If you're doing an epic film, you can't turn up with something academically correct and disappoint people' (quoted in Calhoun 2000).

Whilst all of this might ultimately suggest that we leave *Gladiator* where it sits between the values of high and low concept a lot depends on how we perceive the ideological consequences of mainstream cinema. For the educated – such as Arenas and architect N. S. G. Stern – the film's 'crimes' (such as having a twentieth-century populist plot, or making mistakes in historical accuracy) are forgivable because the film is, after all, a ripping good yarn. The high ground is taken as reviewers stamp their own concern for the protection of realism, whilst engaging in the otherwise base pleasures of cinema. Rather than being high or low concept, then, in an effort to attract as wide an audience as possible *Gladiator* is a high concept film relying on an image of itself as low concept in order to attract the middle-ground. It appeals to the educated *because* they can spot the inaccuracies of postmodern bricolage ('skyscraper Rome', 'Victoria's Secret corsets'), whilst simultaneously dismissing the story ('*Braveheart* in tunics') (Arenas 2001: 6; Stern 2000: 27).

For DreamWorks, the Roman world of *Gladiator* needed the appearance at least of verisimilitude, but also of a classical accuracy that can be taken on trust. All of this suggests a project that prized itself on its attention to detail and fidelity to a lived experience. However, the deep ambiguity that lies beneath the surface of this seamlessness is a result of the production's reliance upon a vocabulary of design *gestures* to create a film that, despite its producer's efforts to avoid clichés, 'wallows in the Roman look' (Thomson 2001: 19). As an unexpected return to a long-passé film genre, *Gladiator* offers crises of masculinity, extreme violence, sexual excess (and/or deviance), military efficiency, democrats and despots, high moral virtue and, of course, the Colosseum itself; everything that we have come to expect of epic films of Rome. As featured in the DVD commentaries, the obligatory Christians-fed-to-the-lions scene (which even appears in Gérôme) only ended up on the cutting room floor because it looked too unrealistic.

Ultimately, the attention to detail is something that is expected of Roman epics, in accordance with the studiousness of the academic painters to whom filmmakers and audiences alike look for visual and even moral inspiration. Fidelity is as much a gesture expected of Roman epics as is Caesar's thumb, verso or not. Here is an ambiguity of obsessive accuracy and cultural interpretation, and acceptance of the new (CGI) given credence by the old (history). In this case, we might ask whether or not the aura of the old, to use Walter Benjamin's concept, arrives from classical antiquity or nineteenth-century Romanticism.

Introduction

So, finally, it is time for an introduction: 'How do we get from Jacques-Louis David to Ridley Scott?' Exhibited for the first time at the 1785 Paris Salon, David's *The Oath of the Horatii* was a rallying cry for the radical pamphleteers who opposed the increasingly desperate French government of Louis XVI. These insurgents would have recognised, according to Thomas Crow, the connection between the control of things (and thus the economy) and the control of language and representation (1985: 222). David's painting spoke as revolutionary a language as the letters of Marat, or the cries on the barricades. This is an element of David's work that is often lost when we view his work with forgetful post-Classical eyes.

The painting's power is in the awkwardness of its representation: its inability to adequately resolve the dreams of antiquity and the passions of contemporary politics. It is scandalously republican because it eschews Romantic representations of the mythical past in favour of pantomime. Dorothy Johnson (1993) suggests that David adopted a radical style of painting, with awkward composition and a use of 'corporal' expression of the body that she describes as 'pantomimic'. This use of the 'corporal' was a unique form of expression not seen in the academy, but one later adopted as an overtly expressive form of body language. This 'corporality' that can be seen in later popular forms such as melodrama, which has always appealed to public rather than elite taste. As melodrama has become depoliticised, it has become accepted as an innocent bromide or sop, with no direct ideological ramifications. However, its overwhelming force lies in its ability to seduce the popular spectator through physical attraction, even if the overtness of the political method is less evident.

As Michelle Henning has noted, the modern-day blending of digital technology and the aura of photographic culture that already exists echoes David's use of academic rhetoric (the history painting) to criticise it (1995: 222). Form and content manage to blend seamlessly in *The Oath of the Horatii*. The radical style frankly opposes the academic style of aristocratic taste, whilst the aura of ancient Rome and its nobility provides this style with the courageous truth of unbending republican nobility. This allows David to revoke the classical themes of the academy but still manage to invoke the heroic themes of classical patriotism. As a source of inspiration, it seems, ancient Rome is infinitely adaptable.

But how does this work in contemporary depictions of classical heroism, and what does David demonstrate about *Gladiator*? Despite having no obvious political message within its text, the easy use of beguiling images of fascism has an obvious danger, whilst the use of design gestures to signify North Africa as exotic and barbarous, for example, echo Gérôme's careless Orientalism. This essay questions the implications of presenting technology and realism as politically and ideologically innocent: *Gladiator* is a seductive and even inspirational film because its historical accuracy and contemporary plot do not quite fit together. *Gladiator* takes its CGI to excess, as David took his gestures of the body, but where the eighteenth-century painter's message was open handed for all to see, the politics of *Gladiator* are as submerged in its contemporary image as is David's to our twenty-first-century eyes. *Gladiator* might ostensibly be based upon Alma-Tadema or Gérôme, attempting to inherit the trust placed in their academic or romantic vision, but in a haphazard way it is closer in fact to David's contorted spectacle and coded politics.

All of this suggests that we should be wary of any perceived difference between the chemical and digital image. Instead we should consider them as a single medium in the same way that they are often employed, seamlessly. Instead we should be prepared to investigate the social or ideological forces that inform the technical image, since it continues to be invested with authority through its abstract use of science. We should be prepared to see all photographic apparatuses, from the camera to the culture and beyond, as a black box, which is how the philosopher Vilém Flusser saw it. Only by admitting this do we stand a chance of breaking free of it, either as creators (Flusser's concern) or as academics, and of understanding its beguiling and seductive ambiguities.

Notes

1   'Pollice Verso' could mean 'thumbs up', but the consensus of opinion is that it means 'thumbs down'.
2   Figures for April 2001 (see Gray 2001).

Bibliography

Ackerman, G. M. (1986) *The Life and Work of Jean-Léon Gérôme: With a Catalogue Raisonné.* London: Sotheby's/Philip Wilson.
Althusser, L. (1971) 'Ideology and Ideological State Apparatuses (Notes Towards an Investigation)', in *Lenin and Philosophy and Other Essays*. Trans. B. Brewster. London: New Left Books, 121–73.
Arenas, A. (2001) 'Popcorn and circus: *Gladiator* and the spectacle of virtue (Re-emergence of Hollywood epics on classical themes)', *Arion – A Journal of the Classics and the Humani-*

ties, 9, 1, 1–12.

Bankston, D. (2000a) 'Death or Glory', *American Cinematographer*, May, 34–45.

_____ (2000b) 'Veni, Vidi, Vici: Interview with Ridley Scott', *American Cinematographer*, May, 46–53.

Calhoun, J. (2000) 'Circus Maximus: Production Designer Arthur Max Takes Filmgoers to the Arena in *Gladiator*', *Entertainment Design*. Available online: http://entertainmentdesign-mag.com/ar/show_business_circus_maximus_production/index.htm (12 January 2003).

Crow, T. E. (1985) *Painters and Public Life in Eighteenth Century Paris*. New Haven: Yale University Press.

Flusser, V. (2000 [1983]) *Towards a Philosophy of Photography*. Trans. A. Mathews. London: Reaktion.

Gray, T. M. (2001) '*Gladiator* reaps Oscar spoils', *Variety*. Available online: http://www.findarti-cles.com/cf_0/m1312/7_382/73236255/p1/article.jhtml (12 January 2003).

Henning, M. (1995) 'Digital Encounters: mythical pasts and electronic presence', in M. Lister (ed.) *The Photographic Image in Digital Culture*. London: Routledge, 217–35.

Johnson, D. (1993) *Jacques-Louis David: Art in Metamorphosis*. Princeton: Princeton University Press.

Magid, R. (2000) 'Rebuilding Ancient Rome', *American Cinematographer*, May, 54–9.

McQuire, S. (1999) 'Digital Dialectics: the paradox of cinema in a studio without walls', *Historical Journal of Film, Radio and Television*, 19, 3, 379–97.

Stern, N. S. G. (2000) 'Great Caesar's Ghost: Whose Version of History is *Gladiator*?', *Architectural Record*, 7, 27.

Thomson, D. (2001) 'The riddler has his day', *Sight and Sound*, 11, 4, 18–21.

Wyatt, J. (1994) *High Concept: Movies and Marketing in Hollywood*. Austin: University of Texas Press.

CHAPTER FOUR

Dangerous Metaphors and Meaning in Immersive Media

Martin Lister

There is a disarming notion that sensory immersion in virtual media environments can be understood as 'entering into' the space of an image. This experience of immersion is also characterised as 'stepping through a window', as the picture frame was conceived by the fifteenth-century theorist of perspective, Leon Battista Alberti. In either case we have a metaphor which immediately seeks to explain the nature of immersion by reference to perspective and the Western pictorial tradition. Yet, however serviceable and compelling this perspectival metaphor for media immersion seems to be, it stands in need of sustained scrutiny to test its explanatory sense. In what follows I attempt to do this and indicate a number of problems raised by this way of thinking about immersive media.

My starting point is the frequent invocation of 'renaissance space' in discussions of the significance of virtual reality (VR). In a much quoted passage, Jonathan Crary (1993: 1) suggests, that the transformations in visuality being brought about by computer-generated imagery (CGI), including virtual environments, are 'probably more profound than the break that separates medieval imagery from Renaissance perspective' and we are witnessing a 'narrative of the end of perspectival space'. It is the experience of this profound 'break' that is captured in one or another version of the phrase 'stepping through Alberti's window', arguably, the main metaphor for characterising immersion. The reference is to a practical method of perspectival depiction formulated by Alberti in 1435–36). However remote this reference to fifteenth-century theory may appear to be in the context of 'new media', we should note that it is also frequently used to contrast VR with media of the modern period: photography, film and television. We find clear Albertian echoes, for instance, when Mark Dery suggests that 'in virtual reality, the television swallows the viewer headfirst' (1993: 6). Margaret Morse also thinks of the television screen as a thin membrane between an immaterial world of symbols, a 'pocket of virtuality', and the material world from which we view it. She suggests entering a virtual environment is like 'being able to walk through one's TV or computer, through the vanishing point … into a three-dimensional field of symbols' (1998: 181) and virtual environments are, 'the last gasp of Renaissance space' where the VR user is a spectator whose 'station point is inside the projection of an image, transformed from a monocular and stationary point of view into mobile agency in three-dimensional space' (1998: 182). By invoking Renaissance space in this way, media immersion is actually being understood by reference to an earlier technology, one that has dominated Western visual culture for five hundred years: that of pictorial perspective. In making this connection between immersive space and perspectival space, perspective is being revealed as, amongst other things, a technology. A technology in the sense that its images were very often constructed with the use of machines and because the very concept of 'technology' strictly includes 'know-how' or the possession of knowledge and skill (see Mackenzie & Wajcman 1999: 26). At the same time, a radical difference or contrast, with perspective as its marker, is set up between all analogue media, ancient and modern, and the (post-modern) virtual and immersive.

The history that highlights such continuity is well known. It commences with the camera obscura as 'the very instrument for the mechanical production of monocular perspective'. Photography itself then becomes the means by which its images 'could be mechanically and chemically fixed, printed, marked and inscribed' (Neale 1985: 20). Camera lenses are designed and engineered to produce perspectival vision and were intended to do so from the very invention of photography. One of photography's pioneers, Nicephore Niepce, explicitly stated his aim as being to discover an 'agent' that would durably imprint the images of perspectival representation. This would no longer be a system of drawing but a machine, in particular, a lens. With the rapid spread of photography in the first decades after its invention, it was possible to conclude that as 'strong as the mathematical convention of perspective had become in picture making before the pervasion of photography, that event definitely clamped it on our vision and our beliefs' (William Ivins quoted in Neale 1985: 21). In short, the photographic camera industrialised perspective and naturalised the Cartesian conception of space which it anticipated. Some fifty years later, cinematography, utilising the photographic lenses in which perspective is inscribed, complicates the picture in many ways. In film the 'centred eye' of Albertian perspective is still at work but it is multiplied and mobile. It is (strongly or weakly) present as we look from our darkened cinema seats at the screen; with the camera in its movement as we look from some place within the 190-degree space depicted by the film itself, or finally, as we share the gaze of a character within the fictional world of the film narrative (as in the subjective shot/reverse shot).

The 'clamping' of perspective onto our 'vision and beliefs' by the once all pervasive photography now continues with CGI and the very software that is used to build virtual environments and the scenes of digital cinema. As Lev Manovich observes, 'the Cartesian co-ordinate system is built into computer graphics software and often into the hardware itself. A designer launching a modelling program is typically presented with an empty space defined by a perspectival grid ... the built-in world of computer graphics is an empty Renaissance space – the co-ordinate system itself' (2001: 254). Indeed, perspective and the related conception of Cartesian space appear with a prototype of VR. In 1968, the computer scientist Ivan Sutherland built a rudimentary apparatus and explained in his seminal paper, 'A head-mounted three-dimensional display', that its basic purpose was to 'present the user with a perspective image which changes as he moves' (1968: 757). The space the wearer of the helmet 'saw' and which shifted as they moved was generated mathematically. It was a three-dimensional Cartesian grid with its three spatial co-ordinates imaged stereoscopically on the binocular television screens held close before their eyes. Sutherland's work was part of the search for the ultimate interface with the computer, a transparent interface in which a seamless connection between the human sensorium and the machine would be established. This is an idea, later translated by pioneers of VR, into the strange notion of 'post-symbolic' communication; of communication without symbols (Lanier 1989: 118). We will need to return to this idea, but first, let us look more closely at the perspectival image which Sutherland took to be a step toward the ultimate human/computer interface, unencumbered by symbolic mediation.

Alberti conceived of vision as a pyramid of rays with their apex at the eye and their destinations at points on the surface of the object seen. He then showed how a perspective drawing or painting could be thought of as a plane intersecting this pyramid. This intersecting plane is both (i) the material surface of the painting, the picture plane, and (ii) a transparent window. The part of the pyramid 'behind' this plane is pictorial space; the world of the picture itself. A space that Michael Kubovy, a theorist of perspective, already calls a 'virtual space' (1988: 140).

In this configuration, the persons and objects that are depicted as occupying the picture space are seen from the precise point of view of the 'eye' where the rays of sight converge. Alberti's system gives this eye a location in the real world and places it at a precise distance and angle from the picture plane. The overall achievement of this system is to give the impression that the represented world behind the picture plane is continuous with the viewer's position in real space.

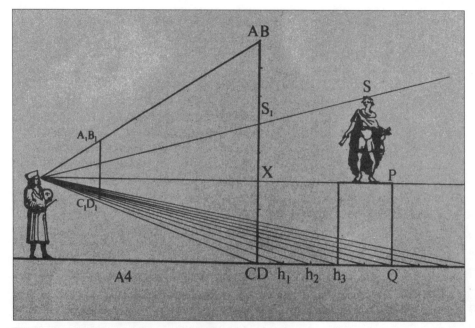

Figure 8 Diagram of Alberti's 'system'

SCREEN METHODS

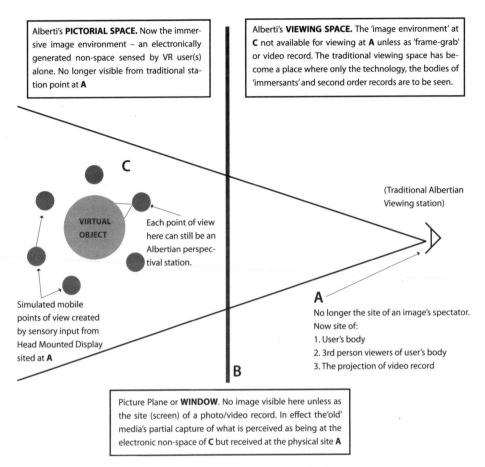

C

VIRTUAL OBJECT

Each point of view here can still be an Albertian perspectival station.

Simulated mobile points of view created by sensory input from Head Mounted Display sited at **A**

(Traditional Albertian Viewing station)

A
No longer the site of an image's spectator. Now site of:
1. User's body
2. 3rd person viewers of user's body
3. The projection of video record

B

Picture Plane or **WINDOW.** No image visible here unless as the site (screen) of a photo/video record. In effect the'old' media's partial capture of what is perceived as being at the electronic non-space of **C** but received at the physical site **A**

Figure 9 The condition of Alberti's 'window' when applied to immersive 'virtual reality'

In many paintings of the period, constructed with the help of Alberti's system, the point where the real space of the spectator meets (and becomes) the picture or virtual space is drawn attention to by placing depicted objects as if they were located at an edge existing between the spectator's and the painting's worlds. This frequently adopted convention is evidence and a kind of display of the painters' acute awareness of the significance of the method they were using.

It is instructive to see what happens if we take the diagram or schema that locates Alberti's window (and therefore the image) in relation to a spectator (see figure 8, opposite) and reconfigure in terms of VR. Figure 9 (above) takes the key elements of Alberti's method: the viewing station of the spectator (A), the picture plane (B) and the image or pictorial space (C) and uses them to consider what sense 'stepping through the window' could hold.

By looking at the three points – A, B and C – marked on the diagram we can observe the following. At point A, the position traditionally occupied by a spectator of an image, the user's or immersant's body remains. But, it is a body that cannot *see* the world it occupies. Its field of vision is wholly filled by the electronic stimulus provided by the small, binocular LCD screens held close to the user's eyes.

They are rendered blind to the world that they stand in and therefore they are also unable to establish their relationship to the virtual world that they see. In terms of the sociality of spectating (sharing the act and occasion of looking with others, especially important in the way we consume cinema and television, and once important in the way that paintings and prints were used as a basis of discussion and conversation) we should also recognise that the immersant is sealed off from others. At point A, there can be other viewers, but they will not be immersed in the image space but an audience for the VR event and apparatus. What they see is the immersant's body moving to the logic of a space that they, in turn, cannot see.

Point B is the site of the old picture plane or window; the material surface or substrate of an image. Nothing is left here. Rather than being 'stepped through' it is more accurate to say that it has dissolved. The extreme proximity of the binocular LCD screens that carry the image to the eyes of the spectator is such that no edge can be detected and no consciousness of the surface of the image be maintained. However, this picture plane or surface may be resurrected for the 'secondary' audience, via 'old' media (video or photographs) which partially capture, compensate for, and put into public space what is individually experienced in the virtual environment.

Point C (this could only be an imagined, notional point inside the traditional Albertian 'picture space') is now an electronically-generated environment; the virtual world itself. In many examples of virtual environments, perspectival images (of Cartesian space) survive here in the immersant's perception. They are mobile and dependent upon the immersant's point of view in a way that is reminiscent of perspectival lines of sight in cinema. This perceived and simulated reality at Point C is being generated and managed by technological extensions and data inputs to the human sensorium taking place at point A. This is the place where the spectator's body remains, and it is this experience of spatial dislocation that gives rise to the untenable idea that the VR user's body is split into two partial bodies! It may be better to entertain the idea that it is its sensorium that is split or, as Brenda Laurel has observed, in VR, you only get to take some of your senses with you (quoted in Coyle 1993). Whatever the case, at point C (within the image) there is no-body, partial or otherwise.

This closer inspection of the sense contained in the metaphor is also a partial analysis of spectatorship as it is structured by perspective (figure 8) and by immersive VR (figure 9). From this analysis we surely have to conclude the following: no 'stepping through' has occurred and no straightforward 'entry into the image' has taken place. However, three other things have happened. The spectator has lost sight of the frame of the image and they cannot gauge their embodied and physical relationship to its surface or the pictorial/virtual space that it carries and opens onto. The image surface, where the media producer deploys his or her symbolic language and conventions (by whatever technological means) has dissolved. Does, then, the act of 'stepping through' a window or 'into an image' makes any sense? VR may indeed lead to a new kind of relationship between spectators and images but it seems to be a very problematic relationship, which raises some difficult questions about immersive media. Let us now begin to define those problems in two ways. First, by considering the crucial question of what may be lost or 'left behind' (Crary 1993: 2) in the radical change that immersion brings. This means asking about the functions of the frame and the surface that immersion dispenses with. Second, we should remember that perspective is both a technology with which a certain concept of space is realised and, in Erwin Panofsky's (1997) phrase, a 'symbolic form'. We have seen that perspectival space, as pictorial space, is inseparable from the frame and surface of an image. What conception of space exits when they are no longer present? Finally, if perspective is a symbolic form – a means of conveying and expressing ideas – how is this function of images translated into a 'post-symbolic' immersion in a virtual world which aims to simulate our direct traffic with the real?

Frames

The physical picture frame begins to appear in the fifteenth century. Frames are coeval with the early development of perspective but also appear for social reasons concerning the ownership and functions of pictures. Pictures began to shift from being literally a part of walls to become smaller portable, often domestic, objects. Framed images or pictures, with their material substrates, are clearly in the same physical world as the viewer. They are a part of the everyday material world while being separated from it, as a special kind of object or event in the world, by the convention of the frame. Frames mark out spaces of representation and surfaces which invite imaginative projection. They are not confined to paintings and photographs, we might also note: the proscenium arch of the theatre, the edges between the cinema screen and the darkness which surrounds it, the physical limits of the television screen, the edge between glass and plastic. Indeed, the covers, title and end pages of a novel perform a similar framing function; within them imagined worlds are represented, outside of them the real world extends. There are also temporal frames: the occasions for telling stories in the communities of oral cultures, the serialised narration of drama on radio, or the allotted 'bedtime' story. We can even think of carnivals and festivals as occasions which are a combination of spatial and temporal frames as, on certain dates and within certain neighbourhoods, identities and behaviours are performed that are discontinuous with those we live in the real world. In all of these cases, the frame functions to distinguish the fictional, possible, rehearsed, imagined or desired (all passing here as currencies of the virtual) from everyday physical and social reality. As Morse, following Christian Metz, reminds us, empathy and identification with the events on a cinema screen depend upon a 'sense of safety and distance in time and space' (1998: 19). It is the frame which marks out spaces in which the unthinkable, the terrifying or the transgressive can be explored from a position of safety.

Surfaces

The oscillation between *seeing the surface* of an image or *looking through it* has been crucial to our experience of visual media. Image-makers of all kinds know that the play and tension between erasing the picture surface and offering it up as a sight of sensual pleasure and reflection is a main source of our fascination with images. In new media discourse this is recognised in Jay David Bolter and Richard Grusin's (1999) twin notions of hypermediacy and immediacy which they see operating in the digital remediation of analogue media. This play between the surface and pictorial space, between the material and the virtual, is not only true of painting even if this is a paradigm case. Consider the acknowledged tension in movies – between the onward drive of a narrative sequence in which each image or shot has to be subsumed to the logic of the narrative, and the iconic image which film can also give us, as in the lustrous images of the modern 35mm print or the now lost technique of black-and-white cinematography of classical Hollywood – the tellingly named 'silver screen'. In the first case, the image passes relatively unnoticed as we are caught up in the temporal unfolding or diegesis of the characters' psychologies and actions. In the second, the narrative is punctured or arrested by the single image held before us on the screen, for as long as a director, with any kind of interest in sustaining narrative or temporal sequencing, may dare. Importantly, the qualities of the image surface, its materiality, its textures, lustres, grain, saturation, contrasts, configurations, design and its intertextualities, are a condition and a source of pleasure and identification for both the reception of art and the consumption of popular media (see Bolter & Grusin 1999: 6).[1]

Space

In its developed form, the pictorial space which perspective constructs is far more than a three-sided, gridded box in which objects can be deployed, diminishing in size in a schematic manner. It has a density, it has a presence between the objects that 'fill' it. As Panofsky understood, 'perspective … creates room for bodies … and yet at the same time it enables light to spread out in space and in a painterly way dissolve bodies' (1997: 67). This kind of space existing on the far side of Alberti's window is not, however, the kind we enter in VR. In VR we are not in Alberti's space but another kind of space, what Panofsky called 'aggregate' space.

Lev Manovich has discussed the usefulness of concepts developed by the early-twentieth-century historians and theorists of art, Erwin Panofsky and Alois Riegl, for thinking about the space created in the virtual worlds of computer games. Using Panofsky's concepts of 'aggregate' and 'systematic' space, and Riegl's notions of the 'haptic' and the 'optic', he asks 'What kind of space is virtual space?' In 'aggregate' space, as exemplified in the remains of fresco images produced in ancient Greece, each depicted object exists, as it where, in its own discrete envelope of space. Space becomes a product of each individual object's rendered presence or a collection of such presences. This is distinguished from 'systematic' space; precisely the kind of represented space achieved by the artist/mathematicians of the fifteenth century, as they developed Alberti's construction of perspective. This is an 'infinite, homogeneous, isotropic' space (Manovich 2001: 254) that is established prior to the objects that are placed within it and whose appearances are determined by it. In Riegl's terms, such space is the result of 'optic perception', which 'unifies objects in a spatial continuum' while 'aggregate space' is the result of 'haptic perception' which 'isolates the object in the field as a discrete unity' (2001: 253). Computer-generated virtual worlds, argues Manovich, 'are actually more haptic and aggregate than optic and systematic'. Such virtual spaces, created by the layering techniques of computer animation or 3D polygonal modelling, have no spatial density, no spatial medium. They are collections of objects outside of whose boundaries there is a vacuum. So what is missing from these virtual worlds is 'space in the sense of a medium' where objects and the space in which they exist are rendered inseparable. This is a concept of space exemplified in the work of many modernist painters where space itself is depicted and 'occasionally hardens into something that we can read as an object' (Manovich 2001: 255).[2] At this time, the development of such an active sense of space, a 'space-medium' is something that computer graphics and VR do not construct or hold.

Symbolic form

Earlier, we met the idea that in immersive VR we enter a realm of 'post-symbolic' communication where no symbolic forms or signifying codes intervene or mediate between the spectator and image. (Or, alternatively, where simulation replaces mimesis as the virtual world in question refers to no prior existing reality.) However, perspective, the technology of representation which immersion is thought to exceed and invert, is more than a technology. In Panofsky's phrase it is also a 'symbolic form'. This is especially interesting in the present context, because as perspectival images achieved a higher level of optical realism or verisimilitude, and rendered the picture plane or surface more transparent than the medieval images they displaced and transformed, they too presented problems for artists. As Panofsky shows in his detailed research, perspective became a symbolic form through the efforts of the fifteenth-century artists *for whom it was a new technology*, to solve these problems in pursuing their communicative and expressive purposes. It is arguable that, in the same way, far from being 'post-symbolic', VR must also find its symbolic means, its conventions and signifiers, whether they be adopted from other media practices (as re-mediations) or are newly developed over time.

It is in 'Perspective as Symbolic Form', originally published in 1927, that Panofsky demonstrates how perspective is more than a geometry or a mathematics of pictorial space. Perspective is not only a way of constructing pictorial space or modelling the processes of vision, but is also a means of expressing ideas in visual form. He begins by noting the expressive or communicative problem which perspective presented to artists. In a second essay, 'Perspective in Early Netherlandish Painting', he shows how the problem arose from the manner in which perspective worked to construct a unified space. A space which begged to be lit coherently and coloured naturalistically rather than according to the logic of symbolic significance, where the size and prominence of depicted objects was determined by their position in the unified and continuous space rather than their conventional, widely understood symbolic importance. In this way, for artists who were skilled at arranging icons and symbols laden with conventional meaning on flat surfaces, and for whom space, depth and volume were treated differently in various parts of the picture, perspective caused considerable representational problems. The problem for painters was how to mark out what was significant in an image when matters such as size, scale and appearance were determined by a degree of perspectival naturalism instead of symbolic importance. For spectators, the other side of the problem was how to discern what was significant and what was not?

There is no space here to even review the solutions that artists found to these problems. Such a task would, after all, amount to an account of a large part of the history of Western representational art. Neither would there be any point. The real point is to note that if media immersion is a profound shift in visuality as important as the emergence of perspective itself, and is as poorly understood as our pressing of the 'stepping through' metaphor suggests, then the range of problems facing meaningful production with immersive media may be greater than those which faced early Renaissance painters. If Alberti's metaphor fails us in one way, in another it at least points us to a body of thought about art, media and images which will have to be emulated in getting to grips with media immersion, actual or promised. While they have been our reference points in this essay, what is at stake here is not a conservative aesthetic judgement on the relative qualities of Renaissance or Modernist art, cinema or emergent forms of immersive media. The question is one of what work images do in a culture and how, quite practically, they will do it.

Notes

1   Yet as Morse notes, complicating matters further, how will new symbolic conventions be discovered? For artists and experimental producers of virtual environments a practical barrier stands in the way of finding solutions to this question. At present, at least, the intense and expensive work entailed in constructing VR, together with their short duration means, amongst other things, that it is difficult to accrue experience from one experiment to another. 'Virtual environments are produced like packages that are designed without knowing what they might hold on the inside. In a field where the lore of veterans is non-existent and where conventions are invented ad hoc as one goes along, even the artists ... could not be sure what to expect once the machine or "environment" ... was finished' (Morse 1998: 200). This is not the only practical problem, for if the massive computing power needed to run a VR work can only be achieved for brief periods and the work subsequently exists only as memory (the users and the computers, and as video documentation) how will we ever arrive at answers?

2   I may have problematised the notion of 'entering into the image' but I must of course accept that immersive VR *does* operate without frames and surfaces. While, in my second category of immersive screen-based forms, images continue to be framed and have perceivable surfaces they are significantly weakened. As noted above, even the surface of the traditional television image is weak, 'a thin membrane' rather than a sensuous surface, and the problems of framing the immense, immersive images of IMAX cinema, with implications for the filmic conventions that can be used, has been noted elsewhere (Allen 1998: 115; Lister *et al*. 2003: 145).

Bibliography

Alberti L. B. (1966 [1435–36]) *On Painting*. New Haven, CT: Yale University Press.

Allen M. (1998) 'From *Bwana Devil* to *Batman Forever*: technology in contemporary Hollywood cinema', in S. Neale and M. Smith (eds) *Contemporary Hollywood Cinema*. London: Routedge, 110–29.

Bolter J. D. and Grusin R. (1999) *Remediation: Understanding New Media*. Cambridge, MA and London: MIT Press.

Coyle R. (1993) 'The genesis of virtual reality', in Philip Hayward and Tana Woollen (eds) *FutureVisions: New Technologies of the Screen*. London: British Film Institute, 148–65.

Crary, J. (1993) *Techniques of the Observer: On Vision and Modernity in the Nineteenth Century.* Cambridge, MA and London: MIT Press.

Dery, M. (1993) *Culture Jamming: Hacking, Slashing, and Sniping in the Empire of Signs.* Westfield: Open Media.

Kubovy M. (1988) *The Psychology of Perspective and Renaissance Art.* Cambridge: Cambridge University Press.

Lanier, J. (1989) 'Communication Without Symbols', *Whole Earth Review*, Fall, 118–19.

Lister M., J. Dovey, S. Giddings, I. Grant and K. Kelly (2003) *New Media: A Critical Introduction.* London and New York: Routledge.

Mackenzie D. and J. Wajcman (1999) *The Social Shaping of Technology.* Buckingham and Philadelphia: Open University Press.

Manovich L. (2001) *The Language of New Media.* Cambridge, MA and London: MIT Press.

Metz, C. (1982) *The Imaginary Signifier: Psychoanalysis and the Cinema.* Trans. C. Britton *et al.* Bloomington: Indiana University Press.

Morse M. (1998) *Virtualities: Television, Media Art, and Cyberculture.* Bloomington, IN: Indiana University Press.

Neale S. (1985) *Cinema and Technology: Image, Sound, Colour.* London: British Film Institute.

Panofsky, E. (1997 [1925]) *Perspective as Symbolic Form.* New York: Zone Books.

Sutherland I. (1968) 'A head-mounted three-dimensional display', *Joint Computer Conference, AFIPS Conference Proceedings*, 33, 757–64.

CHAPTER FIVE

Sound and Empathy: Subjectivity, Gender and the Cinematic Soundscape

Robynn J. Stilwell

When George Lucas remastered and reissued the *Star Wars* trilogy in 1997, most of the media attention was given to additional scenes and improved special effects.[1] Yet in interview after interview, Lucas reiterated that the improvement in sound production was the driving force behind the desire to revisit the films released twenty years earlier. Similarly, Wolfgang Peterson's 'director's cut' of *Das Boot* (1997) not only restores scenes cut from the television mini-series for the original film release, but also has an extensively revamped soundtrack, including all-new sound effects and a new digital underlay of the musical score. Examples like these are proof in action of an extraordinary thing about the film soundtrack – the gap between its importance to the cinematic experience and the development of its technology, and its relative neglect in the reception and study of cinema.

Even the term 'soundtrack' is misunderstood. For most people, 'soundtrack' means a film's musical score. Yet music is only one of the three main constituents of the film soundtrack: the others are speech (generically termed dialogue) and sound effects. Like the red, green and blue which combine to form the process colour of the film's image, dialogue, sound effect and music together form the film's soundscape, an inclusive term I prefer to use because of this misunderstanding of 'soundtrack'. It also lays a connotative substrate for the geography of cinematic sound, while shifting emphasis from the technological to the perceptual, which is the focus here.

Although the study of film sound has been slowly gaining ground in the past twenty years and several useful anthologies have appeared (*Yale French Studies* 1980; Weis & Belton 1985; Altman 1992), alongside several scholarly books on sound's specialised subset, music (of which Goberman 1987 is the first and still most important), the position of sound within the field of film studies is still marginal. It is possible for undergraduate and even postgraduate courses to ignore sound with impunity, and sound is often missing from general texts on the subject (although this is improving year on year). Even more narrowly focused studies of genres or individual films may omit sound and/or music whilst still making some claims to comprehensiveness. At major international film conferences, with multiple sessions over several days, papers on sound – let alone music – can be completely absent, and few people notice. Having dedicated sessions may improve visibility, but it also reinforces marginality by being separate and easy to skip.

My purpose is not to argue primacy of the aural over the visual experience, or even equality, but an importance that is easily the equal of such components as lighting, design, camera angles and editing and therefore needs to be integrated into the study of film as these other elements have been. In this essay, I would like to bring sound back from the margins of Film Studies, at least for the moment; sketch the ways in which sound, subjectivity and gender are mutually implicated (though rarely overtly) in psychoanalytic film theory; and take a particular film, *Closet Land* (Radha Bharadwaj, 1990), in which these factors are unusually foregrounded.

The marginality of sound

While no one would consider separating the image into red, green and blue for study, the separation of dialogue, sound effect and music is marked in film literature. Undoubtedly that analogy is exaggerated; there are fundamental phenomenological reasons why sound is segregated into dialogue effect and music. Although all of them are the product of acoustic waves, just as colour is the product of light waves, they are in some ways less divisible into their constituent parts than colour: red light has a different wavelength than blue light, while a violin, a human voice and a police siren may all occupy the same range of acoustic wavelengths. They may be distinguished by amplitude (volume), direction, timbre (tone colour) and duration. While the first two of these may be erased by the cinematic apparatus – reproduced sound can be manipulated in volume and projected from whichever speaker in the auditorium the sound engineer desires – it is in the continuity of sound, its rises and falls in pitch (wavelength), and its harmonics (the subsidiary vibrations that give a sound its particular timbre) that we identify the source as a musical instrument, a voice or a police siren. As human beings learn to listen to and comprehend sound, not merely receive (hear) it passively, we learn to distinguish and hierarchise sounds. The effect is sometimes referred to as the 'cocktail party' effect – amid the din of voices, clinking glasses and music, we can concentrate on the voice of the person talking to us, or even cue into someone across the room who mentions our name or a subject which interests us.

A similar process allows us to interpret the cinematic soundtrack. Typically, we prioritise the dialogue, as a bearer of the narrative, but the occasional sound effect may catch our attention with new information. Music tends to remain a subliminal signal for most audience members as is intimated by the title of perhaps the most significant book yet on film music, Claudia Gorbman's *Unheard Melodies*. In reality, of course, the music is not really unheard: it is merely not apprehended with the same semantic precision as dialogue or even sound effects.[2]

The tripartite division of the soundscape is replicated academically, as the methodologies are quite divergent: music is the domain of the musicologists. Sound effects are usually taken up by those interested in the technology of sound reproduction in film. Speech can be split into dialogue (taken on by scholars of narrative or other literary or drama-based approaches) and the voice itself, which is primarily the province of the film theorist of a psychoanalytic bent. Very few scholars have taken on the entire soundtrack (Weis 1982 was an early exception), and even then the most prominent of those, sound theorist Michel Chion, has devoted separate books to his study: *Le Voix au Cinéma* (1992), *Le Son au Cinéma* (1994b) and *La Musique au Cinéma* (1995).

Subjectivity, gender and sound

Subjectivity is a complex concept, composed of multiple overlapping meanings, all of which bear, to some degree or another, a cultural coding as 'feminine', if only because of the deeply ingrained binarisms of Western culture that force gendered identifications of opposing terms. The multiplicity of 'subjectivities' can in itself be regarded as a 'feminine trait' because of these binarisms.[3] In experiencing a film, the viewing/listening subject is invited to take a position with regard to the film text. Film theorists Christian Metz (whose writings through the 1970s are collected in Metz 1982) and Jean-Louis Baudry (1974–75; 1975) turned to psychoanalysis to describe this positioning, positing the experience of film as analogous to dreaming. In classical cinema, therefore, the technical aspects of film that reminded viewing subjects (and for these theorists, the subjects were almost always exclusively *viewing* subjects) that they were watching a film – editing, for example, and camera angles – were naturalised to a high degree. Following from this came one of the most influential of film theories dealing with gender, Laura Mulvey's 'Visual Pleasure and Narrative Cinema' (1975), which theorised the 'male gaze' of cinema, stating that the camera creates a male subject position for the viewer, whether biologically/psychologically male or female, through the ego-gratifying identification with the male hero and the libidinal spectacularisation of the female body. One need not even buy the psychoanalytic trappings of such an argument to recognise the camera as an extension of male directors and male cinematographers working for an audience in which the male perspective is not just presumed but assumed to be the norm.

Sight is a means of exerting control; what we look at is an active choice. This is an illusion in film, as we are guided to see what the author(s) of the film text wish us to see. As Mulvey argues, the 'real' gazes of the pro-filmic look of the camera (the camera's framing of the real people [actors], scenery, props and so on being filmed) and of the audience at the screen are collapsed with the gaze of the characters at each other within the diegesis. Sound, on the other hand, forces a surrender of control; we cannot turn away. Closing our eyes only serves to intensify our experience of the sound because of lack of interference from visual input; putting our hands over our ears rarely shuts out the sound completely. The equation of active sight with masculinity and passive sound with femininity is uncomfortably easy, reinforced by the domination of sight over sound in culture, especially film.

According to Freudian theory, the male voice is that of the law; the female voice is reduced to meaningless babble, incoherent sound or – significantly – music. Mary Ann Doane (1999) uses the metaphor of the womb in describing film sound, a 'sonorous envelope' surrounding the spectator. Doane draws on French psychologist Guy Rosolato, who draws on Lacan, who is in turn based in Freudianism. The terminology changes, but the female-identification of the features associated with sound remain.[4]

The psychoanalytic feminine, even in its most benign form, is always shot through with violently negative feelings and irrationality; it is also associated with sound. From biological womb sounds to the mother's voice (replete with music, nonsensical baby-talk and lullabies), to film sound, feminine sound is elided similarly to the way Mulvey describes the collapse of the male gaze. Yet the experience of a film is still dislocated in space, split between the visual image projected on the screen at some distance from us, and the sound which envelops and even literally touches us as the air vibrates in sympathy with the speakers to transmit the acoustic waves which give us 'sound'. This split reinscribes the visual as masculine and the aural as feminine, and this welter of gendered factors works to overdetermine a close relationship between sound and the feminine subjectivity.

The subject position and the geography of the soundscape

Experiencing a strong identification with a character in the film places us in another's subject position, creating an emotionally empathetic response. Film has many ways of coaxing the audience into that position, from character development, narrative discourse and events, to the more 'visceral' point-of-view shot compositions and sound design.

Because of its intimate relationship to our real, physical bodies, via the vibrating air, sound seems more immediate. It does not need the same structuring composition as the image, which is not to say that it is without structure. In a modern cinema, the sound literally surrounds us with speakers all around the auditorium, 'reconstructing' a naturalistic acoustic picture which has direction that can even be partially reproduced by a moderately good home-theatre system. But even before the cinematic apparatus was so adept at creating this acoustic picture, experience of the real world allowed the audience to construct a simulacrum via the image. As Michel Chion has pointed out, the coming of synchronised sound created space beyond the depicted image, by creating a space 'off' from which sound may emanate if we do not see it within the frame (1994a: 83–4).

While vision creates a 'there', locating an object in space separate from (though obviously in relation to) one's own subject position, sound creates a 'here', or rather a 'there' + 'here'. Two points in space, the object and the subject, both separated and connected by the vibrating medium which transmits the sound. We create a geography of sound with our subject position always at the centre; to make an analogy to the visual, it is our 'point of audition'. Chion makes the distinction between the spatial and the subjective senses of this term, and points out that it is often impossible to speak of a precise 'spatial' point of audition (he proposes a 'place' or a 'zone' of audition; 1994a: 89–92), but the exploitation of the point of audition in film is perhaps more common than the point of view, though it is usually just as intermittently used. It is commonly called 'subjective sound' and is frequently associated with female characters. The classic examples cited by most historians are both from Alfred Hitchcock. In *Blackmail* (1929), a young woman who stabs a man who tried to rape her bears only the word 'knife' in an innocuous kitchen conversation; in *Psycho* (1960), the audience eavesdrops on the voices in Marion's head as she drives away from the scene of the crime. Once again, while point-of-view puts us in the subject position of a character in control, point-of-audition puts us in the subject position of a character who has lost or is losing control. The possibility for unease is far greater than with point-of-view because we must relinquish even the illusion of control. It is perhaps significant that *Closet Land*, a film about a woman struggling with a man for emotional and psychological control, is so dependent upon sound for its effect on the audience. It is also a film in which the spatial point-of-audition is unusually precise and reinforced by the extensive use of subjective sound; the two types collude to place the audience in the woman's physical and emotional subject position.

Closet Land

Closet Land has been criticised for being 'uncinematic': by that, the critics mean that it seems too much like a photographed play.[5] After all, it takes place in one room (or does it?); and it has only two characters (or does it?). It is highly stylised, taking place in a nameless country at a nameless time, the characters merely identified as 'the Woman' and 'the Man'. Despite this abstraction, the film seems to have a profound effect on the viewer.[6] I would like to propose that one reason for this is the subject position constructed by the soundscape.

The soundscape is unequivocally cinematic; this is a 'filmed play' that could never take place in real space because there is only one space that the audience can inhabit and that is the Woman's place. Except for one brief moment, the entire soundscape of the film is generated from the female lead character, both from her psychological subject position and her physical point of audition. The power of this positioning may even undercut the psychoanalytically theorised visual spectacle of the passive Woman, which is further undermined by her appearance. Small, delicate, her dark hair pulled loosely back in a braid, her feet bare, she has a Madonna-like quality, accentuated by her simple, white cotton nightgown; the high waist minimises the curves of her slight figure, freezing her in pre-pubescence, a symbol of her arrested sexual development.

As the opening credits are printed in white on a black screen, we are plunged into her physical place by the sound. From the ambient room tone and the echoes of steps and voices, we can hear that is a large room, empty and hard, probably cold; an electrical hum testifies to fluorescent lighting. The Woman is being handed over from a rough, gruff guard to the officer in charge. They are on either side of her, as the stereo effect makes quite clear, even though we will find out that this is an impossibility; an apparently 'realistic' sound is manipulated to deceive us as well as to force us into an unusually close identification with the Woman. The first visual image is also from her point of view. As her blindfold is removed, the light flares in her unaccustomed eyes – a sound of ringing crystal provides an aural homology to this blinding flash, momentarily overpowering other sounds – and gradually the face of her elegantly-clad interrogator resolves into focus. This visual/aural effect is repeated halfway through the film when she is blindfolded again.

Designer Eiko Ishioka created a high-tech interrogation room with classical columns, replete with optical illusions (the room is diamond shaped rather than square, the columns do not extend all the way to the ceiling, the floor tiles appear to have holes in them, the lighting is indirect and hidden). Everything, including the clothing, is in cool shades of black, white and grey – everything, that is, but for the brilliant blue lining of the Man's overcoat, which becomes a telling marker. Outside, a thunderstorm is audible throughout the film.

These are just some of the many symbols in *Closet Land*, a film that virtually demands a semiotic decoding. The film is itself a deconstruction of the act of deconstruction. The Woman is being accused of 'subliminal indoctrination' because her interrogator interprets the children's books she writes as politically subversive. 'Do you object to my interpretation?' he asks. 'No', she replies, 'but that's all it is, your interpretation. I can't control the messages people chose to find in my stories. There are people who get turned on by passages in the Bible.' When she suggests that her story, 'Closet Land', is merely a fairytale in which the usual element of horror – a witch, a dragon, a monster – is replaced by an everyday object – the closet – the Man laughs in disbelief, retorting, 'It's not a simple word, is it?', and proceeds to delineate the myriad possible meanings of the closet. He is right: the closet is not an everyday object in the story but he has got the interpretation wrong. The stereo-typical male=public/female=private split is realised in their interpretations: the story that he has interpreted politically is in fact symbolic of the Woman's sexual torment, brought on at the hands of one of her mother's literary friends when she was five years old and he used to molest her in the coat closet.

This revelation emerges as the two joust intellectually, occasionally physically, and the power gradually shifts. From the outset, the Man lets her know in no uncer-tain, if poetic and patronising, terms that he is in charge:

> I am in a small part of a large mechanism; that goes for you, too, but together we must seek the truth. I will help you to the best of my ability, but the brunt of the responsibility lies with you. Deliberate deceit will not be tolerated, although personally I may find your lies charming; inadvertent blunders will be treated with firm kindness, and you must trust me to determine the ratio of firmness to kindness. Your best hope would be to depersonalise what follows and not to look upon me as a foe, or yourself as a victim. Remember, we are both seekers of truth, and in this quest, I am your friend, philosopher and guide.

He is polite, even friendly, offering her some broth and his suit jacket for warmth; but he also plays cruel tricks on her, calmly taunting her with a cigarette after telling her about prisoners being burnt by cigarettes and playing a tape secretly recorded at her mother's deathbed. As he plays the tape, the sound of an agitated heartbeat pulses like a musical underscore, abruptly ending when he explains such procedures are 'government policy' – it is as if her heart stops when she realises how much trouble she is in. When she reacts by crying, the sound is unnaturally loud, acoustically 'wet' and reverberant, as someone crying would hear within her own head.

Richard Einhorn's underscore is minimal, both stylistically and in the time it takes up in the soundscape. The minimalist style helps create a musical texture which blurs the borders between 'music' and 'sound effect', creating an empathetic depiction of the Woman's emotional and physical states. The first musical fragment, which occurs as the Woman enters the room and offers her wrists to the Man for her handcuffs to be removed, is not highly distinctive melodically, as in a classical film score, but is both a source of musical gestures used throughout the film and almost a physical description of the Woman's sensations. A light heartbeat rhythm provides the bassline. A slightly syncopated arpeggio figure (which might seem accompanimental but which is used thematically in the underscore) may reflect an agitated state of mind, the jangling of nerves. The long-held notes of the flute's descending line create tension, intensified by the long, dissonant suspension of the A flat, finally but briefly resolved.

During the initial stages of the interrogation, the bursts of underscore are what might be described as 'heightened sound effects'. They are more obviously subjective, or empathetic, than the relatively neutral opening music. When the Man asks the Woman if she is menstruating, she is shocked, then outraged and refuses to answer; he calmly swoops in to kneel at her side, pinning her against the chair with one arm, and feels clinically beneath her nightgown. An outbreak of Taiko (Japanese)-style drumming provides an excellent outward expression of her panic and kinetic mimicry of her pounding heart and racing thoughts. Later, when he boxes her ears, a nauseating concoction of chimes, their ringing bent and spatially displaced through recording manipulation, gives a realistic aural depiction of the physical effects of having your ears boxed but is musically created.

But the Man's true deviousness is revealed when he blindfolds her for the second time and 'sends in' the gruff-voiced guard to knock her around. The gruff guard is merely another guise of the officer, as is the frightened fellow prisoner tossed at her feet to convince her to talk to the sensitive interrogator, the one who used to be a university professor, the one who plays the piano – the Man.

He can play all these parts because he is adept at manipulating sound. All three of his personae have distinctly different voices, different accents and different ways of moving. The guard has a rough bass voice and a slow drawl of indeterminate provenance; he wears heavy boots and moves like a bull in a china shop. The prisoner has a quavering, breathy tenor with a strong working-class London accent; he has no shoes and moves by dragging himself across the floor because he has been crippled by his torture. The officer has a clear baritone and a cultured (but not aristocratic) English accent; he is light on his leather-shod feet, at times moving as gracefully as a dancer. To the blindfolded Woman, they sound like clearly differentiated individuals. In one sequence, he is both the guard and the prisoner engaged in a brutal interrogation, swiftly turning from one position to the other (and moving strikingly in and out of a key light which strikes the prisoner like the clichéd lamp in a third-degree but leaves the guard in shadow). In another, he even has a tape of the prisoner being tortured so that he can talk to her in the guise of the guard over the recorded cries and whimpers. Heightening his deception is the technical manipulation of the soundtrack at the beginning of the film, already referred to. As the blindfolded woman is escorted to the interrogation chamber by the officer and the guard, their voices are clearly spaced in the stereo picture – the Woman in the centre, the voices of the 'guard' and the 'officer' on either side. For all the sound tricks in the film, this is the only one which, in retrospect, is impossible; the Man simply could not have moved from one side of the Woman to the other quickly enough – and more importantly, silently enough – to fool her. But it does have the effect of putting the audience off the scent and more importantly, plunging them into her subject position.[7]

Michel Chion has theorised the *acousmêtre*, or acousmatic being, who is heard but not seen; these characters often have striking 'powers' or 'gifts' because of their acousmatic existence: they see all, know all, are omnipotent and ubiquitous. Most acousmatic characters are revealed at some point during the narrative, as are Dr Mabuse, the Wizard of Oz and Norman Bates' mother. In each case the revelation is highly dramatic but also results in a defusing of their acousmatic powers (1994a: 129–31). In *Closet Land*, the security guard and the officer are acousmatic characters to the audience as well as to the Woman, while the prisoner is acousmatic only to the Woman. *Closet Land* may be the exception in which the character's power seems to grow – at least to the audience – with each new revelation, for we come to realise how all powerful – at least over the Woman – the Man is.

The Woman's strength in resisting the Man's interrogation techniques begins to wear him down. As she resists, her words ring in his ears; the one moment in the film in which the point of audition shifts from her to him, he experiences an auditory flashback while we momentarily see him outside the room, driving in his car in the rain. Distantly, he hears a male voice, possibly (one of) his, echoing her words, hinting that he had once been in her situation and had not only been broken but turned, something to which 'the prisoner' had already alluded.

The Woman has psychological walls forged by her experience as an abused child. She can escape his torture into the fantasy worlds she had created then that now provide the inspiration for her children's books, which in turn have brought her to the attention of the authorities. These escape sequences are depicted as animations that look like the illustrations for such books, and the ambient sound changes to delicate wind chimes and soft insect and bird sounds – all very quiet, but creating a definite sense of a change of space. That the Man is making some breach in her defences is indicated in an animation of her character 'the cat with green wings'. As he unfurls his protecting arms to enclose her, the cat's face is suddenly transformed into a fang-encrusted snarl and the insides of his wings turn to electric blue – the same colour as the Man's coat lining. But as she senses that the Man is breaking down, her defences are reinforced, and when the Man pulls out one of her toenails, she is able to call upon the cat, once more with the comforting wings, to fly down and carry her away through a portal that looks like the *trompe l'oeil* tiles in the floor. Unnerved by this escape, the Man drags the Woman into a closet off the main interrogation room. A particularly loud thunder clap emphasises the opening door, and a distinct shift in the ambient room tone changes our perception of the size of the space 'we' are in.

The Man hopes to break her but in fact he reveals himself, again through sound, by singing a nasty children's taunt ('Here comes the candle to light you to bed and here comes the chopper to shop off your head').[8] The nursery gothic of the chant resonates with the Woman's assertion that children's tales all have an element of horror in them. As the Woman recognises the tune and its implications, a man's voice is mingled with the tune played on orchestral chimes, and the whole is put through extensive electronic distortion, echoing and looping, creating an intensely subjective picture of the Woman's reeling mind. It is also the explanation for the flashes of a closet image, the distant sound of a man's voice and the similar playing of the 'chopper tune' on tubular bells during the earlier auditory maelstrom when the Woman's ears are boxed. This time, it is merely emotional shock that brings on the effect. She recognises the Man's singing voice as that of her literary molester, the man whose tortures on the child produce the resistance that the Woman uses to defeat the Man. In the end, on the verge of tears, the Man begs her to sign the confession to save herself. She takes the confession and rips it up, the white pieces showering over them both in slow motion after she tosses them into the air. As dawn lights the strip of windows above the columns, the Man opens the door for her and ushers her out, handcuffed, presumably to her execution. She may be the one to die but he is the one whose spirit is broken.

Preliminary conclusions

Sound – particularly hearing – is historically associated with irrationality and emotion, traits magnified by its subset, music; irrationality, emotion and music have all been associated with the feminine implicit in culture. This alliance is woven deeply into psychoanalytic theory, with positive but also profoundly negative implications for female subjectivity, and therefore into psychoanalytic film theory. Yet these associations, like the recognition of sound in the field of Film Studies, are almost always oblique and marginal to the main argument – much in the way femininity exists in the gaps and margins of masculinity in these theoretical constructs.

Probably because sound in film exists largely in a liminal (even subliminal) position, it can have an uncanny effect on the audience – uncanny in that the 'spectator' is usually less able to recognise and articulate that effect than a visual one. This is particularly true in the case of music, though the cinematic soundscape as a whole has an effect on the audience which is rarely considered. Because most of the major work on sound in academic film scholarship has concentrated on the technology or technological history of sound, or on the abstract, usually psychoanalytical theory of sound on the (viewing) subject, and because music, sound effects and dialogue have tended to be methodologically segregated, we do not have many examples of studies which bring these disparate items together (Fischer 1977 and Weis 1982 being two notable exceptions) and begin to illustrate how we actually experience film. Although we may discern and hierarchise the elements, and some people may in fact be more perceptive of various elements than others as a result of proclivity and training, we do all receive film sound acoustically and then phenomenologically as a dynamic soundscape, interacting within itself and the images and the narrative trajectory.

In the film industry, sound seems to be a greatest concern to those who produce big movies; we have come to expect teeth-rattling explosions and bombastic scores in modern blockbusters. However, sound can be even more intensely felt in intimate, quiet films, where the slightest whisper or silence can have a marked effect. Closet Land is such a film, a political allegory in which the sparse but complex soundscape highlights subjectivity in its multiple meanings, both internally and externally to the film text, and particularly regarding gender and geography and the cinematic soundscape.

Closet Land is a rare film in which the soundscape is equal, if not superior to, the visuals in constructing a subject position for the audience. As it happens, that subject position is quite atypically female. The soundscape is unusual, too, in the considerable overlap in the distinctiveness and function of two elements normally considered separate: sound effect and music. This elision creates sound effects more stylised than objective reality and more representative of subjective reality.

These conclusions are necessarily preliminary because the issues involved are so complex, crossing numerous disciplinary boundaries, from the acoustic to the psychological to the philosophical to the art-historical, and have so rarely been directly addressed. I am not so much interested in theoretical proof or 'truth' as the persistently gendered way in which sound (including music), subjectivity and the relationship between vision and audition are conceived. These are apparently so deeply ingrained in our culture that no amount of theoretical acrobatics can budge them, and thus must necessarily affect the way films are constructed and therefore the way we see and hear them.

Notes

1   This chapter appears in a longer version in K. J. Donnelly (ed.) (2001) *Film Music: Critical Approaches*. Edinburgh University Press.
2   A discussion of music and meaning is clearly out of the scope of this essay, as it one of the most intensely debated subjects in the field of musicology today. I shall therefore simply state my position: music does not have the same strong semiotic connection between signifier and signified as language does. However, there is a cultural consensus that music does have meaning, and there are enduring cultural connections between certain musical gestures and particular meanings, they often have a potential range of meanings that can be and usually are decoded by the listener.
3   For a further exploration of the gendered implications of these binary codes, see Robynn Stillwell (2003) 'Hysterical Beethoven', *Beethoven Forum*, 10, 2, 162–82.
4   Julia Kristeva theorises a womb space which is 'chaos': multiple, without reason but also paradoxically ordering the infant's basic drives and manifesting flashes of energy and rhythm. Kristeva calls this the 'chora', a term borrowed from Plato, yet in our present context it is hardly an 'innocent' choice. The term meant a space, but more specifically one where a chorus was trained or where a choral dance was performed. Music, therefore, sound, is always inscribed in the space (see Oliver 1997: 52).
5   See, for example, Daws 1991, Gilbert 1991, Honeycutt 1991 and Kehr 1991.
6   For strong anecdotal evidence, see the user reviews for *Closet Land* on the International Movie Database (http://www.imdb.com) to get an idea of the impact this film can have.
7   One might argue that Alan Rickman has one of the most distinctive voices in film and theatre, which resonates through the various disguises. However, this was one of his earliest films, limiting his familiarity with the audience.
8   This refrain comes from the children's chant 'Oranges and Lemons' which cites the different church chimes in London. The remarkable specificity of this nursery rhyme seems quite out of character with the rest of this highly abstract text.
9   My thanks to Peter Franklin, Nicolas Cook and Rachel Moseley for their helpful comments on earlier drafts of this essay.

Bibliography

Altman, R. (ed.) (1992) *Sound Theory, Sound Practice*. London: Routledge.
Baudry, J-L. (1974–75) 'Ideological effects of the basic cinematographic apparatus', *Film*

Quarterly, 28, 2, 39–47.

____ (1975) 'The apparatus: metaphysical approaches to the impression of reality', *Cinema, Communications*, 23, 56–71.

Chion, M. (1982) *Le Voix au Cinéma*. Paris: Cahiers du Cinéma.

____ (1994a) *Audio Vision: Sound on Screen*. Trans. C. Gorbman. New York: Columbia University Press.

____ (1994b) *Le Son Au Cinéma Cinéma*. Paris: Cahiers de Cinéma.

____ (1995) *La Musique au Cinéma*. Paris: Librairie Arthéme Fayard.

Daws (1991) 'Review: *Closet Land*', *Variety*, 11 March.

Doane, M. A. (1999 [1980]) 'The Voice in the Cinema: The Articulation of Body and Space', in L. Braudy and M. Cohen (eds) *Film Theory and Criticism: Introductory Readings*. Oxford: Oxford University Press, 363–75.

Fischer, L. (1977) 'Rene Clair, le million, and the coming of sound', *Cinema Journal*, 16, 2, 34–50.

Gilbert, M. (1991) 'Angst Consumes: *Closet Land*', Boston Globe (http://kelclancy.tgsolutions.com/reviews/cl-bgl.htm).

Gorbman, C. (1987) *Unheard Melodies: Narrative Film Music*. London: British Film Institute.

Honeycutt, K. (1991) 'Review: *Closet Land*', *Hollywood Reporter*, 316, 24 March.

Kehr, D. (1991) '*Closet Land*'s political prurience', *Chicago Tribune*, (http://kelclancy.tgsolutions.com/reviews/cl-ctrb.htm).

Metz, C. (1982) *The Imaginary Signifier: Psychoanalysis and the Cinema*. Trans. C. Britton *et al*. Bloomington: Indiana University Press.

Mulvey, L. (1975) 'Visual Pleasure and Narrative Cinema', *Screen*, 6, 3, 6–18.

Oliver, K. (ed.) (1997) *The Portable Kristeva*. New York: Columbia University Press.

Weis, E. (1982) *The Silent Scream: Alfred Hitchcock's Sound Track*, Rutherford, NJ: Fairleigh Dickinson University Press.

Weis, E. and J. Belton (eds) (1985) *Film Sound: Theory and Practice*. New York: Columbia University Press.

Yale French Studies (1980) special issue: Cinema/Sound, 60.

views

theory and method

Introduction

Karen Randell

This section brings together essays that use, to some extent, theoretical practices usual to film analysis such as psychoanalysis and queer theory or to literary theory such as post-colonial theory and adaptation theory. These essays give examples of ways in which these methodologies can be appropriated and re-visioned. In chapter six John Phillips offers an astute analysis of Catherine Breillat's film *Romance* and argues from the psychoanalytic model adopted by Laura Mulvey (1975). He asks whether the film promotes the interests of the female spectator by offering her the pleasures of an active female gaze and if so whether this induces 'fear of castration in the film's male characters'. Through the use of close textual analysis and drawing on the Freudian notions of voyeurism and scopophillia and Lacanian theory Phillips interrogates the film form and narrative of *Romance* questioning its address and exposing its 'potentially liberating' viewing experience for women in its address to the heterosexual female gaze.

Christine Cornea's essay focuses on issues of race in the contemporary science fiction/cyborg/martial art film. She draws on post-colonial theorist Homi K. Bhabha's work to interrogate the image of the cyborg in terms of race. As Cornea points out although there has been much academic discourse around the hyper-masculine white man/machine cyborg, very little attention has been given to racial issues. In particular, she concentrates on the 'straight-to-video' science fiction and cyborg film rather than mainstream works as they present a richer body of research for the representation of race, in the most part that of East Asian characters. This essay also moves beyond ideological discussions of race representation within the text and considers the economic factors of this type of low-budget DVD and video. In particular she considers the notion of 'Techno-Orientalism' within these high technology films in light of the increase in East Asian money in the American film industry. This multi-strand methodological approach enables a broader discussion of the issues around race and the constructed body.

Michael Williams adopts a methodological approach that critiques as it investigates. His reading of *A Room with a View* (James Ivory, 1986) articulates 'the potential for a "queer" reading ... but also the methodological problems that arise in considering such an undertaking'. His work 'privileges the "tingle" over the "actual"', that is, the feel for a camp reading of the film whilst also allowing other readings to be possible. Williams uses newspaper articles and reviews to construct the cultural surround of the film on its release. Combined with close textual analysis of several key moments in the film and an engagement with the critical debates already in existence (Monk 1995; Dyer 2002) this primary evidence suggests that the film has been open to several interpretations – none, as Williams points out, any less valid than the other.

Darren Kerr's essay on literary adaptations moves beyond the notions of fidelity to the original and discusses the character of Mr Hyde in terms of the development of this character over subsequent film adaptations between 1920 and 1942. Kerr considers the cultural and social changes that occurred during this twenty-two year period and in the period between the original publication of *The Strange Case of Dr Jekyll and My Hyde* in 1886 and its film adaptation in 1920. Combining a Cultural Studies methodological approach with close textual analysis of the three films enables a discussion of the construction of the pathological character that we are familiar with today. If Hyde's character in 1942 is not faithful to the book Kerr suggests that one needs to look outside of the adapted texts to discover why.

Monica B. Pearl argues in her essay that although *Philadelphia* (Jonathan Demme 1994) is a film that is concerned with AIDS it is its representation of race that may be more significant, or at least, more progressive. For Pearl the film does nothing to alleviate the common misconceptions about AIDS and HIV but it does, albeit unintentionally, 'combat and confront unaccepting attitudes and prejudices about race'. Through close textual analysis and an engagement with the critical debates concerning AIDS, Pearl constructs an argument that suggests the issues of race in this film displace the issues of AIDS, the very issue that the film seeks to address.

Michael Chopra-Gant interrogates issues of masculinity in his essay within a social framework of post-World War Two 'absent' fathers considering masculinity within a historical model rather than a subjective one. This non-essentialist approach to discussing identity requires a Cultural Studies methodology that takes into account discourses pertinent to the time of the film's release. This essay offers close textual analysis of four Hollywood postwar films combined with a discussion of contemporaneous discourses concerning the welfare and development of the child found in *Dr Spock* (1946) and lifestyle magazines. This empirical research enables a methodology that can move toward a fuller understanding of the issues and anxieties surrounding the integration of the returning veteran after World War Two.

This final essay marks a shift that is continued in the third section of this volume, from the idea of the spectator as generalised subject positioned by the film text to the idea of a viewer from whom opinions are sought and empirical evidence gathered.

Bibliography

Dyer, R. (2002) *The Culture of Queers*. London and New York: Routledge.
Monk, C. (1995) 'Sexuality and the Heritage', *Sight and Sound*, 5, 10, 33–4.
Mulvey, L. (1975) 'Visual Pleasure and Narrative Cinema', *Screen*, 6, 3, 6–18.

CHAPTER SIX

Masochism, Fetishism and the Castrating Gaze: Female Perversions in Catherine Breillat's *Romance*

John Phillips

Romance, directed by Catherine Breillat and released in 1999, has arguably been one of the most influential French films to obtain international distribution in recent years. Its reputation is largely due to the explicit representation of sado-masochistic activities, and also of male as well as female nudity, to the extent that it has been described as containing hard-core elements. While the film's focus on male genitalia may invite negative responses, especially from feminist critics, it may also be described as both novel and potentially liberating for the female spectator, in that it facilitates a heterosexual female gaze within the narrative. It may be said to generate a point of view, with which heterosexual women in the audience may identify. I want to explore this claim here.

On the surface, the film depicts a woman's quest for erotic fulfilment. However, unlike most previous treatments of this popular theme of male-centred erotic cinema, of which Just Jaeckin's *Emmanuelle* (1974) is probably the best known if not the best crafted example, the point of view represented appears to be unam-biguously feminine. With few exceptions, the film is shot in a succession of interiors, reflecting the inner world of the heroine, Marie (Caroline Ducey), whose internal monologues fill the voice-overs that accompany most scenes. These voice-overs provide direct access to Marie's point of view. This helps to distance the heroine and us from events surrounding her and to reinforce the role played in eroticism by fantasy. Certainly, then, the presence of this narrative voice enables women but also men in the audience to identify with the female protagonist on psychological, emotional and sexual levels.

But does Marie have a gaze as well as an orally expressed point of view? We remember that for Laura Mulvey (1975) only the male spectator experiences pleas-ure, through visual enjoyment of the female star, as he shares the voyeuristic gaze of the camera and the male star, with whom he identifies. Through this process, the male spectator is able to neutralise the castration anxiety that the female image always evokes: his sadistic voyeurism demystifies the female body, while his fetish-istic scopophilia turns it into a substitute for the missing phallus. The female spectator, on the other hand, has nothing to look at and no one to identify with. Since Mulvey's seminal essay, however, feminist film critics have repeatedly problematised the pleasure of the female spectator. 'Cinema' declares Mary Ann Doane, for example, 'is about woman, not for her. She is assigned a special place in cinematic representation but denied access to that system' (1992: 760). This is true also of one of the dominant critical discourses in Film Studies, psychoanalysis, which places the phallus at the centre of interpretation.

So the questions we need to ask at the outset are, does *Romance* promote the interests of the female spectator by offering her the pleasures associated with the female gaze, and secondly, if so, does this gaze induce fear of castration in the film's male characters? Emma Wilson certainly has no doubt that the film offers the female spectator a gaze with which to identify: *Romance*, she maintains, 'shows a woman, Marie, actively looking: the subject of her own desire' (2001: 151). The implication here is that the feminine point of view is determined by camera shots which at times represent the gaze of the female director and at other times adopt the gaze of the female protagonist. It is true that there are a number of seemingly voyeuristic shots of good-looking young men sporting erect penises. However, evidence of an explicit female gaze within the diegesis is problematic. This is hardly surprising since the voyeurism on which the erotically motivated gaze depends is essentially a masculine activity. As Louise J. Kaplan observes in her study of female perversions, 'Very few reported cases of compulsive sexual voyeurism are of women' (1991: 30).

Although the diegesis appears to construct Marie's relationship with her lover, Paul (Sugamore Stévenin), along active/passive lines, with Marie playing the active role and indeed assuming the voyeuristic position, in fact, her gaze is singularly unerotic, accompanied by little in the way of sexual excitement. She may seem to look at her male lovers, but displays no real enthusiasm for looking. In stereotypically female fashion, on the other hand, she is seen to privilege the tactile over the visual. She wants to touch her boyfriend Paul's penis, which denies even the female spectator a proper look, playing hide and seek, peeping shyly above the sheets and popping back into the safety of his boxers at the earliest opportunity. In the scene in which she has sex with Paolo (Rocco Siffredi), the Italian stud she picks up in a bar, his penis is erect and in full view, and Marie fondles him briefly to help keep it so, but her gaze remains downcast and pensively distant throughout. As for Robert (François Berléand), Marie's middle-aged and unprepossessing boss at the school where she teaches, bondage-fetishist and proud seducer of many thousands of women, his appendage stays mercifully out of sight.

In contrast, Paolo, Robert and any interested spectator are afforded plenty of lingering opportunities for the scopophilic enjoyment of Marie's pretty elphin looks and nymphet body (her tiny breasts and narrow hips suggest the vulnerability of a pubescent girl). Wilson concedes that the physical representation of Marie has voyeuristic potential, although she does her best to intellectualise a commercial imperative: 'This exhibitionist complicity itself works to trouble active and passive roles in viewing relations' (2001: 151).

Romance actually functions on one important level as a metatextual commentary on the very problem of the gaze: Marie's enchanting nakedness indeed represents complicity, but it is a complicity with male spectatorial pleasure. At the same time, Marie does not so much 'look at' as 'look for': she is positioned by the film narrative as a searcher. Marie's quest for sexual fulfilment which structures the entire diegesis becomes also a metaphorical quest for the missing phallus and an object lesson in the voyeuristic male perception of woman's castrating potential. As indicated in the discussion of Mulvey above, in a psychoanalytic perspective, the female body may always unconsciously evoke the threat of castration for the male. Marie's nymphet body augments her image as victim of castration. As we shall see shortly, Paul's negative responses to Marie seem to imply castration anxiety.

So the camera, the spectator and Marie herself look for the missing phallus as antidote to the castration threat posed, above all, by her biological identity as a woman. The fetish, suggests Freud, is a fantasy substitute for the missing penis in women (1977b: 351–2). In Marie's case, it is not any particular part of her body that the camera fetishises (perhaps because the director is a woman, not a man), but her entire body. Caroline Ducey's Kate Mossish figure, her small breasts and long slender legs, together with her frequent vertical positioning (especially in the bondage scenes), serve only to make her more phallus-like. But being the phallus is not enough for Marie, who wants to have it as well. In phrasing strongly reminiscent of Lacanian discourse, Marie teaches her class the difference between the verbs 'to have' and 'to be': 'to have is not at all the same thing as to be. You can be without having. You can have without being.' For Lacan, women are the phallus but cannot have it, while for men the reverse is true: in the Oedipal phase, as reinterpreted by Lacan, the boy goes from being the phallus to having it, thereby separating himself from the mother and identifying with the father.[1] Marie and the film itself set out to disrupt the system of sexual difference that this linguistic difference symbolically represents, but both are ultimately forced to recognise the impossibility of doing so. Marie is the phallus both physically and symbolically, but yearns to have it too by appropriating that of the men she encounters. In an obvious reversal of stereotypical gender positions, Marie 'hates guys who screw her', but is fixated on their cocks, which must be thick and hard – 'a thin cock's ignoble,' she declares. The contempt that Marie expresses for the less well-endowed male immediately foregrounds castration anxiety.

Marie's boyfriend, Paul, a male model played by an actor with girlish good looks, is shown as symbolically vulnerable to castration in the first scene of the film. There is a suggestion of his feminisation in the opening shot as he is made-up in a stereotypically feminine way for the photo-shoot. He is playing a matador, a sexually ambivalent figure: the bullfighter is phallically vigorous and erect, on the one hand, but his stylised movements, skin-tight pants and general theatricality introduce feminine notes. Perhaps to compensate for this undercurrent of femininity, Paul is instructed by the photographer to adopt an even more erect (or phallic) posture, whilst the female model at his side counterfeits a submissive feminine attitude. There is an implication here of uncertainty in Paul's gender identity. Moreover, the constructedness of this image of polarised sex roles is foregrounded to the point of parody, hinting that such gender fixity might be challenged in this film. Moments later the scene moves to Marie's and Paul's bedroom, which closely resembles a hospital ward, all brilliant white paintwork and antiseptic minimalism. The bed itself looks like a hospital bed. In it, Paul reclines watching television, while Marie sits demurely at his side, caricature of a visiting sweetheart. Paul wears a shapeless, short-sleeved white top, that looks more like a patient's nightgown than a T-shirt.

He initially refuses to remove this garment when invited to do so by Marie. This refusal, puzzling in realist terms, on a symbolic level suggests fear of the castrating female gaze. When Marie tries unsuccessfully to bring his penis to life by fellating him, Paul shrinks away from contact, and eventually restores his penis to the safety of the covers as if apprehensive of what might happen, blocking Marie's gaze. Her disparaging reference to his smallness, comparing his penis to a little bird that, by implication, she could so easily crush, further reinforces the impression of the man's feminine positioning and of the woman's castrating potential.

The hospital-like setting appears to present us with an anxious patient facing the castrating knife and who in watching male athletes on the wall-mounted ward television is attempting to reassure himself that he and they still have the phallus. Paul's preoccupation with the male athletes leads Emma Wilson to view Paul as a repressed gay. Certainly, the very name recalls St Paul, the father of sexual repression in Christian mythology, but it is Paul's gender that is presented as vulnerable rather than his sexuality, and in this bedroom scene, his behaviour is motivated by an unconscious fear of being feminised further by Marie's castratory attentions.[2] Paolo, on the other hand, has no such anxieties. Paul's exotic and virile alter ego, Paolo is the Italian stallion with all the right equipment: a rigid body, rippling with muscles and barely contained lust, a volcanic phallus on the brink of eruption (he tells Marie that it is four months since he last had sex).

However, even he seems to have difficulty staying erect, and he is obliged to rub himself constantly. In any case, Marie seems unexcited by this hard-core display. It is as if the failure of her gaze with Paul has definitively destroyed her aspirations to visual eroticism. When she and Paolo do have intercourse, visual signifiers of pleasure are less important than a soundtrack that emphasises his pleasure over hers. A prick both literally and metaphorically, Paolo is only interested in his own orgasm. Despite a few perfunctory moans, Marie seems passive, impassive and largely unfulfilled. Paolo was never in any danger of castratory loss at the hands of an active, rampant female: his phallus, shielded first by his own hand, then by the condom he wears for intercourse, remains his.

In contrast, the man who later offers Marie money to perform cunnilingus on her, then ends up raping her, is responding to the unconscious imperatives of castration fear. This is a strikingly unstereotypical request on the part of a predatory male, seeking sexual gratification in the street, such a male being far more likely to pay a prostitute for fellatio. As such, the scene invites largely symbolic rather than realist readings. The act of cunnilingus promises to satisfy Marie's rather than the man's sexual cravings, asserting her sexual subjectivity over his. Her moans of pleasure, signifiers here of a female sexual agency unwished for by the male street predator, symbolically (though not literally) return his own gaze. At the same time, he is visually confronted with the wound of castration. His violent act of rape might therefore be read on the one hand as an aggressive response to Marie's self-assertive sexuality, and on the other, as the expression of an unconscious desire to punish the castrated woman and in so doing, assuage his castration anxiety.

Marie decides to stop seeing Paolo, ostensibly in order to avoid emotional involvement. Thus when the headmaster offers her extracurricular activity, which lacks the emotional complications of a conventional love affair in the weekly ritual of bondage, she takes the opportunity to retreat into masochism, positioning herself in what at first appears to be the stereoptypical female passive role. In other words, she stops looking to have the phallus and returns to the position of simply being the phallus, as her phallic body is rendered even more phallic in the vertical attitude of a crucified Christ, hands and feet tightly bound. It is beginning to appear as if Marie wishes to be a sex object, not a gazing subject. Her own gaze has in any case been mostly directed at images of herself throughout the film, as in the early bathroom sequence, in which we watch her watching herself in the mirror brushing her teeth. During her first bondage lesson with Robert, Marie again confronts her own image in the mirror, a gesture that draws attention to the self-focus of masochism (as opposed to the other-focus of sadism). Significantly, on this occasion, it is not her teeth, signifier of castrating power, but her exposed pubic hair that catches our attention, signifier of the castrated hidden female sex. Yet the vagina is henceforth valorised as a source of pleasure, not as a sign of castration. Mediated by the specular image, the pubic triangle seems soft and downy, rather than Medusa-like. Later in this scene, Robert carefully cuts a hole in her knickers to open up access to the vagina, inserts his finger-tips and withdraws them glistening with the signifier of female pleasure. The camera from now onwards focuses increasingly on Marie's vagina, abandoning its earlier preoccupation with the phallus.

These scenes are open to criticism, especially from feminist critics. The problematic may be summed up as follows: is there a sadistic objectification of the woman here that is politically unacceptable, or are Marie's masochistic responses potentially liberating for the female viewer? Given both the portrayal of Robert as a caring and sensitive man and his role in the masochist scenario it would be hard to view this character as a true sadist. He portrays what Gilles Deleuze calls the 'pseudo-sadist of masochism', a sadism staged for the benefit of a subject, who has contracted for this to happen (1967: 108). He merely seems to have an interest in the aesthetic potential of bondage. After painstakingly tying Marie up, he stands back like some proud artist or artisan and declares that it (not she, we note) looks beautiful.

As for the possibility that masochism affords women more sexual freedom and therefore pleasure, this is confirmed by the Deleuzian view, according to which it is not the father but the oral mother that could be the primary figure of identification and power. For the Deleuzian masochist, the law passes metaphorically and symbolically from castrated father to phallic mother. The father loses the phallus, while the mother symbolically and figuratively acquires it. Similarly, the feminine is seen to be dominant over the masculine and ultimately to destroy it. Admittedly, Deleuze's masochist follows Severin Sacher-Masoch's own hero in being male, while *Romance* presents us with images of a more politically troubling female masochism. But as Gaylyn Studlar (1992) argues, the masochistic scenario makes opposite sex identification not a problem as it is in Laura Mulvey's analysis, but a pleasure available to both sexes. Thus, Breillat's male spectator can identify with the masochism in Marie, just as the female spectator can identify with Robert's pseudo-sadistic position.

Gender role reversal is in fact a dominant feature of the film. Paul occupies the stereotypical feminine position in refusing to have sex, and Marie takes on the active masculine role as she sets off at night in search of sexual excitement. In the bondage scene itself, Robert's masculinity is undermined by his somewhat effeminate manner and submissive attitudes to Marie. He readily defers to Marie's wishes with regard to the bondage procedures. The contract with Robert is very definitely an ambivalent one, as the submissive position is occupied explicitly by Marie but implicitly by Robert. The result is a fluidity of gender positions, as Marie plays the masochistic male in search of erotic pleasure, while Robert adopts the Deleuzian role of the good mother, who, for Deleuze, is also the phallic, pseudo-sadistic mother:

> The theme of the bad mother certainly does appear in masochism, but as a marginal phenomenon, the centre being occupied by the good mother. In masochism, it is the good mother that possesses the phallus, that beats and humiliates, or even prostitutes herself. (1967: 94)

Deleuze was the first to argue against explaining masochism in terms of a father-complex, suggesting that, rather than being the 'reverse side' of a 'father-identified' sadism, as Freud had posited, masochism has its roots in the symbiotic relationship between the male child and the oral mother of the pregenital stage. For Deleuze, in masochism, the good mother has supplanted the father, taken over his role, and it is on this symbolic level that she is perceived by her willing victim as having the phallus: signifier of authority and the law. Robert fulfils the good mother role so well that he later supportively attends the birth of Marie's child.

Although initially perceiving herself erotically as a hole, Marie moves to adopt a far more positive self-image: the vagina may be a hole, but it is a productive, fertile hole, the sign not of emptiness but of plenitude. So, in the end, Marie's quest for the phallus is abandoned and the vagina enthroned in its place. Not, however, before we are shown how men try to make the vagina their own when it becomes a passage for childbirth. This is demonstrated in two scenes. When Marie falls pregnant by Paul, he develops a proprietorial interest in her, and indeed makes love to her for the first time in months after the scan that confirms the pregnancy. Marie's condition fetishistically restores the missing phallus for Paul, who nevertheless remains a prick himself, behaving disgracefully towards her in a nightclub scene, flirting with other women and displaying a total callousness towards her condition. In the second scene, Marie is subjected to an internal examination by a succession of trainee doctors who are seen to clumsily insert their fingers into her vagina, a symbolic and literal display of male control of the female body. The scene carries an erotic charge, as Marie lies with her legs wide open, offering herself as much to the male spectator as to the male doctors, who appear embarrassed by the intimate contact required of them. Reality is here seen to lack the honesty of fantasy. Unlike the fantasy brothel scene with which this gynecological examination is juxtaposed, the erotic pleasure that men derive from vaginal penetration is here concealed, passing itself off as medical treatment: the pornographic potential of the scene is thus undermined by its ironic frame.

The recuperation of the vagina from male control is graphically enacted, again in two scenes, one fantasised by Marie and the other a piece of *cinéma vérité* depicting the birth of her baby son. In the fantasy brothel sequence referred to above, Marie imagines her body as fragmented for the pleasure of men. This fantasy is a visual enactment of her erotic desire to be nothing more than a cunt, the Lacanian hole for men to fill. The separation of the female genitals from the upper part of her

body, which constitutes her identity as an individual, is effected in Marie's imagination by a kind of guillotine without a blade. It powerfully suggests the irrecon-
cilability of female sexual desire in which rape fantasy can play a powerful part
and women's need in the real to be loved as well as fucked. In the birth scene the
enlarged and engorged vagina is seen to fill the entire screen and opens up for the
first time in full view, a hard-core uterus to match the hard-core phalluses of earlier
scenes. Marie's baby provides her with the substitute for the phallus she has been
vainly seeking and Paul becomes immediately dispensable.[3]

Romance, then, enacts movement from the ubiquitous visibility of the phallus
to the gradual unveiling of the hidden vagina as entrance to the womb. Thus is
the feminine-maternal laid bare, while the masculine is laid to rest in a final fantasy scene, in which Marie imagines a horse-drawn hearse bearing Paul's coffin. The
coffin is lowered into the ground watched by a heroically-postured Marie, cradling
her new-born baby. The Mother supplants the Lover, the uterine gash in the earth
swallows Paul's corpse-phallus, and the film ends with a final voice-over in which
it is made clear that the baby boy is a new Paul: bearing his father's name, the son
has been exchanged for the father. In the fruit of her uterus and vagina, Marie has
finally found the unconditional love and perhaps the erotic fulfilment she has been
seeking all along.

With its middle-class Victorian decor and costume, the final scene takes us back
into a nineteenth-century romanesque world. Unlike Emma Bovary, however, the
adulterous Marie does not allow her sexual misdemeanours to kill her, she kills her
husband instead. As in so many nineteenth-century novels, death is countered by
rebirth, and Breillat's film ends with the positive image of a baby, pointing perhaps
towards the utopic vision of a future women-centred cinema in which the uterus
and vagina have replaced the phallus as principal signifiers of female desire. Some
might object that to represent the female body in terms of substitutes for the phallus keeps us trapped in a phallicist economy. In clear illustration of Freud's contention that the birth of a male child gives the woman the penis she longs for, the
final scene is certainly open to powerful criticism for helping to perpetuate what is
perceived as a masculinist construction of femininity.[4]

In conclusion, then, *Romance* boldly addresses the representation in film of
female pleasure, demythologising the sight of the erect penis on screen. On the
other hand, non-sexist pornography is not just a question of displaying erect
penises. Desire must be shown as operating outside a phallicist economy altogether, and Breillat's film regrettably falls short of this objective. The film does,
however, suggest that masochism offers the spectator, male or female, an alternative non-phallic position from which to experience scopic pleasure. Indeed, regardless of gender or sexuality, the spectator may move between different positions,
identifying sometimes with Robert's pseudo-sadism, at other times with Marie's
masochism, and even with her fertility, shifting from active to passive as much as
from male to female positions.[5] Masochistic and even sadistic fantasy might also
be thought of as liberating for women in that, as Linda Williams suggests, 'it may
represent for women a new consciousness about the unavoidable role of power in
sex, gender and sexual representations and of the importance of not viewing this
power as fixed' (1990: 228). As I have argued here, the loosening of sexual/gender
identification in the cinema that *Romance* promotes and the consequent creation

of multiple viewing positions for the female as well as the male spectator are, in the end, far more valuable gifts than the suggestion that the answer might lie in a crudely staged and essentially phallocentric female gaze.

Notes

1   See Jacques Lacan's seminars on 'The formations of the Unconscious', summarised by Jean-Bertrand Pontalis in *Bulletin de Psychologie*, 10 and 11, 1956–57.
2   Other names seem to carry a transparent symbolism: Marie in her virginal white dress (except in the second bondage scene) is all sexual innocence and victimal passivity. Robert is a self-avowed authority on 10,000 women, a veritable dictionary of eroticism, the voice of male sexual wisdom, who condescendingly claims to listen to women, but actually lectures them (like Mario in *Emmanuelle*).
3   Paul has progressed from his earlier feminine role to become a literal father to her child, but exasperated by his selfish behaviour and lack of support, Marie kills him by causing a lethal gas explosion in their flat as he sleeps. This symbolic castration removes the father's phallic law along the lines of Deleuze's theory, and paves the way for the triumph of the feminine-maternal.
4   See Freud 1977a: 296–302, and Mitchell 1974: 101–4.
5   Laura Kipnis restates this argument succinctly: 'Identification is mobile, unpredictable, and not bound by either one's gender or by practical reality … as a male you can identify with a female character and vice versa' (1996: 196–7). See also Adams 1988 and Williams 1990: 215.

Bibliography

Adams, P. (1988) 'Per Os(cillation)', *Camera Obscura: A Journal of Feminism and Film Theory*, 17, 7–29.
Deleuze, G. (1967) *Présentation de Sacher-Masoch. Le Froid et le cruel*. Paris: Éditions de Minuit.
Doane, M. A. (1992 [1982]) 'Film and the Masquerade: Theorising the Female Spectator', in G. Mast, M. Cohen and L. Brady (eds) *Film Theory and Criticism: Introductory Readings*. Oxford: Oxford University Press, 758–72.
Freud, S. (1977a [1917]) 'On Transformations of Instinct as Exemplified in Anal Eroticism', in *On Sexuality: Three Essays on the Theory of Sexuality and Other Works*. London: The Pelican Freud Library, 294–302.
_____ (1977b [1927]), 'Fetishism', in *On Sexuality: Three Essays on the Theory of Sexuality and Other Works*. London: The Pelican Freud Library, 351–7.
Kaplan, L. J. (1991) *Female Perversions: The Temptations of Emma Bovary*. New York: Anchor Books.
Kipnis, L. (1996) *Bound and Gagged: Pornography and the Politics of Fantasy in America*. New York: Grove Press.
Mitchell, J. (1974) *Psychoanalysis and Feminism*. London: Penguin.
Mulvey, L. (1975) 'Visual Pleasure and Narrative Cinema', *Screen*, 6, 3, 6–18.
Studlar, G. (1992) 'Masochism and the Perverse Pleasures of the Cinema', in G. Mast, M. Cohen and L. Braudy (eds) *Film Theory and Criticism: Introductory Readings*. Oxford: Oxford University Press, 773–90.

Williams, L. (1990) *Hard Core: Power, Pleasure, and the 'Frenzy of the Visible'*. London: Pandora Press.

Wilson, E. (2001) 'Deforming Femininity: Catherine Breillat's *Romance*', in L. Mazdon (ed.) *France on Film: Reflections on Popular French Cinema*. London: Wallflower Press, 145–57.

CHAPTER SEVEN

Techno-Orientalism and the Postmodern Subject

Christine Cornea

This essay argues for more attention to be given to issues surrounding race in the science fiction/cyborg film. The essay specifically focuses upon the depiction of 'oriental' images in recent science fiction films from the early 1980s through to 2003. After setting the films briefly within an economic and cultural context, reference to post-colonial theory is made to suggest ways in which these images may be understood. I open with a discussion of examples of mainstream American science fiction films, but then move on to provide close filmic analysis in conjunction with a number of straight-to-video, what I have come to term, martial art/cyborg films. The straight-to-video examples that I use have been taken from a cluster of martial art/cyborg films, which emerged in the early to mid-1990s. I have chosen to concentrate my brief analysis on these films partly because they more directly engage with issues surrounding race and the cyborg than their mainstream predecessors and, I would suggest, can also be seen as low-budget forerunners to the later wave of mainstream martial art/cyborg films – probably peaking with *The Matrix* trilogy (Andy and Larry Wachowski, 1999/2003).

Emerging in American science fiction cinema in the 1970s, with films like *Demon Seed* (Donald Cammell, 1977) and *Star Wars* (George Lucas, 1977), the figure of the cyborg has become the site upon which ideas of postmodern experience and identity are played out. In the 1980s the cyborg became central to the film genre and mainstream cinema bombarded the viewer with images of white hyper-masculinity, in characterisations like the Terminator, RoboCop and the universal soldier. However, largely inspired by Donna Haraway's (1985) seminal piece, 'A Manifesto for Cyborgs', early academic work recognised this hybrid formation as important due to the challenge it offered to traditional models of sexuality and gender. Criticisms of the way in which received notions of gender (in particular masculinity) may or may not be disrupted by the representation of the cyborg were certainly pertinent in the 1980s and early 1990s but very little attention was given to racial issues in conjunction with this figuration. After all, classifications of human identity have referred to racial markings, as with the markers of sex/gender, as 'evidence' of an essentialised being that is necessarily separate and divided from other modes of being and have been used as a premise to support racial and sexual inequalities. So, in the last few decades academic studies have turned their attention toward challenging and disrupting this 'evidence' and more recently the concept of hybrid-ity has been used to draw attention to the falsity, both conceptually and literally, of traditional paradigms involving clear-cut division.

Post-colonial theory has been one of the main academic areas that has explored and developed ideas surrounding hybridity, and the notion of racial and cultural hybridity has been central to the growth of theories that aim to counteract con-cepts of purity and exclusivity as the necessary components in a claiming of self-hood. This approach has been greatly influenced by the leading theorist, Homi K. Bhabha. By drawing upon a mixture of Lacanian psychoanalysis and post-structur-alist theory Bhabha expounds a model of hybridity as based upon 'a kind of "dou-bleness" in writing: a temporality or representation that moves *between* cultural and social processes' (1990: 293; my emphasis). In addition, Bhabha has stated that it is necessary to 'open the way to conceptualising an *inter*national culture, based not on the exoticism or multiculturalism of the diversity of cultures, but on the inscription and articulation of culture's *hybridity*' (1988: 22; emphasis in original). Gail Ching-Liang Low reads Bhabha's strategy as 'a discourse of partiality which works against the colonial reproduction of (unitary) meaning' (1996: 197). She goes on to point out that in an application of the terms of hybridity to the colonial subject, 'neither the desire for racial and historical originality nor the demand for absolute obedience – based on this origination – will be met' (ibid.). In this way, the notion of hybridity extends not only to the colonised but also to the coloniser. For instance, if the racial Other is culturally hybrid, having taken on aspects of the coloniser's culture, then the traffic goes both ways – meaning that the coloniser, in an appropriation of an-Other's culture, can also be understood as 'de-purified'. As Nikos Papastergiadis has pointed out: 'Bhabha's strategy is not a redemptive one' (1997: 279). In other words, it does not attempt a return to some imagined 'before' of colonialism; it does not assume that the colonial subject can regain some kind of lost innocence or purity. Instead, the post-colonial subject, much like Haraway's feminist cyborg, is not innocent, but 'the illegitimate offspring of militarism and patriarchal capitalism' (1985: 68).

Given the body of work very briefly outlined above, the relative paucity of academic analysis focusing upon issues of race in the cyborg film is surprising. Even though racial issues may not always have appeared prominent, in terms of the representation of the cyborg, they have undoubtedly been present in these films.[1] Certainly, Claudia Springer (1999) has brought race into the equation with her study of the way in which African or Afro-Caribbean/American characters have functioned in several examples of the genre. Nevertheless, I would suggest that the figuring of the 'oriental' (in particular, I am referring to representations associ-ated with the Pacific Rim countries) in cyborg films is of particular interest. As far back as *Blade Runner* (Ridley Scott, 1982) the 'oriental' has been seen in conjunction with new technologies in science fiction cinema.[2] Although the oriental charac-ters in this film are dominated by a white elite, as Richard Dyer says of Tyrell and Sebastian: 'both the representatives of white creativity in the film are pale creatures leading attenuated lives, devoid of human interaction, dead and dying' (1997: 214). So, there is a sense that these figures of supremacy are dying out, which may well suggest that a new kind of being, one that is associated with the oriental, is about to take over.

One way of explaining this new kind of being is purely in terms of the ideological and nationalistic underpinnings that may be evident in American science fiction films. For instance, at the time of *Blade Runner*'s release certain Eastern economies were growing fast and countries like Japan and Korea were well known for their manufacture of computer components and other cutting-edge technologies. Prior to this, it might have been that these nations were understood as suppliers for the West, but over the course of the 1980s it became apparent that the, so called, 'Tiger Economies' were growing fast and that they were moving from being the copiers/providers of Western-led technology to becoming the inventors/initiators of new technologies. It is possible then that economic and industrial shifts may have altered the way in which these territories (Taiwan, South Korea, Hong Kong and Singapore) were perceived by the West, or more specifically by the USA, at this time, which could indicate a sort of 'econocultural' rationale behind the use of oriental images in *Blade Runner* and more recent science fiction.[3] In addition to this, a certain amount of Eastern money has recently been poured into the American film industry (for example Columbia Pictures' take-over by Sony and Japanese investment in Disney), which may also account for the manifestation of certain cultural references. Alongside Eastern financial intervention in the US film industry has come the exploitation by the US of various Asian markets for the American film product. Although numerous multiplex screens were built in new geographical markets (Japan proved to be one of the most lucrative markets in this respect), growth for the US film industry has also been aided by video, pay TV technologies and, more recently, the production of DVDs.[4] It may be, then, that oriental images have also been consciously built into many mainstream films as a way of addressing those markets as well as reflecting their increasing cultural prominence due to economic growth and technological innovation. While it is difficult to argue for some kind of direct link between these economic, political and national positions and the images in question, it is well to bear in mind the historical backdrop to the emergence of specifically East Asian characters and imagery that connotes East Asian cultures in the cyborg film.

There is surely more to these images than a simple reflection of world economic trends. For instance, David Morley and Kevin Robins suggest that evident within cultural representations of 'high technology' there exists something that they have come to call 'Techno-Orientalism' (1995: 147–73). Back in the 1970s, Edward Said's groundbreaking book, *Orientalism*, explored how Western cultural representations constructed the oriental Other. By drawing upon his ideas, Morley and Robins argue that the association of what they term 'postmodern technologies' with images of the Orient can be understood as a continuation of an orientalist practice in the West. In an application of their ideas to the cyborg film, it seems that the depiction of postmodern technologies is often located in the creation of a kind of virtual Orient – an exotic space in which the 'tourist' can be freed from Western rationalism and taste the 'mystic essence' of the East. This kind of formation seems particularly evident in recent movie versions of computer games like *Streetfighter* (Paul Anderson, 1994) and *Mortal Kombat* (Steven De Souza, 1995). Both of these films present the audience with a markedly fictional space; a space that can be read as corresponding to the type of cyberspace in which the games may be played; a space which is most definitely signalled to be oriental in nature. *Mortal Kombat* accomplishes this by heavily referencing *Enter the Dragon* (Robert Clouse, 1973) and, indeed, features an oriental hero (played by Robin Shou – a Hong Kong martial artist/actor) who is pitted against an evil overlord (played by Cary-Hiroyuki Tagawa – a Japanese-American actor). *Streetfighter* sets its action in a fictional oriental country – complete with images that resemble both those seen of the Vietnam War and the first Gulf War. Although there are oriental characters present in these films, aspects of a now popularised oriental culture are appropriated by the Western characters – in particular their consistent use of martial arts in the action sequences of the films.[5] In fact, increasingly, the martial arts content of a science fiction/action film is not directly associated with oriental characters, but has become a kind of free-floating signifier of the interaction between human and computer technologies. An even more recent example of this can be found in *The Matrix* (1999). Here the Western protagonists are all represented as adept at forms of martial art that, in conjunction with actual computer graphics and computer-altered images, give them super-human capabilities. It is as though these characters become oriental-ised in their interaction with these 'postmodern technologies'. Indeed, the camera/computer techniques along with the wirework displays in this film are sutured to the oriental, as though the actors and the characters they play were orientalised as well as cyborgised, in becoming immersed in such technologies. The mystique of various forms of martial art to a Western audience is here co-opted to underpin, or account for, the splendour of the graphics on display and, in particular, those which allow the human actants to perform extraordinary feats. These characters are both literally and diegetically cyborgised; they operate on the borderline between fantasy and reality and between the real and technologically-created world. Yet even though this seems to suggest the continuation of an orientalist tradition in Western filmmaking, it is my contention that some of these charactersations could also be read alongside Bhabha's post-colonial subject – as if they were the embodiment of his 'in between' state; a state that can be understood as connoting a hybrid identity in terms of race, nationality and technological interaction.

The 'high'/'low' feedback loop

Although there is a need for more attention to be given to the racial issues present in the mainstream films mentioned above, I have chosen to concentrate my brief analysis on the spate of low-budget, straight-to-video, martial art/cyborg film that appeared in the 1990s. Straight-to-video releases like *Knights* (Albert Pyun, 1992), *Cyborg Agent* (Richard Franklin, 1992), *TC 2000* (T. J. Scott, 1993), *Heatseeker* (Albert Pyun, 1994), *Techno Sapiens* (Lamar Card, 1994), *Cyber Tracker* (Richard Pepin, 1994) and Albert Pyun's *Nemesis* series (1993–96) have been ignored by Film Studies. This is a mistake because, even though they may be considered 'poor', they often offer unconventional visions/enactings in association with the cyborg film. This differ-ence in approach may, in part, be due to the fact that these films more often fea-ture central characters of Asian origin and are frequently directed, produced and/or written by Asian-Americans or Americans with some Asian heritage (for example, Albert Pyun, Ashok Amritraj, Don 'The Dragon' Wilson). Perhaps, given the authorial control that the low-budget film more readily allows for, some of these filmmakers have attempted to articulate the specificity of their racial/cultural hybridity. Whilst some may be attempting to break into the Hollywood mainstream, they might also, simultaneously, be working through racial and cultural issues in these films. In this respect it is particularly interesting that many of these straight-to-video films serve to reveal much about the higher-budget, mainstream films. In fact, intertextual readings are encouraged, quite blatantly, by a number of straight-to-video, martial art/cyborg films – as is apparent sometimes in the similarity of their titles with more familiar films and in the way in which they heavily reference plots, scenes, even dialogue, from mainstream films of the genre.[6] Of course, I am not the first to recognise the lower-budget or straight-to-video film as important. For example, Carol Clover's (1992) and Linda Ruth Williams' (1993) work concentrates on how lower-budget films may be appropriated and altered for more popular, mainstream consumption. However, what I am, in part, suggesting is that many of the lower-budget, martial art/cyborg films also answer to earlier or existing main-stream films and, it could be argued, have gone on to inspire later mainstream films of the genre.

In order to illustrate my points, one of the clearest examples of a martial art/cyborg film that outwardly encourages an intertextual understanding is *Grid Runners* (Andrew Stevens, 1995). The title is, of course, reminiscent of *Blade Runner* and, whilst it draws upon this seminal film, it also refers to the 'computer game' films mentioned above. *Grid Runners* concentrates on the complications of living in a hyperreal city environment and, like *Blade Runner*, sports a number of 'repli-cated' humans. The 'Grids' refer to geographically policed areas, which are, in turn, represented by computer grids located in a central Police Station: surveillance and control is centrally guided from here. In this panoptic environment the bounda-ries between urban Grids (which could be read as symbolically representative of wider, national boundaries) and between the diegetically real and virtual world, are patrolled by the 'Runners'. The Runners, like border guards, make sure that no one crosses between urban grids without permission or between the virtual and real world without payment. The narrative revolves around the illegal cross-ing of these boundaries and the central protagonist. David Quarry (played by the actor/kickboxer, Don 'The Dragon' Wilson), as a Grid Runner, is the oriental 'meat' in this particular sandwich. When two virtual, female porn stars are brought over into the real world it is up to Quarry to track them down and return them to their 'Cybersex' program. At the same time, a further male character, Dante (played by Michael Bernardo), manages to escape from a virtual, martial art game called 'Lethal Combat'. Initially Quarry takes his orders directly from the policing force that employs him, but upon the murder of his partner, by Dante, divorces himself from this authority, in his quest to avenge the killing.

Interestingly, it is within the virtual world of 'Lethal Combat' that we are first introduced to Quarry. The film opens with martial art fighting scenes in which Quarry faces a number of opponents and it is not until he requests a move to another 'level' of the game that the viewer is alerted to the fact that this is not a 'real' environment. Having succeeded through levels five, six and seven he asks to be 'transported' to the final level ten, where he faces the 'demon' Ninja, Dante, who is able to predict Quarry's movements and fighting tactics. One of the main tropes of recent orientalist discourse has involved the idea that the oriental Other does not 'play' by the same rules of conduct as the West. This has, for example, been used to underpin a notion of Japanese business techniques as 'unfair' and has been extended to encompass the idea that 'they' are essentially and culturally very different.[7] During the level ten battle Dante, in a telepathic communication with Quarry (represented by the speaking of dialogue in voice-over whilst the camera shot concentrates on Dante's unmoving mouth) states: 'I don't play your rules.' The use of this voice-over device could certainly indicate that it is Quarry who imagines what his adversary is actually thinking. However, if Dante were meant as the embodiment of an oriental threat then the racial reversal, due to Bernardo's more Western appearance, may simply suggest a role reversal – in which the oriental character is good and the Western character evil. Nevertheless, this is complicated by the fact that Dante appears as the most proficient, amongst the virtual fighters, in martial art combat and by the way in which there are various references to a more intimate connection between these two characters. Although the Bernardo characterisation could be read as less authentic, in a comparison with the characterisation of Quarry (a reading which could be underpinned by Wilson's past career as an international kickboxer) at one point Dante communicates: 'You can't kill me, it would be like killing a part of yourself', which implies that he represents an aspect of Quarry's own character. If Dante is meant to represent the manifestation of the oriental aspects of Quarry's character (aspects that may have become repressed due to his involvement with American culture and underlined by his positioning as an agent of the American law machine) then it is interesting that this is embodied by a character of more Western appearance. Several configurations arising from this play upon racial positionings are possible, but suffice to say what the film succeeds in doing here is thoroughly confusing what is seen as self/us and what as Other/them. Indeed, both these characters could be construed as racial and cultural hybrids, articulated through their meeting within a technologically-produced environment.

The use of weaponry and fighting techniques used in this film also deserve a mention, as there are a number of visual allusions to the psychical temperament of both Dante and Quarry. The idea that the fighting images are expressive of their inner state is underlined by the way in which the weapons are posited as extensions of their bodies, as opposed to separate technological aids. This is literalised in the film when Dante is able to *grow* both a new hand and sword after Quarry cuts away his arm, thus foregrounding the connection between body and weapon. Of course, the notion of weaponry being brought into close association with a bodily referent is not new to cinema. There has been much written about the phallic nature of armaments and whether phallic power can really be understood as separable from its bodily referent, the penis. But what is particularly notable in martial art/cyborg films is the way in which the weapons are so often dispersed throughout the body. For instance, unlike the classic Hollywood action film where guns are carried at hip (genital) level, Quarry chooses to conceal a knife in his shoe at one point. In addition, the fighting techniques themselves, when compared to sequences featured in classic American films, also utilise many more parts of the body. Wilson's kickboxing skills are displayed when Quarry is shown to use his legs, arms and hands in fighting opponents. This is a gymnastic display that proposes a much more de-centralised version of the fighting body than has been commonly seen in American action films – where emphasis has classically been placed upon the upper body in aggressive/defensive displays. Further to this, during his initial, virtual battle with Dante, Quarry uses the split stick (known as 'Screamers' due to the noise they create when wielded) against Dante's single stick ('Bo'), in what appears to be a visual metaphor of his inherent duality as compared to Dante's more singular manifestation.

Having stated that Dante is represented as a more 'singular' character this is also extended to the virtual porn stars, Leanna and Greta. Both of these women are blatantly one-dimensional and sexually stereotyped: Leanna being submissive and obliging stands for a kind of 'soft' or passive femininity as opposed to the threateningly active Greta, who is dressed in leather and sports a Dominatrix whip. They are each driven by singular motivations and perform very particular functions for the male characters and also in terms of the game/plot of the film. Having escaped their virtual worlds Dante, Leanna and Greta are heavily marked as fictional and therefore set up in direct contrast with Quarry. It is almost as though these virtual characters (who are all Western in appearance) represent the types of narrative agent commonly found in American action films. This suggests that Quarry's *hybrid* positioning is being advanced as more 'realistic': a racially and technologically-inflected hybridity here is sutured to a more complex characterisation.

The seemingly ramshackle narrative of this film, and of many of the straight-to-video martial art/cyborg films, can be understood as an attempt at a more detailed account of how race and technology can be seen to interact. They can also be understood to be playing out a particularly post-colonial form of hybridity, as encouraging an 'in between' reading, or, alternatively, can be seen as part of an ongoing tradition of Orientalism in Western culture. In some respects these films appear to reverse arguments that have been made about the relationship between lower-budget films and mainstream counterparts – in particular the way in which the lower-budget movie may pare away and simplify what is at stake in later mainstream versions. These straight-to-video, martial art/cyborg films, although fore-grounding more latent elements of some mainstream cyborg films, are relatively complex. In this sense, they do not necessarily offer a *simpler* accounting of what is at stake, but seek to play out the paradoxes and complexities associated with post-colonial hybridity. This kind of 'complexification' is also evident in the sheer number of characters that get an airing in these films. Whereas, in previous mainstream films the spectator may be offered a couple of central and opposing characters, in the martial art/cyborg film it is more common to have a multitude of central characters.[8] In addition, within the conventions of the straight-to-video genre at least, the classic dualism of 'good versus bad' is often broken up by the introduction of a third, in between, positioning or grouping. For instance, in *Prototype* (Philip Roth, 1992)[9] a band of martial artists, called 'Protectors', attempts to halt the devastation caused by the 'battle of the sexes' between the male Prototype-cyborg and the female Omega-cyborg. Although male performers represent the Protectors, they are positioned both literally and figuratively 'in between' the sexes/genders and appear to offer up a hope for the future in this film. Likewise, *TC 2000* features an orientalised band of renegades, called 'Breakers', led by Sumai (played by Bolo Yeung). The Breakers primarily live on the streets and are positioned between the warring factions of the dominating Underworld and a mafia-like, criminal group, whose headquarters resemble the Tyrell Corporation's central offices. In all these straight-to-video films it is as though the filmmakers had taken familiar images and tropes used in mainstream science fiction films but re-focused the narrative to bring out the racial issues. For instance, the *Blade Runner* elements (which are a common reference in the straight-to-video cyborg film of the time) may serve to remind the audience of the futuristic vision at play in this seminal film, but what is magnified in *TC 2000* is the oriental, street-level existence. So, although the central character of Jason (played by the martial artist/actor, Billy Blanks) can be seen as an alternative stand-in for Deckard, the story is effectively re-focalised, thereby bringing into sharp focus the complex racial issues implied in the former film.

Given this brief discussion of the straight-to-video, martial art/cyborg films, it becomes apparent that racial issues are foregrounded in these films in interesting ways. Vivian Sobchack has pointed out that in a postmodern America 'we are hard pressed to locate where, what, and who is either "all-American" or "ethnic"' (1991: 331). She goes on to look at examples of many mainstream science fiction films that, in her estimation, trivialise racial and cultural difference in the vast array of cultural references and depictions of difference on offer. For instance, she says that in *Blade Runner* 'the Oriental domination of Los Angeles ... is effectively defused and diffused by the impression the *mise-en-scène* gives us of a cultural crazy quilt, of an ethnic pastiche (1991: 338)'. Certainly, it is possible to read the kind of complexification evident in many of the straight-to-video, martial art/cyborg films alongside the sort of updated American 'melting pot' scenario that Sobchack sees in mainstream science fiction films. However, it is my contention that in many of these films this device does not operate in this way. On the contrary, these films very often insist upon an engagement with issues surrounding ethnic and cultural difference, however complex this becomes within the context of a postmodern America.

Notes

1   For instance, cultural/ethnic hybridity in early figurations of the cyborg were often conservatively signalled via star persona: Arnold Schwarzenegger's Austrian heritage or Jean-Claude Van Damme's persona as 'the muscles from Brussels'. A notable shift can be seen in the use of the Keanu Reeves persona in both *Johnny Mnemonic* and *The Matrix*: Reeves being understood as a more literal racial and cultural hybrid given his parentage and upbringing (Reeves' mother was English and his father Chinese-Hawaiian, and he has dual Canadian and American citizenship).

2   Of course, there are earlier instances in science fiction and action films. For example, the 'Ninja' characters in the James Bond films reveal that this is hardly a new phenomenon. Along with these examples aspects of the robot-gun slayer (played by Yul Brynner) in *Westworld* (Michael Crichton, 1973) and *Futureworld* (Richard T. Heffron, 1976) can be read as oriental. Having hailed, originally, from Vladivostock (situated in the east of Russia – very close to East Asia), Brynner's heritage appears to have been drawn upon to make of him a kind of Westernised, oriental persona. In addition, more obvious references appear in the thinly disguised, orientalised Jedi characters of the *Star Wars* films – the 'force' referring to the mystical *chi* energy associated with the martial arts.

3   Roland Robertson uses the phrase 'econocultural' to denote a 'clashing' between two opposing cultures based upon the economic dynamics of a particular historical context (1991: 186–7).

4   Richard Maltby (1998) gives a concise account of this growth and dispersion of Hollywood films – in particular, the early 1990s growth in Eastern markets for American films.
5   This is also reminiscent of the many low-budget martial arts films that emerged in the 1970s and from which some of these films appear to draw their imagery – as opposed to directly referencing Hong Kong action movies or Chinese films.
6   This can also be understood as a device that exploits the mainstream market. However, this does not belie the fact that a number of these films engage in active and interesting intertextual comment.
7   For instance, Roland Robertson describes how since the 1960s, and especially during the 1980s, economic clashes between the two nations 'have ramified into a conflict over the core cultural features of the two societies'. He goes on to describe how these came to be played out in terms of assumed, essential differences between the two races (1991: 186–7).
8   I would suggest that a similar complexification is also evident in *The Matrix Reloaded* (2003). For instance, alongside the deliberately complex and dense narrative structure of this film, we see a further profusion of central characters. In the case of this film, this structure plays to a 'fan' audience as well as allowing for the marketing of multiple 'spin-off' narratives (for example, *Animatrix* and the spin-off computer game) and can be aligned with what Thomas Elsaesser and Warren Buckland refer to as the 'video game logic' evident in recent film narratives (2002: 161–7).
9   Released in the US as *Prototype X29A*.

Bibliography

Bhabha, H. K. (1988) 'The Commitment to Theory', *New Formations*, 5, 5–23.
_____ (1990) *Nation and Narration*. London and New York: Routledge.
Ching-Liang Low, G. (1996) *White Skins Black Masks: Representation and Colonialism*. London and New York: Routledge.
Clover, C. (1992) *Men, Women, and Chain Saws: Gender in the Modern Horror Film*. London: British Film Institute.
Dyer, R. (1997) *White*. London and New York: Routledge.
Elsaesser, T. and W. Buckland (2002) *Studying Contemporary American Film*. London: Arnold.
Haraway, D. (1985) 'A Manifesto for Cyborgs: Science, Technology, and Socialist Feminism in the 1980s', *Socialist Review*, 80, 65–107.
Maltby, R. (1998) 'Post-Classical Historiographies and Consolidated Entertainment', in S. Neale and M. Smith (eds) *Contemporary Hollywood Cinema*. London and New York: Routledge, 21-44.
Morley, D. and K. Robins (1995) *Spaces of Identity: Global Media, Electronic Landscapes, and Cultural Boundaries*. London and New York: Routledge.
Pastergiardis, N. (1997) 'Tracing Hybridity in Theory', in P. Werbner and T. Modood (eds) *Debating Cultural Hybridity: Multi-Cultural Identities and the Politics of Anti-Racism*. London and New Jersey: Zed Books, 257–81.
Robertson, R. (1991) 'Japan and the USA: The Interpenetration of National Identities and the Debate about Orientalism', in N. Abercrombie, S. Hill and B. S. Turner (eds) *Dominant Ideologies*. London: Unwin Hyman, 182–92.
Said, E. (1978) *Orientalism*. New York: Vintage Books.
Sobchack, V. (1991) 'Postmodern Modes of Ethnicity', in L. D. Friedman (ed.) *Unspeakable*

SCREEN METHODS

Images: Ethnicity and the American Cinema. Urbana and Chicago: University of Illinois Press, 329–52.

Springer, C. (1999) 'Psycho-Cybernetics in Films of the 1990s', in A. Kuhn (ed.) *Alien Zone II: The Spaces of Science Fiction Cinema.* London and New York: Verso, 203–18.

Williams, L. R. (1993) 'Sisters under the Skin: Video and Blockbuster Erotic Thrillers', *Sight and Sound*, 3, 7, 105–14.

CHAPTER EIGHT

To Release Himself at the Last Moment: Constructing the Sexual Deviant in Hyde on Screen

Darren Kerr

'The story has been movie-molded almost to the obliteration of its individual character.'
  – *New York Times Film Review*, 29 March 1920 (quoted in Amberg 1971: 17)

'The industry was less concerned with the adaptation of a work than with its adaptation to a set of external political conditions.'
  – Richard Maltby (2000: 82)

'The photographic image was never just about seeing; it was also about knowing.'
  – Isabel Tang (1999: 119)

The simplicity of Isabel Tang's quote above opens up the problematic beginnings of studies in adaptation. There is often an obligatory assertion that links literature and film with reference to D. W. Griffiths' and Joseph Conrad's claims that both forms aim to make you see. It is this visual connection between the forms that initiated studies in adaptation but has, as I will discuss, led the study of screened literature into a methodological blind alley. Adaptation is not about seeing. Adaptation is about making you think and for the film scholars that have long ignored this area of screen study it is about making you re-think.

My aim in this essay is to address the concerns of adaptation study as a screen method and to open up the approach to the shift from text to screen by offering a case study based on film versions of R. L. Stevenson's *The Strange Case of Dr Jekyll and My Hyde* (1886). In this the area of adaptation study converges on how the literary Hyde, who kills an elderly statesman and tramples on a small child, was established on screen as a cinematic sexual sadist through John S. Robertson's silent film of 1920, Rouben Mamoulian's celebrated 1931 film and the 1941 adaptation directed by Victor Fleming and starring Spencer Tracy and Ingrid Bergman.

The critical and commercial success of adaptations have long influenced the field as a topic of study particularly in measuring success through fidelity, that is, how well the screen translates the source text's narrative and 'universal' meanings. This faltering formation of the topic of study illustrates the narrative common ground shared between forms but proves to establish a misguided reading of the cinematic image. The fidelity issue also ensures a lack of consideration for wider influences in adaptation despite this latter approach being a staple methodological feature in film analysis. Imelda Whelehan notes how contemporary methods lead adaptation studies 'into the speculative realms of authorial intention and "appropriate" textual readings' (Cartmell & Whelehan 1999: 17) rather than recognition within the cinematic and other intertextual links.[1] Such marginalisation of methodology will fail to acknowledge the significance of history – as a product of its time certain discourses influence a film's conception and production – and of film language itself. This is where the strongest subversion of traditional adaptation study may emerge.

What has to be confronted is the assumption that the written word has within it a greater symbolic resonance that the screened image. Brian McFarlane explains how literature has low iconic value (a word on a page) and a high symbolic function whilst cinematic signs are of high iconic value (the presentation of an image) and 'uncertain symbolic function' (2000: 47). This reflects on the conceptual and perceptual natures of film and literature and whilst it may be agreed that literature functions *con*ceptually and film *per*ceptually this is too limiting and simplistic, adversely impacting on adaptation studies. The perceptual mode for literature is, by its form, limited (the image of the word/s on a page, for example 'her face was fearful'), but film functions both perceptually and conceptually. The very perceptual mode (*seeing* that face) which denotes – critics of film versions would say limits – meaning is itself made conceptual by the choice of actor, the use of *mise-en-scène*, and the roles of montage and cinematography. Images on the screen, like words on the page, do not function independently. Adaptation studies have too long rested on the assumption that the perceptual nature of images on screen does not afford the space for understanding that literature's conceptual mode does. The moving image gives us the perceptual only to repeatedly expose our perception to the conceptual through film language. What is therefore necessary is to embrace the conceptual mode in adapted texts that demands an awareness of external factors, influences and contexts.

The process of re-imagining a literary text for the screen then becomes an investment of ideas that transcend a critique based on verisimilitude and fidelity because to adapt requests a consideration of ideological, industrial and cultural contexts. This necessitates a multi-perspectival approach.[2] What I hope to demonstrate is how reading adaptation does not have to determine the reduction of literature but in fact does quite the opposite. Adaptation can open out a literary text as its words, actions and themes are imagined across film, its industry, culture and contemporary mores. Rather than reduce, diminish and simplify, adaptation enhances, credits and critiques. Clearly most adaptation studies consider, in Walter Benjamin's terms, the aura of the original source text as dissipated but the film version carries with it a degree of like-originality as it demands understanding in the space of new determinants. Robert R. Ray notes that 'far from destroying the literary source's meaning, adaptation "disseminates" it in a process Benjamin found democratising' (2000: 45). In the case study that follows this notion of adaptation as democratising is illustrated through a close consideration of Hyde and why this literary character became such a specific sexual monster on screen.

Stevenson's novella of 1886 demonstrates many instances of a visual affinity with what later became the cinematic imagination. Examples include the recognition of small but significant detail in close ups ('the silent symbols of the after dinner face'), its montage imaging ('He would be aware of … a nocturnal city; then of the figure of a man walking swiftly; then of a child running from the doctors; and then these met') and dream sequences ('in the darkness … Mr. Enfield's tale went by in a scroll of lighted pictures') (1979: 29; 37). Its narrative structure, however, based on independent and inter-dependent chapters, do little to ease adaptation to mainstream cinematic form. The novella is a combination of conflicting testimonies, witness statements, wills and reports that shift back and forth in time. The character of Hyde denies any ease of adaptation altogether as he is sketched through the voices of various fallible narrators who collectively fail to provide a coherent image. Hyde has a 'deformity without nameable malformation', appears 'particularly small and particularly wicked' and is 'an extraordinary-looking man and yet [is] nothing out of the way' (1979: 40; 48; 34). Those that encounter Hyde are determined by their need to define Hyde, to *see* him and unravel him and whilst they singularly fail to do so they do reveal what he *means* rather than who he is or what he looks like.[3] Along with trampling a small girl and killing an elderly member of Parliament Hyde does little more than stimulate desire through hate, violence and attraction. Most importantly though, he embodies something that is not explained or articulated. This does not mean he *cannot* be explained but that the various narrators who attempt to define him for the reader are unable to do so. The implication is that Hyde provokes a silence which prefigures language and emerges in the form of aborted conversations, the guarding of certain knowledge and the failure to speak of his vices. Like an uncanny moment, language fails to contain or capture Hyde whose very image is recognised but illogical. This inability to articulate also provides a thematic space for the (almost absent) presence of both sex and women in the story.

The Strange Case of Dr Jekyll and My Hyde locates women in a space of difference where they are heard but rarely encountered or spoken of. Their role in the novella is to function through hysteria, to bear witness and to be innocents subject to violence. Again, as they are encoded through inarticulation women are, like Hyde, something of an enigma that needs to be unravelled, classified and ordered. This hidden-presence of women elides with the sexual and for Stephen Heath's seminal essay on Jekyll and Hyde, male sexuality in particular; simply put, Hyde's monstrosity is the 'creation of a civilised sexual morality' which leaves 'male sexuality as problematic' (1986: 100). Heath draws attention to the new sexology of Krafft-Ebing's *Psychopathia Sexualis* (1886) looking at the pathology of the sexual that considers how the act of sex is displaced in favour of violence. For Heath this *perversion* becomes one way of conceiving of 'men's narrative and their story' (1986: 104) around sexuality. Male sexuality, articulated in the silent space of the subtext, allows us to then read Stevenson's literary Hyde as the hidden male, yet to be defined and presented, but alive in a form of desire and perversion as the will to hate, commit violence and embody attraction.

The visual affinity with filmmaking in Stevenson's tale is no surprise as early cinema's turn to narrative forms of telling emerged out of literary-theatrical forms and influences. A recognisable form could capitalise on a growing audience as films moved from sideshows to emerging cinemas which ensured economic growth for this new commercial industry. The filmic narrativising of Stevenson's penny dreadful has its roots in Thomas R. Sullivan's stageplay that provided the blueprint for the early screen adaptations. The play, first performed in America in 1887, ran in the autumn of the following year at London's Lyceum theatre and adapted the cryptic narrative to a linear form. The most basic tenets of classical narrative promoted character, desire and conflict as cornerstones of dramatic progression. The use of this form then opened up an ideal space in which Hyde could now be *seen*.

Each of the films under consideration follow a similar narrative trajectory of cause and effect with six stages to mark the dramatic progression. The introduction offers an insight into Jekyll and his work through the 'human repair shop' (1920) helping the lame to walk in 'free wards' (1931) and saving the mentally unstable from the narrow minds of conventional medicine (1941). Jekyll's work ethic, his sense of altruism and commitment, is questioned at a dinner party held by his future father-in-law where he is reprimanded for his unorthodox views and open affections for his fiancée. It is this critique and reproach that motivates the next stage which turns to how the desire for change is manifested. Jekyll encounters a sexually provocative woman who stimulates the, already present, carnal desire within him. A brief flirtatious exchange is brought to a halt but proves critical in the next sequence that begins with Jekyll's first transformation and his living as Hyde. Returning to the music hall where Jekyll first encountered his fiancées flirtatious alter ego Hyde now coerces her into his company and subsequently brutalises and rapes her. This continued maltreatment is carried through the next stage that plays out the consequences for Jekyll. Temporarily estranged from his fiancée Jekyll ceases to take the vial, and resolves to wait for his impending marriage. The penultimate episode sees Hyde re-emerging without the use of the chemical draught, becoming stronger than Jekyll and provoking Jekyll's death in the narrative dénouement. The death does not, however, signal Hyde's success but rather his degeneration and Jekyll's salvation as the doctor dies as a Promethean figure.

Through the three adaptations the extent and excess of Hyde's sadism and sexual violence becomes more apparent. John Barrymore's Hyde (1920), a vampiric spider with a distended head, negotiates with the music hall manager to have the exotic Italian dancer 'Miss Gina'. His sadistic degeneration is manifested through performance and expression as his sharp gestures and physical ageing mark his time with Gina whose own physical and psychological deterioration is notable when he sends her out onto the street saying he is done with her. Hyde's attraction and repulsion towards the dancer is made manifest on entering a bar and encountering two women. One is clean, attractive and flirtatious towards Hyde who responds by moving his cane along her leg. The second female, slovenly, dirty and an alcoholic, interrupts Hyde, also offering a sexual encounter. Interestingly both are rejected as Hyde forces them to gaze upon their reflections, an illustrative action that marks the women with shame. Whilst most obviously signifying and supporting the story's foremost theme of duality the scene more interestingly articulates Hyde's pleasure in constructing the women's humiliation and ignominy. It is at this point that he takes a room and is presented with a girl who in articulating fear and aversion proves a more suitable sexual partner for Hyde. This associative bond between lust and cruelty is further imagined through Frederic March's performance in Mamoulian's 1932 adaptation.

March energised Hyde's paraphilia both physically and verbally by explaining away his violence as an expression of love for Miriam Hopkins' singer Ivy Pearson. Hyde, made up as a Neanderthal primitive, gives us a male sexuality that belongs to a pre-civilised being who is a model of primary narcissism. Hyde's sexual violence sees Ivy beaten and raped until suicide appears to be her only release. Again he can only be gratified once the woman has been prostituted, in this case her complicity coercively exchanged for champagne, silk and jewellery. In having to perform this role (out of fear) Ivy not only endures a humiliation that excites Hyde but ultimately condemns her own life. In one of several bedroom scenes Hyde assaults her, desperately demanding she speak of the loathing that clearly consumes them both. Whilst this can be seen as a lucid moment on behalf of the Jekyll/Hyde conflict and their mutual torment, it is carefully coloured by Percy Heath and Samuel Hoffenstein's script that has Hyde admit that his attraction to Ivy is stimulated by provoking her in her heightened emotional states. Ivy's death provides a logical conclusion to Hyde's screen sadism, as the sex is finally completely displaced by violence, leading to a murder in which suffering is deemed both arousing and exciting. In this scene Mamoulian has Ivy offering herself to Hyde on her knees moments before he strangles her next to the bed.

The most disturbing quality in Fleming's 1941 remake of Mamoulian's film is how it moves towards naturalising the sadism through Hyde and Ivy's relationship that now mirrors an abusive marriage rather than an illicit relationship. Spencer Tracy's performance sees Hyde's sadism become internalised and a more carefully implicit expression of how power and control are sexually accentuated.[4] The sadism is written through symbolic gestures in how his influence bares down upon Ingrid Bergman's barmaid Ivy. Her appearance, dress and hair are altered along with her speech that is often reduced in his presence to yes/no responses and diminished by his interjections. An important exchange between Hyde and Ivy's friend Marsha indicates that she too can change the way she thinks of Hyde's inappropriate sexual gesturing just as Ivy has done. The master-slave paradigm central to sadistic relationships is again not just illustrated through the violence Ivy is subjected to but is also enforced through his demanding she 'perform' the music-hall song. The scene, unlike Mamoulian's that demonstrated Hyde's power and control, now intimates his need for her to *become* the flirtatious girl to justify his treatment of her.

This stronger sense of hidden domestic violence in Victorian culture, typified through upper-body injuries and 'shaming, polluting gesture[s]' (D'Cruze 1998: 75) is in Fleming's film carried beyond Hyde's world of professional gentlemen. The sense of hidden domestic violence is typified in the upper-body injuries Ivy later exposes to a companion. In having to explain the bruises and whip-marks across her back she implicitly exposes the 'shaming polluting gestures' of such violence in Victorian culture. These 'gestures' of control manifested in violence that demands intimate proximity are expressed beyond Hyde's world of professional gentlemen. Prior to raping Ivy, Hyde delivers a line ('The world is yours my darling. The moment mine') that becomes the first line of the next scene in an exchange between two working-men that Hyde passes on his return to the laboratory.[5] The notion that Hyde's *being* extends to all is further expressed in the lack of make-up applied to

Tracy in the transformation sequences which has become the staple cinematic gesture of conceiving of the change as less physiological and more psychological. With Hyde now portrayed as a dishevelled Jekyll the division between the two is greatly reduced. Jekyll can no longer hide behind an extended visual metaphor – Barrymore's spider, March's ape – but rather gives us an unruly and uncivil body that implies contagion, deterioration and appears diseased. On gazing at his first mirrored reflection as Hyde, Jekyll claims 'change, but no change' signalling his freedom that gives us a return of the repressed in his own recognised form.

If Stevenson's Hyde is the hidden male then the early cinematic Hyde is the hidden male made present and revealed. The adapted versions do this through a notion of Victorian sexuality informed by medico-moral panics. This draws a correlative narrative between sex, disease and dis-ease in society. Frank Mort notes how male sexuality in the late nineteenth century was conceived of as being subject to instinctual forces that required 'physical and mental gratification through semen discharge in the act of copulation' (2000: 61). Outside of this other sex acts were perceived as illegitimate forms of gratification that compromised the restraint demanded of professional gentlemen; a concept belonging in the same discursive field as hard work and intellectual control. Both homosexuality and masturbation were immoral acts, the former described as 'the paramount sexual sin' (Hall 1991: 32) and the latter legislated against 'all forms of … contact' (Mort 2000: 101). What is important here is how discourses around medico-moral panic and the film adaptations use the role of women to both legitimise and construct Hyde for the screen in order to define the problematic male sexuality that governs both Jekyll's decision to take the id emetic and Hyde's sadism.

Whilst Victorian society's 'respected gentleman' was virtuous on account of his sexual activity and restraint, the respected wife and eventual mother was defined through the 'absence of sexual desire' (Mort 2000: 61). This absence perceives a lack in sexual desire as a morally sound deficiency that defines the 'pure woman'. The sexually active woman who refused to deny the presence of sexual desire was then read as a depraved figure and morally vacuous contagion. This polarisation of female sexuality served illicit male desires at a time when advances in the photographic image saw the market for pornography expand.[6] By polarising women thus, it not only served to define and legitimise aggressive male sexuality (in being the *doer*) but also justified the degradation of women (in being *done* to). This is especially so of the 'prostitute' whose sexuality, culturally constructed as illegitimate, became the Victorian locus of attraction, hate and violence; the very qualities that define the literary Hyde and encompass the notion of men's problematic sexuality.[7] Hyde's screen sadism is written out of this notion of medico-moral panic and appeared on screen at the time psychoanalytic theories became popular cultural currency for Hollywood narratives.

Hyde's move onto the popular screen mirrors Hollywood's use of Freud in its narrative and characterisation. It is not Freud in particular that is of significance here but how the adaptation to Hollywood narrative form makes demands upon characterisation. The classic narrative style, in which Hyde's sadism emerged, is fixed on explorations of causality, particularly through psychological motivations and the overcoming of various obstacles to achieve resolution. Sexual neuroses and pathological behaviour see Hyde on screen governed by a narcissism and self-preservation, which overwhelms Jekyll's ability to enact the restraint that would stabilise his identity. More obviously presented is the Hollywood narrative's common use of Oedipal rivalry as Jekyll battles personally and professionally with his fiancée's father before Hyde eventually kills him. Jekyll's sexual frustrations are then vented violently through sadism on the flirtatious girl from the music hall.

Whilst the use of Freud and the instability of identity have been integrated into Hollywood narrative it is still predominantly 'defined as a conservative system because it practically guarantees that the existing order will prevail' (Strinati 2000: 30). Each film sees Jekyll punished for his transgressions, which restores order and leaves his respectable colleague, Lanyon, to orchestrate Hyde's demise and Jekyll's necessary salvation. Jekyll's atoning suicide in Clara Beranger's 1920 script places Lanyon as protector in telling Jekyll's fiancée that Hyde has murdered him. Hoffenstein and Heath's script for Mamoulian sees Lanyon lead the police to Hyde's laboratory where he is shot dead by a police officer. In Fleming's film John Mahin wrote Lanyon as the killer of Hyde increasing his agency in reinstating order. Despite this conservative reading of restored order it is not difficult to reveal an anti-Victorian sentiment in the adaptations that subvert any such notion of resolving the 'enigma' central to classic narrative form.

Guy Barefoot's work on gaslight melodramas noted Fleming's opening church-scene sermon showed how the 'values of morality, the family, capitalism, progress and Christianity – values that are explicitly characterised as Victorian – become less clear' (2001: 90). Hyde is firstly a reaction to these Victorian values that see to it that he does not succeed. Culture suppresses the revolt and its reasons for happening but despite filmmaking codes that demand the restoration of order the revolt against Victorian values is significantly given a voice. Hyde's sexuality and shift in adaptation (into overt sadism) becomes a reaction to the values that create the *perverse* in this representation of male sexuality. Hyde's sadism then (rightfully) must not succeed. What is important here in the adaptation is that problematic male sexuality is given voice. So despite the narrative restoration of (Victorian) social order an anti-Victorian discourse and consideration of perverse male sexuality is opened up by how the films have adapted Stevenson's text.[8]

Finally, a brief comment should address how significant *reading* adaptation is in illustrating the shift from Stevenson's hidden male to Hyde's murderous sadism. Foucault's *The History of Sexuality* (1978) identifies a societal need for locating power in certain forms of knowledge and recognises how sexuality itself has been used to shape modern consciousness. Assuming legitimate forms of bourgeois power repress sex, Foucault notes how political and sexual liberation is deemed possible through engaging more fully in discourses on sexuality. Whilst Foucault is more concerned with how this repressive hypothesis was formed, such an example of liberation is demonstrated through not just the films but through the *adaptations* of Hyde.

Reading the adapted Hyde becomes a means of exploring male sexuality through a narrative of perversion. This begins to reveal the hidden male (or hidden sexuality) of Stevenson's source text. The sadism of Hyde is clearly not proposed as an answer to living without repressing but proves a most effective and dynamic way to enforce discussion and debate about this area (the criminal-sexual, the lust-murder) of male sexuality. Cinema does after all invite you to look and Hyde is gazed upon and finally recognised.

Adaptations operate within new contexts that disseminate meaning whilst simultaneously re-functioning it. This process of democratising the source material consistently provides a means of exploring its central themes and characters without being limited to the concerns of fidelity. Only in the shift from text to screen is *The Strange Case of Dr Jekyll and My Hyde*'s problematic male sexuality given the vocabulary to speak for the novella's profound silences. The burden of adaptation has been that it is too often considered as an impure form of cinema and so has itself been suppressed. The methodology of adaptation as democratising denies this and reminds us that 'things repressed (objects, groups, signs, questions) return in displaced forms' (Ray 2000: 48). The historical compulsion of film is to continually reveal that there iss always more to show and more to see and adapting literature to cinema's narrative and generic conventions cannot suppress this.

Notes

1   In his preface to *Novel to Film: An Introduction to the Theory of Adaptation* (2000) Brian McFarlane acknowledges such marginalisation of methods.
2   What is not accounted for in this essay is detailed contextual influence for each film but a broader consideration of an evolving monster in Hyde.
3   Collectively, Hyde appears small, hairy and physically repulsive.
4   A further explanation for a more implicit expression of Hyde's sadism in 1941 can be related to the major studios' compliance with the Hays Code's focus on restricting scenes of sex and crime. Mamoulian somewhat escaped the rigours of the production code for whilst it was produced in 1930 it was not enforced until 1934 with the introduction of the Production Code Administration.
5   The line delivered is 'an I says to her, I says the world may be yours my darling…'
6   Pornography saw art's idealised nude become the naked woman of the common classes. For more on this, see Tang 1999: 94–118.
7   For more on this see Mort 2000: 53–61 and D'Cruze 1998.
8   Barefoot sees this anti-Victorianism as part of a wider debate concerning the rise of popular culture in Britain and America and its respective film industries (2001: 93–106).

Bibliography

Amberg, G. (1971) *New York Times Film Reviews 1913–1970*. New York: Arno Press.
Barefoot, G. (2001) *Gaslight Melodrama*. London: Continuum.
Benjamin, W. (1970) *Illuminations*. London: Jonathan Cape.
Cartmell, D. and I. Whelehan (1999) *Adaptations: From Text to Screen, Screen to Text*. London: Routledge.
D'Cruze, S. (1998) *Crimes of Outrage: Sex, Violence and Victorian Working Women*. Manchester: Manchester University Press.
Foucault, M. (1978) *The History of Sexuality, Volume One: An Introduction*. London: Penquin.
Hall, L. (1991) *Hidden Anxieties: Male Sexuality 1900–1950*. Cambridge: Polity Press.
Heath, S. (1986) 'Psychopathia sexualis: Stevenson's *Strange Case*', in C. MacCabe (ed.) *Critical Quarterly*, 28, 1/2. Manchester: Manchester University Press, 93–108.

Krafft-Ebing, R. von (1886) *Psychopathia Sexualis*, trans. C. G. Chaddock. London: F. A. Davis.

McFarlane, B. (2000) *Novel to Film: An Introduction to the Theory of Adaptation*. Oxford: Clarendon.

Matlby, R. (2000) 'To Prevent the Prevalent Type of Book: Censorship and Adaptation in Hollywood 1924–34', in J. Naremore (ed.) *Film Adaptation*. London: Athlone Press, 79–105.

Mort, F. (2000) *Dangerous Sexualities: Micro-moral Panics in England Since 1850*. London: Routledge.

Ray, R. B. (2000) 'The Field of Literature and Film', in J. Naremore (ed.) *Film Adaptation*. London: Athlone Press, 38–53.

Stevenson, R. L. (1979 [1886]) *The Strange Case of Dr Jekyll and My Hyde and Other Stories*. London: Penguin.

Tang, I. (1999) *Pornography: The Secret History of Civilisation*. Oxford: Macmillan.

CHAPTER NINE

Room with a Gay View?: Sexuality, Spectatorship and *A Room With a View*

Michael Williams

Introduction

A Room with a View (James Ivory, 1986), the story of the romantic awakening of a young Englishwoman while staying in Tuscany, has an established critical appraisal.[1] It is generally viewed, along with other heritage films produced in Britain since the early 1980s, as an idealised and somewhat reactionary escape into the nostalgic past of the authorial classic. The opening titles proudly proclaim the quality of the production, as flowing regency script seamlessly segues between the names of Merchant/Ivory and E. M. Forster and a veritable Who's Who of British character actors. The music is opera; Italian of course.

The film's introduction is at once classic and conservative, all allusions, both specific (the author) and general (the 'feeling' or sensibility) point to high-art values and period authenticity. It all seems very earnest. If we respond to these signals seriously and take them at face value, we would cringe, like Alan Hollinghurst of the *Times Literary Supplement*, at the pretence of the opening titles, and nit-pick over historical specificities. The film's central theme, he notes, the Puccini aria 'O Mio Babbino Caro', was written a decade after the film is set and, moreover, it is included merely for 'the noise and tingle of the scalp, not for what it is actually saying' (1986: 395). I suggest that to respond to this text with such humourless sobriety is to close a closet door on alternative readings. However, Hollinghurst does inadvertently suggest the potential of a camp reading of the film, for what is this 'tingle' he describes but an emotional enjoyment of excess?

I wish to privilege the tingle over the actual in this essay. That is, to try and take an active look at the text beyond its classic reception as a pseudo-high-art arte-fact of middle-class heterosexual romance. This is not to argue for the assertion of an 'alternative' reading against a dominant or mainstream one, and thus to simply replace one monolithic approach with another, but to highlight those tingling and enticing agitations within and without the text. By using textual analysis and exam-ining its critical reception, I shall argue that the film sustains a variety of readings in simultaneity. While my primary emphasis is on the sexual machinations of the

Merchant-Ivory film, there are of course many other areas of interest – nationality, race, gender and, indeed, class – that will be necessarily neglected. I will seek to indicate the approaches that might be taken to articulate the potential for a 'queer' reading (perhaps in its broadest sense) of *A Room with a View*, but also the methodological problems that arise in even considering such an undertaking.

A starched text?

Many critics, regardless of their opinion of the film, assume a reverential tone in their accounts, as if it were necessary to doff their hats before such 'vivid and lovely' art, as the *Daily Mirror* put it (Marshall 1986: 46). It seems hard to get away from the perception that this is a film solely about the (upper) middle class and for the middle class. Andy Medhurst, for example, perceives something almost demonically oppressive about the white lacy ruffles of the blouse worn by Helena Bonham-Carter in the film, citing it as yet another example of the '"white flannel" texts that infested' British cinema in the 1980s (1995: 17). Even E. M. Forster himself once apologetically ascribed a certain Home Counties ethos to his novel in describing it as 'a slight sketch of bourgeois life in an Italian Pension and at home in Surrey' (in Lago & Furbank 1985: 117).[2] While Medhurst may be broadly right in terms of the class ethics often pervading this film and others in the 'deadening and unforgivable' Merchant-Ivory oeuvre, surely he misses the point when he argues that 'pure, prim and high-necked, it stands for all the starched, body-hating bookishness that makes this genre into film-for-people-who-hate-cinema' (1995: 17). As Andrew Higson has pointed out, the starchiness of the garment is 'actually an important signification of Lucy's character, and especially her buttoned-up attitude towards sexuality' (2003: 41). Indeed, for she will later witness lively scenes of full-frontal male nudity, which presents something of a challenge to the film's apparently 'body-hating' aesthetics.

Higson's re-assertion of the character motivation of Bonham-Carter's costume highlights another tension he observes in the heritage film, that of the ostensibly conflicting demands of spectacle and narrative. Higson has found ambivalent campness within the 'nostalgia and pastiche' of the heritage film and has highlighted the 'diversity of interpretations' facilitated by these texts (see Higson 2003: 74 and 2006). A key critic in pushing such interpretations further is Claire Monk, who argued that *A Room with a View* was positively 'simmering with feminine, queer and ambiguous sexualities' which makes the film much more sexually 'radical' in comparison to its eponymous and apparently more sexually transgressive counterparts: *Maurice* (James Ivory, 1987), *Carrington* (Christopher Hampton, 1995) and *Orlando* (Sally Potter, 1992) (1995: 33).[3]

I wish to follow Monk and examine *A Room with a View* as a film highly conducive to a gay reading. It is no more (or less) appropriate to impose a monolithic 'gay' reading of the film than it is to describe a 'straight' one; identities (to employ that slippery concept for a moment) are more complex than that, as are other factors that determine the experience of the spectator. I also hesitate to conjure up the spectre of 'representation' here; not only is the term itself archaic and highly problematic in relation to contemporary theory, but it could be argued that it is exactly and paradoxically the *absence* of overt gay representation that affords the film a radical edge. To discover this edge, I will argue, requires not 'reading against the grain' or even the stripping of period veneer to 'reveal' latent meanings, but to explore the openness of the text and approaches to it. The importance of this difference is that it does not imply a denigration of either the text or status of the spectator in the act of (mis)reading.

One early scene set in the Pensione Bertolini (where the central characters reside while in Florence), depicting Lucy's piano practice being discovered by Mr Beebe (Simon Callow), a Surrey vicar, not only offers the period spectacle expected of the heritage genre but also functions as a metaphor of the kind of 'camp' reading strategies I am discussing. We first see a wide shot of a rather dark, richly furnished and rather claustrophobic drawing room, complete with red silk damask wallpaper, wherein Lucy is passionately playing Beethoven on a piano on the far side of the room. Dominating a rather flamboyant *mise-en-scène* stands a ridiculously substantial piece of Victorian furniture in the centre of the room, consisting of circle of four upholstered seats surrounding a central wooden pillar crowned with a planter. The camera remains motionless for a moment in order to take in the room before it begins to track towards Lucy. However, as her playing becomes more passionate, we notice Mr Beebe lean forward from his concealed position on the opposite side of the furnishing, much to the surprise of Lucy and the viewer, who were both unprepared for his appearance. Cutting to a medium close-up, Beebe then pronounces – evoking the florid prose of romantic novelist Miss Lavish (Judy Dench) – that 'if Miss Honeychurch ever takes to live as she plays, it will be very exciting both for us and for her'.

This brief scene appears to demonstrate precisely the kind of aesthetic submission before period ornamentation criticised by Medhurst, a 'tension' which Higson also notes:

> It is hardly of narrative significance that Mr Beebe is eventually revealed sitting on the far side of this item of furniture, watching Lucy play the piano: it is not as if the revelation of Mr Beebe has created suspense or mystery. Rather, the camera seems more concerned to play over the paintings on the wall, Lucy's dress, and the particular quality of light in the room. (2003: 38)

Higson underlines the way that part of the pleasure of the heritage film is that it offers more than just narrative, which can be subordinated to the degree that 'views' such as the one above are 'displayed for the cinema spectator alone' (ibid.). However, I would argue that there *is* narrative significance in the revelation of Beebe in this scene, exactly in respect to the spectatorial views it facilitates in metaphor. The voyeuristic position that Mr Beebe adopts (and perhaps the spectator) in observing Lucy, and 'discovering' her hitherto concealed passion will later be reversed in the Sacred Lake sequence that it in many ways anticipates. In that sequence, while it is Beebe – and the other bathers, but most comically Beebe – that is hidden from view and then literally exposed, it is Lucy that voyeuristically discovers not only his nudity, but his hidden passion for life (and who knows what else). Moreover, what the ostensibly conservative period ornamentation functions to do in the Pensione Bertolini scene, is to conceal an 'out' gay actor within the fabric of the *mise-en-scène* – 'Callow being famously gay', as Claire Monk observes

(1995: 34) – which casts a certain queer perspective across both scenes. Both use settings designed to give a false sense of privacy to accommodate two of the most 'revealing' emotional expressions in the closeted Edwardiana of the film. Moreover, the way that the spectator is also implicated by the shared voyeuristic gaze of Mr Beebe determines an active hermeneutic of discovery/exposure that underscores the film. This is signified by the tracking shots that present a 'way in' to the scene whether that be peering round furniture screens or the gaps between the trees that surround the lake.

The tingle and the actual: approaching the Sacred Lake

I have made references above to the importance of the spectator and 'camp' readings of the film, so it is necessary to try and determine what is meant by this problematic term. Definitions of camp are legion, but usually revolve around it being a 'site of debate' and act of 'critical labour' as Fabio Cleto puts it in his overview of the theory; the critical tensions between the tingle and the actual, perhaps (1999: 4, 6).

When approaching a text in terms of queer readings, one has not only to think about the question of whether those 'meanings' are there, but also run the gamut of gay, lesbian, queer and, more recently, anti-gay methodologies and contemplate why there should be a desire to locate them in the first place. Thus critics who seek to 'out' what have been perceived to be coded mainstream texts are matched by those who problematise such an activity. On the 'outing' side we have the likes of Moe Meyer, whose edited collection, The Politics and Poetics of Camp (1994), attacked what he saw as the dislocation of camp from the queer in popular culture, not least through Susan Sontag's influential 1967 essay on the subject. The task of the critic, he argues, is to relocate an essentially queer 'substance' to camp style, performance or sensibility (1994: 7). Meyer has been widely attacked for essentialism in arguing for queer authenticity (authentic to what, we may ask), and thus limiting the very performative freedoms that he celebrates in the concept of camp. Indeed, Higson finds Sontag's understanding of camp highly conducive to the study of the heritage film: 'camp art is often decorative art, emphasising texture, sensuous surface and style at the expense of content' (1967: 278). Even the tinglingly sensuous surface constitutes the beginning of a relationship with the text, one where 'content' is very much present through the viewer's projected experience. And who is to say that one film is more or less 'full' of meaning than another?

While critics including Fabio Cleto and Brett Farmer highlight the problems inherent in Meyer's monolithic concept of queer readings and performance, they also warn that the turning tide against essentialism has its own dangers (see Cleto 1999; Farmer 2000). As Farmer explains, if we take the anti-essentialist deconstruction of identity to its extreme one runs the risk of de-gaying gayness entirely, leaving 'an acritical, utopian reading of spectatorship as unbounded and voluntarist, with subjects gleefully partaking of a panerotic smorgasbord with no regard for the structuring materialities of social, sexual and psychic organisation' (2000: 39). Quoting from Eve Kosofsky Sedgwick, Farmer points out that to a large degree the project of gay and lesbian studies rest on '"promises to make the invisible possibilities and desires visible; [and] to make the tacit things explicit"' (2000: 1).[4]

Farmer thus proposes a framework that accommodates gay-identified readings in a psychosocial context on a non-prescriptive, provisional and performative basis. However, the 'anti-gay' movement has challenged the reductive and self-ghettoising tendencies of gay and lesbian culture to seek queer 'representation' in texts rather than delighting in the pleasures implicitly offered by the cinema (see Burston 1996). As Bruce LaBruce and Glenn Belverio irreverently conclude, 'there's a lot more room in the closet' (LaBruce & Belverio 1996: 140). Indeed, the primary reason I am so drawn to A Room with a View is exactly for the way that it is full of possibilities that just would not be available if lingering glances and sequestered impulses were 'outed' within the text. However, shutting up about queer readings of such texts would make discussing them in a sexually politicised context impossible.

The sequence that I wish, perhaps obviously, to concentrate on, is the male bathing scene where Lucy's potential beau, George Emerson (Julian Sands), her brother Freddy (Rupert Graves) and Mr Beebe romp nakedly in the inviting waters of a secluded wooded pool known as the 'Sacred Lake' until they are discovered by Lucy, her mother and her bookish fiancé Cecil. The scene perplexes some reviewers and is ignored by many more, despite being one of the most striking sequences of the film. Indeed, the Today newspaper rather wonderfully points to the existence of a sub-text as it condemns the 'ridiculously protracted bathing scene' by wondering whether E. M. Forster was a 'closet naturalist' (Billsun 1986: 24). I think the intended term was naturist, but what they really should have identified is the nature of this text as a work of Forster the closeted homosexual. Gay cultural commentators such as Thomas Waugh have been more direct in making this link, suggesting that Merchant-Ivory 'succeeded in keeping some of Forster's gay sensibility' intact in their version of the text, 'something that went considerably deeper than the skinny-dip sequence, immortal as it was' (2000: 188). Ironically, the name E. M. Forster thus subverts rather than legitimises the 'classic' authorial status of the text.

The comic utopian fantasy of the bathing scene allowed Forster to write romantically on an oblique level without revealing too much of the nature of his own object choice. Similarly, gay songwriters such as Cole Porter found an ideal outlet for their romantic lyrics about men through the simple device of a female vocalist/narrator. In this way Lucy herself becomes a fluid and 'exchangeable' figure of identification and this lack of a name, a label, is part of the freedom of the bathing scene for different audiences. Without making an issue out of sexuality, which would thereby create a narrative problem, the scene is open and even liberating.[5] Gay men and straight women can enjoy this rare spectacle of unproblematic male nudity, while others (are straight male spectators least catered for in this scene?) can laugh with or perhaps at the men, facilitated by the farcical dénouement of the sequence. As Judith Mayne has observed, film theory has often neglected the possibility that 'one of the distinct pleasures of the cinema may well be a "safe zone" in which homosexual as well as heterosexual desires can be fantasised and acted out' (1993: 97), although we should remember the limits of utopia highlighted by Farmer, above (2000: 35).

It is, then, something of a paradox that the sexual freedom contained within the Sacred Lake sequence is only feasible by keeping this subtext securely closeted. On the one hand this makes the bathing scene very repressive for the homo-erotic imperative of the scene is silent and cannot be openly acknowledged. Equally, however, by refusing to label and therefore problematise this 'love that dare not speak its name', homosexuality does not become an issue that would stand in the way of the utopian dream. 'Naming it' would surely also invoke a '15' rather than a 'PG' certificate, highlighting the commercial expediency of silence. The scene is endearing rather than rude because of its bare-cheeked innocence. Produced in the era of Thatcherite conservatism and as AIDS was beginning to hit the headlines, this 'PG'-rated spectacle seems truly exceptional. If the spectre of 'HOMOSEXUALITY' had been directly enunciated by the film, the naked threesome in the woods would evoke significantly less 'tasteful' connotations. It would have seemed like the 'holy trinity' in white linen had interrupted the men 'just in time', before they did anything that might really end up in the tabloids.

Aside from crudely revealing that George is a less inhibited suitor to Lucy than Cecil, and thus marking something of a sexual 'revelation', there is little apparent narrative justification for the lengthiness of the scene. The dialogue it does contain is limited to shouts and shrieks or snatches of Coleridge's 'Kubla Khan', which merely adds a note of mystification. But if the three characters stopped moving, splashing and shouting for a moment, not only would they stop having fun, but they, and the audience would start to think about what they were doing. Looks and glances would become conscious rather than subliminal. As Richard Dyer and Steve Neale have discussed, the spectacle of the nude male is a rather paradoxical phenomenon in the visual media; evidently displaying the body as an object while at the same time attempting to disavow its objectification, often through physical action to legitimate its 'exposure', especially by the male spectator (see Dyer 1992; Neale 1992). Continuous movement thus 'changes the subject' in more ways than one, it glosses over the potential subtext and in so doing accommodates multiple viewing positions.

Problematising the male nude

No attempt is made to hide genitals at the Sacred Lake, when it would have been so easy to have done so in editing and composition. Indeed the camera position, and the shallow depth of the (artificially created) lake (see Callow 1986: 38), greatly facilitates genital display, though we are of course spared anything too close up. One gay-run internet fansite dedicated to the film contains a link to the article 'A Little Peek: Male Nudity in the Movies', suggesting that this scene is one of the main pleasures of the film (Jones 2002). For Pauline Kael, however, such display creates a 'problem of tone': 'what's awkward about this scene, which is rather long (though not as protracted as it is in the book), is that we know it's supposed to demonstrate natural, unrepressed good fun, but frisking around with no clothes on can't feel natural to the actors when the camera is rolling' (1986: 115). Kael's conclusion that Lucy's little giggle of amusement 'rescues the scene, gives it a point, and gets Ivory off the hook' (ibid.), carries the implicit connotation that there is even more to the scene than meets the eye, despite the *Daily Mirror*'s astonishment at 'everything waving in the wind' (Marshall 1986: 46). This innuendo may have been compounded for audiences viewing the film's theatrical trailer. Taking the nude bathing scene out of context, we first witness a scene of Lucy's hair being rather briskly combed by Charlotte who opines of George: 'I have met the type before, they seldom keep their exploits to themselves.' With Lucy's understandable query, 'exploits?', the trailer immediately cuts to a shot of the naked threesome romping in the water. The implication of this juxtaposition is that these are the 'exploits' to which Charlotte refers, establishing a sense of innuendo to the scene even before audiences reached the film itself.

The element of 'getting off the hook' is similar to the 'getting away with it' factor that I have been discussing. Is there really something that queer and dubious about this scene? The aspect of this scene that perhaps sits most uncomfortably with the rest of the film, is its connection with iconographic sources far removed from the classic terms by which the text is generally appreciated. Claire Monk hints at the nature of this alternative cinematic register in *A Room with a View*: 'The rarity of the spectacle of the male body, outside films aimed at a gay audience, clearly places these movies somewhat outside the mainstream; it also makes them likely sites of anxiety for straight male spectators' (1995: 34).

In other words, what Monk suggests is that in this sequence, this 'PG'-rated British heritage film has more in common with gay pornography than its respectable outward appearance would indicate; which would present an almost sacrilegious clash of high and low-art sensibilities. How can *A Room with a View* be compared to what *Sight and Sound* calls 'the rock-bottom cheapest (and most despised) form of cinema' (Newman 1997: 28)? It is an idea that would be shockingly alien to the *Daily Mail*, which sees the film as the antithesis of porn when pondering the success of the Merchant-Ivory movie in America: 'In the country that virtually invented the commercial side of the permissive society, making cinema porn into mass entertainment with epics such as *Deep Throat*, what chance would there be for a film whose overt sex is restricted to a single kiss exchanged by fully clothed lovers?' (Usher 1986: 7). While also suggesting the possibility that there might be 'covert' sex in the film, the connection to pornography brings into question not only the prestige status of the text but also the spectator that watching it under a high-art 'cover', hence perhaps the awkward squirming of the critics. Although it should be remembered that images of the male nude pervade the gay scene, which somewhat de-centres dominant conceptions of sexual morality and 'decency' with regard to the display of the body. As Thomas Waugh puts it: 'nude bathing has been one of the most obsessive motifs of gay male narrative since its beginnings' (2000: 187).

'The oddest people, the queerest people ... full of possibilities...'

Alan Hollinghurst describes the bodies of the young men on display as 'sleek and attractive' (1986: 395). While this account fits the svelte torso of George, it is certainly not true of poor Mr Beebe. It is the physical incongruity of Beebe that acts as a catalyst in the sequence. Literary criticism of the novel has dwelt upon Beebe as a closet gay character, whose celibacy has affinity with the Platonic love that embraces physical beauty without consummation. Beebe was shocked yet delighted by the homo-erotic imperative of Freddy's summons to 'come and have a bathe', and follows him and George into the woods entirely uninvited, as Monk notes: 'The transgressiveness of the bathing scene is sealed by Beebe's participation ... his only motivation for accompanying the two young men to the pond is voyeurism' (1995: 34). Being 'famously gay' thus opens up the scene to the kind of knowing reading proposed by Barbara Klinger in discussing the (retrospectively) 'droll response' evoked by the queer presence of Rock Hudson in Douglas Sirk's melodramas, where 'camp audiences may be cognisant of the substantial artifice behind romantic conceits' (1994: 151).

However problematic notions of the 'progressive' may be, the presence of an identifiably gay actor in the threesome is an expedient move; it helps provide and access points for different identifications and brings humour to the scene. Callow details how insistent Merchant-Ivory were to cast him as Mr Beebe in his account of the making of the film for *The Sunday Times*. Amid tales of taking Julian Sands to transvestite clubs in Florence 'frequented by gay German dwarfs'; Callow quotes Ismail Merchant as saying to him 'you're the only person in the world who could bring it off', while James Ivory claims that the character would be 'boring' if played by anyone else (1986: 38). Callow embellishes the scene with extra-textual camp-ness; indeed, he himself has noted the strategy of the 'camp-hound' in making queer readings of films partly through the presence of gay performers or directors, spectators who look for 'the hidden innuendo, marvelling at the outrageous excess' (Callow 2003: 16).[6] Moreover, Merchant and Ivory are cited by Boze Hadleigh and Thomas Waugh as themselves being a gay couple, at least by implication of their cohabitation; 'let's take the liberty of bestowing on them henceforth the honor-ary label of "gay filmmakers"', the latter suggested in 1987 (see Hadleigh 2001: 244; Waugh 2000: 190). Despite the speculative nature of such labels, it is clear that the extra-textual personas of cast, crew and Forster as author are deployed as if circum-stantial evidence (or gossip) to support the readings highlighted in this chapter. Indeed, there has been persistent speculation on the internet and in the press as to whether another of the bathers, Rupert Graves, might be gay, although the actor has now married.

The 'voyeurism' of Callow's Mr Beebe, highlighted by Monk, also textually situ-ates a position of identification for the spectator, whether gay or not, facilitated by the structure of the Sacred Lake sequence as a whole. With the threesome absorbed in dizzy abandon, we suddenly cut away from the main arena to a long-shot that echoes that of their approach to the pool. This shot, as if from the position of an unseen and unknown onlooker, is highly voyeuristic and facilitates an ontology of exposure by visually enabling the possibility of discovery (like the tracking camera in the Pensione earlier). As Simon Callow is 'actually' and famously gay, the anxious glances he casts into the bushes as he disrobes have even greater significance. The threat is not only one of being found naked, and with other men, but of meaning being attached to it.

Conclusion

Clearly, disparate approaches can be brought into play when approaching the Sacred Lake scene and there evidently exists a perceived need when making queer readings to subject films to particularly close textual analysis as if to prove that 'something' is 'in' there. As Paul Burston points out, 'a critic who adopts this kind of approach is often accused of "reading against the text", of taking an "oppositional" or (better yet) an "alternative" view' (1995: 120). Yet such allegations are 'founded on the assumption that all cultural production is, by its very nature, straight, unless it proclaims itself otherwise' (ibid.). Indeed, why should a 'gay' or 'straight' reading of *A Room with a View* be more or less valid than the other within a film that flaunts a *mise-en-scène* of every sort of excess? Such defensive strategies link back to the distinction between the 'tingle' and the 'actual' and assumptions about what a text 'really' means.

As I have illustrated in this case-study, *A Room with a View*'s 'vivid and lovely' façade of apparent cultural and sexual conventionality might conceal (and enable the possibility to reveal) other, homoerotic discourses, that can be accessed, or politely ignored, depending on who is watching. If arguing for a queer interpretation of any text one calls upon the same strategies as for making a so-called 'straight' one, albeit perhaps with an added emphasis on the implicit. This includes lingering gazes that express otherwise unarticulated desires, awkward moments that hint at something suppressed, along with extra-textual knowledge about stars, directors and authors. All this might be placed under that elusive heading of camp, whether that be understood as a excess of surface artifice indicating layers concealed beneath, or as a screen onto which a camp audience can project queer meanings themselves. The performative process, or methodology, is thus as significant as the outcome, although some texts provide more explicitly queer starting points than others, including that playful 'tingle' in the tone of *A Room with a View*, perhaps. A gay friend of mine told me about the first time that he saw the film. He was with his family, and needed some viewing material that was suitable for all, and would offend no one. The film entertained all, though he confessed: 'I think we all got something very different out of it.'[7]

Notes

1 A simplified synopsis of the film's plot follows. While in Tuscany with her aunt Charlotte, Lucy Honeychurch meets and falls in love with a young man by the name of George Emerson, kissing him in a country field, an incident that must be suppressed. On returning to England she discovers that her prudish fiancé 'Cecil' has invited George and his father to stay in their village and after a series of comic incidents and misadventures (as when she witnesses George bathing in the nude with her brother and the local vicar, Mr Beebe) she calls off the marriage for Cecil and is eventually united with George.

2 Letter sent by E. M. Forster to Teodor de Wyzewa, dated 3 November 1910.

3 See also Richard Dyer's discussion of 'Homosexuality and Heritage' in *The Culture of Queers* (2002: 204–28).

4 According to Ismail Merchant's sumptuous 'making of'/cookery book about the film, the chair was found *in situ* at the Villa Maiano where the scene was filmed in Florence (Merchant 1994: 99).

5 I have explored the classical framework of the scene and how this both legitimised and sexually codifies the display of nudity elsewhere; see Williams 2005.

6 Callow is here reviewing Richard Barrios (2003) *Screened Out: Playing Gay in Hollywood from Edison to Stonewall*. London: Routledge.

7 Thanks to the many colleagues and postgraduate students who commented on this and earlier versions of this paper at the University of East Anglia and the University of Southampton, in particular Andrew Higson and Richard Shenton.

Bibliography

Billsun, A. (1986) 'Just too Charming for Words', *Today*, 11 April, 24.

Burston, P. (1995) 'Just a Gigolo?: Narcissism, Nellyism and the "New Man" Theme', in P. Burston and C. Richardson (eds) *A Queer Romance: Lesbians, Gay Men and Popular Culture*. London and New York: Routledge, 111–22.

_____ (1996) 'Confessions of a Gay Film Critic, or How I Learned to Stop Worrying and Love *Cruising*', in M. Simpson (ed.) *Anti-Gay*. London: Freedom Editions, 84–97.

Callow, S. (1986) 'To Beebe or Not to Beebe', *The Sunday Times*, 6 April, 36–8.

_____ (2003) 'Nowt so Queer as Hollywood', *Guardian* (Arts section), 8 February, 16.

Cleto, F. (1999) *Camp: Queer Aesthetics and the Performing Subject – A Reader*. Edinburgh: Edinburgh University Press.

Dyer, R. (2002) *The Culture of Queers*. London and New York: Routledge.

Farmer, B. (2000) *Spectacular Passions: Cinema, Fantasy, Gay Male Spectatorships*. Durham and London: Duke University Press.

Forster, E. M. (1987 [1908]) *A Room with a View*. London: Penguin.

Hadleigh, B. (2001) *The Lavender Screen: The Gay and Lesbian Films – Their Stars, Makers, Characters and Critics* (revised edition). New York: Citadel Press.

Higson, A. (2003) *English Heritage, English Cinema: Costume Drama Since 1980*. London: Oxford University Press.

_____ (forthcoming, 2006) 'Re-presenting the National Past: Nostalgia and Pastiche in the Heritage Film', in L. Friedman (ed.) *Fires Were Started: British Cinema and Thatcherism* (second edition) London: Wallflower Press.

Hollinghurst, A. (1986) 'Detached about Attachments', *Times Literary Supplement*, 11 April, 395.

_____ (1987) 'Suppressive Nostalgia', *Times Literary Supplement*, 6 December, 225.

Jones, M. (2002) 'A Little Peek: Male Nudity in the Movies'. Available online: http://www.bjornsmestad.com/rwav/littlepeek.html.

Kael, P. (1986) 'The Current Cinema: Twits, Turtles, Creeps', *The New Yorker*, 24 March, 112–15.

Klinger, B. (1994) *Melodrama and Meaning: History, Culture, and the Films of Douglas Sirk*. Bloomington and Indianapolis: Indiana University Press.

LaBruce, B. and G. Belverio, G. (1996) 'A Case for the Closet', in M. Simpson (ed.) *Anti-Gay*. London: Freedom Editions, 140–63.

Lago, M. and P. N. Furbank (1985) *Selected Letters of E. M. Forster: Volume One 1879–1920*. London: Arena.

Marshall, W. (1986) 'The Lazy, Hazy Way We Were', *Daily Mirror*, 11 April, 46.

Mayne, J. (1993) *Cinema and Spectatorship*. London: Routledge.

Medhurst, A. (1995) 'Inside the British Wardrobe', *Sight and Sound*, 5, 3, 16–17.

Merchant, I. (1994) *Ismail Merchant's Florence: Filming and Feasting in Tuscany*. New York: Harry N. Abrams.

Meyer, M. (ed.) (1994) *The Politics and Poetics of Camp*. London and New York: Routledge.

Monk, C. (1995) 'Sexuality and the Heritage', *Sight and Sound*, 5, 10, 33–4.

Neale, S. (1992) 'Masculinity as Spectacle', in Steven Cohen and Ina Rae Hark (eds) *The Sexual Subject: A Screen Reader in Sexuality*. London and New York: Routledge, 277–87.

Newman, K. (1997) 'L – Low Budget', *Sight and Sound*, 7, 5, 26–9.

Sontag, S. (1967 [1964]) 'Notes on Camp', in *Against Interpretation and Other Essays*. London:

Eyre and Spottiswoode, 275–92.

Usher, S. (1986) 'The Gentle English Conquering America', *Daily Mail*, 14 July, 7.

Waugh, T. (2000) *The Fruit Machine: Twenty Years of Writings on Queer Cinema*. Durham and London: Duke University Press.

Williams, M. (2005) '"Come and Have a Bathe!": Landscaping the Queer Utopia', in Robin Griffiths (ed.) *British Queer Cinema*. London: Routledge, 105–19.

CHAPTER TEN

Messy, but Innocuous: *Philadelphia*'s AIDS Case

Monica B. Pearl

This essay aims to interrogate the discrepancies between what the film *Philadelphia* (Jonathan Demme, 1994) seems to be doing – in terms of presenting a convincing and sympathetic portrait of homosexuality and HIV infection – and what it actually does: underscores the very misconceptions about gay identity and AIDS that it pretends to alleviate. Along the way, however, the film manages, I argue, to present a fairly progressive representation of race.

Philadelphia can seem unfamiliar to the very audience it pretends to include and therefore to address (namely, a gay audience, an HIV-infected audience). While the cast includes characters that some gay and marginal audiences might be expected to recognise (Michael Callen, the singing group the Flirtations, Quentin Crisp, the off-Broadway performers Ron Vawter, Anna Deavere Smith, David Drake and Karen Finley), as well as some of the real symptoms and medications, the film's viewpoints, *mise-en-scène* and themes suggest that the fundamental audience identification will be with those characters who are ambivalent or intolerant of AIDS and homosexuality, not those who are gay, infected and ill. We in the audience identify with the sympathisers, with the tolerant; if we are mean and closed-minded, or even just ambivalent about homosexuality, we identify with Joe Miller (Denzel Washington), who is homophobic and taught over the film's narrative to be a little less so; if we are magnanimous and goodhearted we might identify with Andy's mother (which is to say, with Joanne Woodward), who cannot help crying when she is on the phone with, in the court house with, or at the bedside of her always-dying son.

Philadelphia: accommodation

Philadelphia accommodates anxiety about homosexuality and illness by claiming to challenge, but actually reinscribing, popular misconceptions about AIDS. Gabriele Griffin comments that 'the film has to pander to the anxieties of those who regard homosexuality as deviant' (2000: 189). *Philadelphia* has been described by Amy Taubin as a 'women's picture crossed with a courtroom drama' (1994: 24), in which a young successful attorney is fired from his position with an important Philadelphia law firm when the partners discover he has AIDS. Indeed, *Philadelphia* attempts to resolve the tension of three genres: courtroom drama, romantic melodrama and family melodrama. Rather than challenging popular ideas about AIDS and homo-sexuality, *Philadelphia* exploits these genres to re-create and reinscribe the public's attitudes and misconceptions, for example, that AIDS is exclusively a gay illness (and conversely that it is not, but that only gay people bear responsibility for their illness; others are innocent), that HIV is contagious (rather than infectious), that you can tell who has AIDS (and conversely that you cannot tell, but ought to be able to), and that there is no gay community (see Schulman 1998: 49). What the film does do success-fully and unintentionally, I propose, is combat and confront unaccepting attitudes and prejudices about race. It does this indirectly and passively, mainly through the audience's expected identification with Joe Miller in a way that erases the need for any racial identification (or dis-identification). The film's unspoken preoccupation with race displaces and attempts to rewrite conceptions of AIDS and homosexuality.

The gestures in *Philadelphia* that could be seen to combat or confront unac-cepting attitudes among the public about AIDS and homosexuality only serve to confirm these attitudes. Because *Philadelphia* is itself an exception ('the first major Hollywood movie to deal with AIDS since the disease was first recognised in the US in 1981' (Taubin 1994: 24)), and because the gestures and images and speeches valorising homosexuality and explaining AIDS are highlighted as anomalies and exceptions, the audience is treated to nothing more than an example of what some few exceptional homosexuals or people with AIDS might be like. Although 'much of the success of Philadelphia depends on marrying the audience to Tom Hanks's character as he transforms himself into the good through suffering' (Als 1994: 6), the movie actually succeeds in marrying the audience to Joe – Andy's homophobic lawyer – who moves but inches in his disrespect for homosexuals. By the end of the film he feels for Andy (Hanks) – feels sorry for him – as probably does the audience, but as an anomaly. There is no reason provided by the film narrative to believe that Joe would behave any differently if someone made a pass at him, as the young ath-lete does one night in the drugstore, which disgusts him and incites him nearly to violence, or if given a hard time in a bar by his buddies, as occurs in the film when Joe's friends tease him about turning queer (a little 'light in the sneakers', his associ-ate Filco seems to be mockingly accusing him of). Joe responds, 'Yeah, I am, Filco, I'm changing. I'm on the prowl, and I'm looking for a hunk, not just any hunk, but a man, a real man like you', and then pretends to refer to the sex they enjoy together. Filco is angered and embarrassed at Joe's innuendoes. Finally, earnestly, Joe says, 'look, these people make me sick, but a law has been broken. You remember the law, don't you?' And so the film returns to its theme of justice, always balancing and justifying homosexuality with civil liberties. But not before the bartender can have his say: 'At least we agree on one thing, Joe.' 'What's that?' Joe replies, looking up from his drink. 'Those tutti-fruttis make me sick, too.' Thus homophobia has the final word. When Joe is enlightened enough at the end of the film to adjust the dying Andy's oxygen mask, this is meant to stand for the development and maturity of this intolerant main character, and thus asks for such small measures from the viewing audience.

Double message: virulence and harmlessness

Philadelphia continually turns on images and phrases that restate what the film is supposed to be about. Among the first words in the film, and the word by which

Joe remembers how he and Andy know each other, is 'innocuous'. They are arguing a case in front of a judge about the pestilence of dust manufactured by the construction work of a company that Andy's firm represents. 'Messy', Andy says, holding the white substance in his hand, 'but innocuous'. The film, throughout, considers whether AIDS is dangerous or harmless, starting with the most questionable substance, semen, for which this white powder can be read as a cinematic surrogate. On one hand, it is possible to read, especially through the film's use of multifarious babies, and particularly through Andy's holding and feeding his brother's baby at his parents' wedding anniversary celebration, that AIDS is harmless. But the narrative also takes pains to voice every single misconception and bigotry about AIDS – Walter (Robert Ridgely), one of the law partners, mutters at the trial, for example, 'he asked for it' – without contradicting them. This same law partner exonerates a presumably more 'innocent' victim of AIDS by expressing sympathy for a former colleague with HIV 'who contracted the disease through no fault of her own'. Near the end of the film Joe is allowed an extended homophobic tirade in the guise of 'informing' Andy about 'what the general thinking [is] out there' about homosexuality. After a party that Andy and Miguel have thrown (in lieu of, but in anticipation of, Andy's memorial service), Joe and Andy are going over Andy's testimony for the trial the next day, when Andy is going to take the witness stand. Andy congratulates Joe, as they sit across a table late in the night, for attending what Andy presumes to be his first 'gay party'. In response Joe laughs and reiterates the 'truth' of what America thinks about homosexuality:

> Let me tell you something, Andrew. When you're brought up the way I am, the way most people are in this country, there's not a hell of a lot of discussion about 'homosexuality', of, uh – what do you call it? – alternate lifestyles. As a kid you're taught that queers are funny, queers are weird, queers dress up like their mother, that they're afraid to fight, that they're a danger to little kids, and that all they want to do is get into your pants.

To this Andy replies, 'thank you for sharing that with me'. This conversation is followed by Andy's melodramatic moment, his aria of life and death and hope and struggle, which is itself then followed by Joe's far more normative (and, to a mainstream cinema-going audience, far more recognisable) family setting. The crazed life and dying of Andy (bathed in red light, clutching his IV drip and channeling Maria Callas) is juxtaposed with the ordinary heterosexual life of Joe. Joe holds his baby. He clutches his wife. The strategy to put all perspectives on screen emphasises a liberal acceptance of all points of view without attempting to resolve the contradictions between prejudice and compassion, between queer and common.

While the recognition between Andy and Joe revolves around the word 'innocuous', Joe is at the same time visibly anxious and upset as soon as he learns that Andy has AIDS, and focuses, as the camera directs us, on Andy's head, his baseball cap, his hand, as though each thing he touches is now going to be infected. That same afternoon Joe sees his doctor to reassure himself about his own immunity to AIDS and cinematically creates in the doctor an educator for the audience who reassures Joe that AIDS is not casually transmitted. Joe's doctor, as the teacher for the audience, explains, 'the HIV virus can only be transmitted through the exchange of bodily fluids, namely, blood, semen and vaginal secretions'. But, Joe insists, what if they find out later that it is casually transmitted? Joe then flees the office, both insulted and warily amused when his doctor wants to give him a blood test. If he is worried that AIDS can be spread casually, then why is he so alarmed at the prospect of a blood test? Joe embodies the contradiction common to anxiety about AIDS: that it can be spread casually (which means a blood test would be practical) or only gay men and drug users can get it (which would render a blood test for Joe insulting). Thus it is the paradoxical paranoia about AIDS – that you can get it casually and that you cannot unless you are a homosexual or a drug user – that the movie reinforces and does not dispel. For every reassurance or piece of education in the film there is another accompanying image of danger or virulence to negate it. Printed on Joe's office window, backwards to the audience, is a sign reading 'toxic torts', exaggerating once again the movie's concern with infection and toxicity. Sitting in front of this sign Joe refers to Andy's 'dreaded deadly infectious disease'. This is a long way from 'innocuous', and much nearer to the general fear of deliberate and stigmatised infection.

Masculinity, male sexual identity and AIDS

Philadelphia focuses on the ways men relate to each other around issues of sexuality and identity, and exposes a cinematic ambivalence regarding representations of men and of male sexuality, particularly in the context of AIDS. There are no women in the film who think the disease is disgusting or harmful, no women, that is, who harbor misconceptions about AIDS. Even the defense attorney (Mary Steenburgen), defending the firm that fired Andy, mutters under her breath toward the end of the trial, 'I hate doing this case'. The film can have it both ways here: it shows equal opportunity in who is bad – and who are the topflight lawyers – but still women are sympathetic and veritably, underneath it all, good. Only men end up being homophobes or villains in this movie.

Indeed, Joe's homophobia is a sign of his masculinity. In Joe's kitchen rant against homosexuality, the audience is expected to relate to his confusion and alienation and unexamined contempt. Hilton Als writes of this sequence: 'One of the more unintentionally painful scenes in the film is when Denzel Washington … explains why he's a flaming homophobe. His wife – regardless of her well-intentioned speech about how aunt so-and-so and cousin doodah are gay – embraces him nonetheless for his valour' (1994: 6). In defending his hatred of gays, Joe says to his wife – in the privacy of their kitchen, while wielding a turkey leg, enacting the role of primal man, while knocking the fowl's appendage against the baby bottle he is holding in his other hand, bashing, in effect, what is feminine and domestic – 'You can call me old-fashioned, you can call me conservative, just call me a man', implying that to be a man is naturally conjunctive with disgust for homosexuality. 'Besides', he adds, 'I think you have to be a man to understand how really disgusting that whole idea is anyway.'

In a film that disallows any evidence of gay sexuality, Andy's interaction with the film's myriad metonymically phallic cigars is telling. He fondles his cigar when the law partners smoke theirs. He finally gets to light his cigar only when he is alone and after he has finished writing up an important complaint for the firm and leaving it late at night on the desk in his office. He cannot light his cigar in front of others. He also is never seen smoking a cigar with his lover, which would make the imagery too suggestive, as suggestive as a kiss: 'Philadelphia stops short of confronting straight viewers (to whom it is primarily addressed) with the kind of images that might trigger their homophobia' (Taubin 1994: 24). The next scene in which we see Andy fondling a cigar is when he fondles Joe's. Andy has come to Joe's office to seek legal counsel; Joe looks on horrified and afraid when he learns Andy has AIDS and watches closely – as the camera shows us – Andy's hand as he picks up a cigar from Joe's desk. Joe watches in horror as Andy handles his cigar. The next scene has Joe rushing to his doctor to see if AIDS can be contracted from 'casual' contact.

Confusions of sexual and gender identities in Philadelphia result in effeminising gay characters, particularly Andy, by adhering to cinematic genre conventions that render Andy's role a traditionally female one, thereby asserting Andy as effeminate and further reinscribing public misconceptions about homosexuality. The film also (implicitly) makes a distinction between masculine men and feminine men (Joe wields a turkey leg and grunts; Andy wears make-up to cover his lesions), thus effeminising the gay men in this film. For a film that might be seen to be representing a gay man with AIDS authentically and unstereotypically, it does a lot to undermine its efforts. Besides that, Andy holds a baby at his parents' anniversary party, as only women do in the entire film, and the fact that due to the evidence of his Kaposi's sarcoma lesions he has to learn to put on make-up, the film effeminises Andy by adhering to genre mechanisms that make Andy's role feminine. Andy is effeminised, for one thing, simply by dying so melodramatically. The film also makes Andy's role feminine because 'cinematically, disease has usually been a female complaint … A different scenario attends the male body, which is more likely to be wounded than it is diseased' (Dargis 1994: 10). And in the scene that most closely suggests a sexual encounter between Andy and his lover Miguel (Antonio Banderas), Andy gets penetrated by Miguel. The only sexual intimacy between Andy and Miguel can be read symbolically in the 'penetration' scene: Miguel pushes a needle into a catheter in Andy's arm. When he pushes the needle through, Miguel lets out a sigh, a groan, 'ahh…' But the needle is blocked, it needs to be flushed out; there can be no consummation. Later, Miguel scalds his hand on something burning on the stove in a symbolic gesture of frustrated desire.

Finally, after Charles Wheeler (Jason Robards) and his partners in law are served with a summons the camera watches their backsides: they are made into vulnerable (homo)sexual prey after being slapped with a discrimination suit that will require them to prove their manliness. By looking at the men as sexual objects, this scene betrays an anxiety, particularly aroused by an AIDS narrative, that all men can be (made) gay. Charles refers to the 'pathetic gay bars' that Andy might have frequented and knows that they are on Chestnut Street, while Bob Seidman (Ron Vawter), one of the partners, ever so discreetly cruises a man that is passing by 'into' the camera, thereby 'cruising' the viewer, making the viewer a (homo)sexual object for a moment as well. The focus on their backsides as they walk through a nether canal of the stadium is a reminder of 'what we're talking about here', as Joe eloquently manages to remind us in the court scene (everyone 'is thinking about sexual orientation, who does what to whom and how they do it') lest we forget that AIDS is everywhere and always about homosexuality.

Immediate families

Philadelphia is a film of wedding rings and babies, as though the weight of homo-sexuality is so strong that it needs dramatic overcompensation to give the film a sense of balance. The film loses no opportunity to include a wedding band in a scene, as long as the wearer is heterosexual. We see Charles Wheeler's wedding ring at his first appearance and then it fills the whole frame when he places his hand on the Bible to testify; we see Joe's as he picks up his baby after the terri-fying opera scene (in which Andy takes on a satanic red glow and practically lip synchs – though he is actually translating – Maria Callas singing the death scene from Umberto Giordano's opera *Andrea Chenier*), we see his wife's ring when he crawls into bed with her; we see Andy's mother's wedding ring in her first appear-ance when she picks up the phone; we see Joe's during the trial. The film abounds with them. Strangely, Andy himself wears a ring starting a few scenes into the film, but after that most scenes that have a shot of his hands obscure that finger (par-ticularly when he is holding the baby). There is one moment in the film where the camera renders visible Andy's ring on his left hand when he is also in an intimate connection with Miguel; this is when Andy is dying and looking up at his lover from his hospital bed. He can be 'married' to Miguel now that he is dying. The scenes in which Andy's left hand is actually bare of a ring are the establishing scenes: in his office, when he is at the doctor's giving blood, when he is in the emergency room with his lover. Andy's 'marital status' seems to fluctuate according to how threaten-ing his sexuality might be to the viewing audience.

The film also employs all of its women of childbearing years to either bear chil-dren, to be pregnant, or to hold their newborns. Even the woman with AIDS who testifies at Andy's trial contracted HIV from a blood transfusion during childbirth. Joe and his wife are shown happy in bed in the hospital with their newborn baby. Andy's sister gives birth between Andy's death and his memorial service. Andy gets to borrow his brother's baby at the celebration of his parents' wedding anniversary. Douglas Crimp comments, 'I didn't actually count them, but it seemed to me that there were more babies than queers in *Philadelphia*' (2002: 256).

There are no other gay couples in this film. The *mise-en-scène* of the party man-ages to show only one figure of a couple dancing or to show a complete couple from above so it is not clear what the gender configuration of the couple might be. The camera manages to avoid showing any other couples just as it avoids showing Andy's ring when this can be overtly connected to his being in a gay relationship, especially in the party scene when he is wearing gloves. No gay stereotypes are broken in this film. They are only reinforced by the portrayal of the relationship between Andy and Miguel as an exception. There are no other couples to act as a context, so their relationship just ends up looking unusual – like a singular gay relationship. *Philadelphia* shows no gay person with a job and a home and a life aside from Andy.

Conclusion

As the first (and arguably the only) mainstream film about AIDS, *Philadelphia* does little to change public misconceptions and prejudices about AIDS and about gay men. However, I would like to close by suggesting that even a movie at its most convincing would not effectively change the sentiments of its viewing audience.

The movies, even polemical movies, do not change people's minds, at least not in the way their creators might intend them to and not in the way we expect or hope them to. When a pervasive public trauma upsets our fastidiously achieved (and delicately illusory) equilibrium about sex and death, pleasure and mortality, we must construct cultural paradigms of reassurance. *Philadelphia* is such a film, in which AIDS is featured but made palatable; Sarah Schulman is scathing in this regard when she writes that in mainstream representations of AIDS, 'viewers are protected from seeing people who are really sick, really angry, and really abandoned by the general public – the same public that the distributors feel dependent on for the film to make a profit' (1994: 228). Motion pictures – for their pure intentions to entertain and occasionally (and safely) to challenge less than tenaciously-held conceptions within the public psyche, and because of their mass consumption (through actual ticket sales, widespread advertisements, trailers and universal reviews) – are one of the primary vehicles for expressions and representations of societal, that is, collective, if personal, anxiety and for the formulaic and steady flow of reassurances. Mainstream movies are expressions of and passing antidotes to cultural and sociological trauma. Hollywood offers us an unfailing prescription of palliatives: love conquers evil (or quells it) or we learn that there are far worse problems and they have to do with other people, people who are in no way like us.

Pity can be a great antidote to cultural anxiety. Feeling sorry for someone else (which often translates as feeling relieved for yourself) is antithetical to feeling sorry for or afraid for yourself. However didactic a film may be – and however successfully the music swells to evoke sympathy and pity – no long-lasting shifts in political or cultural beliefs are wrought as long as the viewer continues to believe the trauma is happening – and can only happen – to someone else. I therefore argue that nothing in film will actually relieve anxiety. Melodrama is only ever entertainment; it does not function as motivation toward greater civil consciousness much less revolutionary fervour, and it is working most effectively as entertainment, and least as political provocation, when you cannot stop crying.

Bibliography

Als, H. (1994) 'Since You Went Away', *The Village Voice*, film supplement, May 24, 6.

Crimp, D. (2002) *Melancholia and Moralism: Essays on AIDS and Queer Politics*. Cambridge, MA and London: MIT Press.

Dargis, M. (1994) 'AIDS Against the Grain: Bodies at Risk from Everything but HIV', *The Village Voice*, film supplement, May 24, 10.

Griffin, G. (2000) *Representations of HIV and AIDS: Visibility Blue/s*. Manchester and New York: Manchester University Press.

Schulman, S. (1994) 'Fame, Shame, and Kaposi's Sarcoma: New Themes in Lesbian and Gay Film', in *My American History: Lesbian and Gay Life During the Reagan/Bush Years*. New York: Routledge.

_____ (1998) *Stagestruck: Theater, AIDS, and the Marketing of Gay America*. Durham, NC: Duke University Press.

Taubin, A. (1994) 'The Odd Couple', *Sight and Sound*, 4, 3, 24.

CHAPTER ELEVEN

Representing the Postwar Family: The Figure of the Absent Father in Early Postwar Hollywood Films

Michael Chopra-Gant

The idea that men (at least in Western capitalist democracies) in the late twentieth and early twenty-first centuries have been beset by a 'crisis of masculinity' has become a common theme of both journalistic and academic discourses concerning gender in contemporary society. And although the concept of the 'crisis of masculinity' has recently been the subject of well-aimed criticisms by, for example, Bill Osgerby (2001) and John Beynon (2002), its appeal as a vehicle for generalising about the masculine condition appears little diminished. However, in the absence of greater specificity as to the dimensions of the masculine crisis – its causes, how it is manifested, its historical context – the concept offers little purchase for analysing representations of masculinity. The idea of 'crisis' is just too vague, too malleable to enable much critical insight and to allow scholars to move beyond a tendency – which has limited the insights of film criticism, and psychoanalytic film criticism in particular – to see crisis everywhere and to essentialise it. This notion overlooks masculinity's historical dimensions, reducing it to a manifestation of psycho-sexual anxieties which are assumed to plague all men in all places and at all times. In this essay I want to depart from this essentialising tendency and move beyond the assertion of the existence of a masculine crisis in order to examine one historically specific aspect of discourses relating to the position and role of men in society and particularly in the family. I will look at how this discourse was registered in some of the most popular films released in America as it emerged from the Second World War and began to confront the enormous task of rehabilitating its population – and especially its men – to civilian life after the war.

If there was ever a good time for masculinity to be in crisis, the period after the Second World War was it. Although America's entry into the war had put an end to the challenges presented to the traditional male roles of worker and provider by the years of the great depression, this was achieved in a way which did not return men to their traditional central role in the socio-economic order. This distanced an extremely large number of men even further from 'normal' society by inducting them into the strange, artificial, almost wholly masculine world of the armed forces. The postwar civilian economic boom – which continued the expansion created by the war economy – provided conditions which would prove favourable for the ulti-mate reintegration of these ex-servicemen into civilian roles. This was achieved in both the workplace and the family and was more an unplanned corollary of the economic dynamism of the war and early postwar years than a result of careful stra-tegic planning. As the war moved towards its end, therefore, uncertainties about America's strategy for reconversion to civilian life developed into a major issue for American society, and the question of what to do with the veterans after the war became the subject of vigorous debate in the United States.

One of the key areas on which this debate was focused was the family, which was particularly disrupted by the removal of men from civilian life and by the demands that the war economy made on women. John P. Diggins argues that the war placed almost unprecedented pressures on the family and suggests that changes in family structure were linked to a rise in juvenile delinquency and thus became a major source of anxiety during the 1940s:

> In the early 1940s the American family experienced stresses and dislocations unknown since the civil war. With fathers in the armed services, children were being reared by mothers alone. Many children even felt deserted after being dropped off at a stranger's house as their mothers went to a USO agency to serve coffee and doughnuts to GIs. Many teenagers without parents drifted into juvenile delinquency. (1988: 24)

Concern about the impact of paternal absence on children is evident in numerous publications of the period. Noting that 'war forces a change in the entire peace-time system of family living', Willard Waller expressed concern over the 'great damage to the pattern of family life' caused by the need for the family to 'give up members to the army, to war work', as a consequence of which it 'loses its hold on the minds of the young' (1944: 83). The absence of fathers in particular destabilised the family, leading to a 'rise in juvenile delinquency' (1944: 84). In a lengthy article published on 8 April 1946, *Life* magazine also acknowledged the existence of a link between the rise of juvenile delinquency and the absence of fathers. In an article published in the *Annals of the American Academy of Political and Social Science*, Ray E. Baber predicted a difficult period of destabilised family life after the war and also linked this instability to a high rate of delinquency and lapsed sexual morality:

> The family is in for a hard time ahead … Individual families will be so broken that they can never be mended … Divorce will increase after the war. Juve-nile delinquency will remain high for a time, and in many homes family discipline and parental authority will not be re-established. Sex standards, already lowered, will be extremely hard to raise. (1943: 175)

Hollywood movies released soon after the war registered the enormous pressures that the war placed on family life in various ways. Writers such as Sylvia Harvey (1998) and Vivian Sobchak (1998) have noted the absence of images of the family and the family home in film noir. In some of the more popular films of the early postwar years, however, a different tendency is detectable. In these films it is specif-ically the father, rather than the family, who is absented. This absence takes a more positive form than a simple lack of images of fathers: the absent father is a positive entity in these films – akin to what Susan Faludi describes as 'the nonpresent presence of paternal ghosts' (1999: 597) – an absent presence structured into the text.

The structured absence of the father is exemplified by films such as *Notorious* (Alfred Hitchcock, 1946) and *Saratoga Trunk* (Sam Wood, 1945), both among the highest revenue earners of 1946. Following the pattern of discourses of the period which linked paternal absence to a rise in delinquency, in both films the absence of fathers is explicitly linked to the descent of the films' young female protagonists, Alicia Huberman and Clio Dulaine respectively (coincidentally both played by Ingrid Bergman), into delinquency. In *Notorious*, the conviction of Alicia's father for treason in the opening scene of the film, and his subsequent suicide, establish the definitive physical removal of the father. However, it becomes clear later in the movie that the loss of paternal authority (the real focus of discourses linking paternal absence to a rise in delinquency) had occurred considerably earlier, when Alicia discovered her father's role in a Nazi plot against her adopted country. This loss of paternal authority is framed, by the film's narrative, as the cause of Alicia's descent into a life of drunken excess and sexual promiscuity.

The absent father is also a key figure in *Saratoga Trunk*. In this movie, Clio's father is not even glimpsed momentarily in the movie, since his death has taken place in the film's diegetic past, but a strong sense of his absent presence inhabits the early parts of the film. Like Alicia in *Notorious*, Clio is characterised by her deviation from norms of femininity, particularly in her possession of a similarly aggressive sexuality. So, once again, a link is made between the breakdown of traditional family structures, especially the absence of paternal authority, and the development of delinquent behaviour. In both films the 'solution' to this 'problem' of female delinquency is the same; both women are 'saved' by accepting a position of subordination to their male partners within romantic couples, thereby restoring patriarchal authority. In *Notorious*, the woman's 'salvation' is portrayed quite literally. Alicia's activities as an agent of the American secret services are discovered by the Nazi activist who she married in order to spy on his group. Under his mother's instruction, he begins slowly poisoning Alicia and, in the film's closing scenes, she appears doomed until Devlin (Cary Grant), another American agent, enters her bedroom and carries her to safety, simultaneously saving her life and restoring her to a more normative femininity. The feeling of salvation is less marked in *Saratoga Trunk* but the restoration of patriarchal authority is even more clearly inscribed, with Clio accepting, in the film's closing moments that Clint (Gary Cooper) will 'wear the pants' in their relationship.

Another of the most successful movies released just after the war, *Margie* (Henry King, 1946) follows a similar pattern to *Saratoga Trunk* and *Notorious*, although it lacks the element of sexual promiscuity in the character of its eponymous female protagonist. *Margie* is particularly notable for presenting the absent father as a positive presence in the diegesis. Unlike *Notorious* and *Saratoga Trunk*, the father appears throughout *Margie* and so is not literally absent, although he is a shadowy, mysterious character in the early parts of the film. Despite his literal presence, the narrative positions this character in such a way that he performs the symbolic function of an absent father. Following the death of his wife, Margie's (Jeanne Crain) father has relinquished responsibility for his daughter's upbringing, and he has placed her in the care of her maternal grandmother (Esther Dale). As with Alicia in *Notorious* and Clio in *Saratoga Trunk*, the loss of paternal authority which follows this move is accompanied by the daughter's deviation from feminine norms. In *Margie* this does not involve promiscuity or criminality, but takes the form of a threat of female incursion into a public sphere conceptualised as masculine, under the influence of Margie's grandmother. The grandmother is a former suffragette, who displays over her fireplace the chains with which she once bound herself to the railings of the White House. She has political ambitions for Margie, hoping she will become the first female president of America, and she encourages Margie's engagement with politics through the young woman's membership of the school debating team.

Margie herself apparently shares few of her grandmother's political ambitions. Although she does participate in the debating team, she has a far greater interest in attracting the romantic attention of the school's latest heartthrob, the new French teacher, Mr Fontayne (Glen Langan). A romance does ultimately develop between Margie and this obvious figure of masculine authority, and this provides another clear example of the narrative strategy of replacing the absent father with a romantic partner, which is also present in *Notorious* and *Saratoga Trunk*. The function of this male partner is, at least in part, to substitute for the father as the source of patriarchal authority, regulating the conduct of the female protagonist and ensuring her return to conformity with norms of femininity.

In *Margie*, this restoration of normative equilibrium between the sexes is made apparent by the structure of the film's narrative as well as the events it portrays. The opening and closing scenes of the film are the only scenes set in the diegetic present, the remainder of the film being depicted as an extended flashback. In the opening scene Margie, now a married woman, and her teenage daughter sort through a trunk in their attic. Key items in the trunk – a pair of bloomers, a heavy chain, a photograph album – serve as a cue for the film's flashback section in which the significance of these items is revealed. In the closing scene the film returns to Margie and her daughter in the attic, now replacing items in the trunk and awaiting the imminent arrival of Margie's husband. The arrival of this character, whose identity is withheld until the very last moment, confirms Margie's marriage to Mr Fontayne. Significantly, Margie's husband's arrival in the attic coincides with the replacement of items, which have connotations of transgression against feminine norms, into the trunk where they are safely contained. The chain is that with which Margie's grandmother had attached herself to the White House railings; the bloomers those which at moments of impending romantic engagement in the film's flashback section would fall around Margie's ankles and undermine any impression of graceful femininity. Just as Margie's transgressive potential is contained by her marriage to an unambiguous figure of patriarchal authority, so the film's own account of Margie's potentially transgressive past is safely contained within the flashback structure of its narrative.

The elimination of Margie's transgressive potential is confirmed in the film's closing scene by an article in the newspaper which Mr Fontayne shows to Margie. The report relates to the appointment of Margie's father as ambassador to Nicaragua. In an earlier scene, in the middle of the film's flashback section, Margie's father's interest in American military activities in Nicaragua had been stimulated by the argument which Margie had put forward during a high-school debating competition. In a number of scenes after the debate, Margie's father repeats the arguments she had put forward, in a rather comical, uncomprehending manner. Whilst the father's appointment as ambassador may, at one level, function as a joke concerning the competence of politicians, it also signals the restoration of normative gender roles. Margie as a housewife in the domestic sphere, her father having gained an important role in the public sphere by appropriating a political stance which was originated by his now depoliticised, domesticated daughter.

Although *Notorious*, *Saratoga Trunk* and *Margie* are all very different films with a diverse range of generic affinities, each relies on the figure of the absent father as a key element of its narrative. All three films construct femininity as problematic in some way, and in each case this 'problem' is related to the absence of fathers and resolved by the involvement of the woman in a heterosexual romantic couple which operates to normalise the woman's character. The foregrounding of woman's transgressive potential as a central element in the narratives of these films has a certain resonance with the problematisation of femininity which has been noted as a key element of film noir, linked particularly to the figure of the femme fatale. If the femme fatale can be understood as an expression of some of the anxieties about gender roles that troubled the popular consciousness in America during the period of postwar readjustment, then the absent father can be viewed as a different way of articulating those concerns. The popular films I have discussed do not generally share the concern of the film noirs with the punishment or destruction of the transgressive female. Although this is certainly an element in *Notorious*, the most 'noirish' of these films, the impetus to assert male power and restore patriarchally structured norms of gendered behaviour is equally strong. While this positions these movies as politically regressive, and suggests that the figure of the absent father should be seen as an element of conservative discourses, this was not the only use of this figure in early postwar discourse or Hollywood's contemporary films.

The pleasures of fatherhood

In addition to its position in discourses concerning juvenile delinquency, the figure of the absent father was also an element in another early postwar discourse concerning the pleasures of fatherhood and the development of a more active role in childcare for fathers. The absence of fathers from the family may have been exacerbated by the war, but the war was not its only cause, since it was also part of the institutionalised, gendered segregation of parenting roles which was already a well-established pattern for family life long before the war. In *Baby and Child Care*, which was first published just after the war, Benjamin Spock provided a vivid account of the exclusion of fathers from the birth of their children which was, at the time, standard practice in maternity units: 'The poor father is a complete outsider. He has to wait around alone for hours while the baby is being born, feeling useless and miserable' (1946: 13). Spock also noted an ingrained belief in some fathers that they had no active role to play in childcare: 'Some fathers have been brought up to think that the care of babies and children is the mother's job entirely'; he also observed that some fathers 'would get goose flesh at the very idea of helping to take care of a baby' (1946: 15). Against these ingrained attitudes towards parental roles in child care, Spock argued for greater involvement by the father, although he conceded that 'there's no good to be gained by trying to force them' (ibid.).

Male detachment from parenting may have been the conventional pattern in American society, but Spock was not alone in emphasising the benefits which followed from a greater degree of paternal involvement in parenting. The views expressed in Spock's writing at this time suggest a more general shift in these entrenched attitudes, away from the tradition of a low level of paternal contribution to childcare, and towards the more involved, domesticated masculinities which became increasingly important in the decade following the war.[1] An article by Juliet Danziger, published in the *New York Times Magazine* in 1944, gives an account of the experiences of her family following her husband's departure for the war. She recounts a different experience of the families of absent fathers from that suggested by discourses which linked paternal absence to juvenile delinquency. Danziger's article did not suggest a family which fell apart, the children turning to lives of crime or promiscuity in the absence of a paternal authority-figure. On the contrary, Danziger emphasised how well the family coped without a father. The need to continue everyday life as normally as possible led to her discovery of new skills and abilities as she was forced to take on tasks which would usually have been undertaken by her husband. Danziger even noted distinct advantages to family life without a male partner: 'From a cold and calculating point of view, there are definitely points on the credit side of this wartime ledger' (1944a: 16). She concluded that 'after a year of life without father, I have discovered that we can make things go, that I can live alone, and – well almost – like it' (1944a: 47). Despite the advantages of the situation, Danziger emphasised the importance for the children of maintaining a sense of their father's presence in the home:

> Leaving things where they've always been makes the children feel strongly that they still have a Daddy … It preserves some of the masculinity in the household … They don't have that insecure sense of 'Daddy's gone. He may never come back.' Daddy isn't gone. He's away for a while. (1944a: 16)

In another article, published later in the year in *Parents* magazine, Danziger's emphasis had shifted and she placed greater importance on the role of fathers in the home: 'Everyday living with no man about the house is essentially an unnatural way of living.' She also discusses the idea that the father should play an active role in parenting: 'Daddy should take an active part in the going-to-bed rites. He can read to them before they go to sleep, or tell them something about what he does on his field or in his camp or on his ship' (1944b: 78).

In the popular films released in 1946, this discourse concerning male participation in childcare focusing on the figure of the absent father, is registered less often than the concerns over juvenile delinquency in fatherless families already discussed in this essay. This discourse of involved fatherhood does, however, provide one of the most affecting scenes in another of the year's biggest box-office successes: *Blue Skies* (Stuart Heisler, 1946). So far as it is relevant to the use of the figure of the absent father in the film, the narrative tells of the development of a romance, and eventually a marriage between Johnny (Bing Crosby) and Mary (Joan Caulfield). The marriage is an unequal partnership, and is marred by Johnny's constant failure to discuss with Mary important decisions which affect the family. Johnny is a night-club owner, and his repeated buying and selling of different night-clubs, which each time involves uprooting the family and relocating to another city without even mentioning his intentions to Mary, is a mounting source of conflict between them. Even before their marriage breaks up, then, Johnny displays considerable detachment from his family, refusing to involve Mary in important decisions. He really becomes an absent father, however, when Mary, who can no longer stand the upheavals, finally leaves Johnny, taking their daughter with her. His status as an absent father is clearest in a scene near the end of the film, in which he pays a late-night visit to see his daughter, Mary Elizabeth (Karolyn Kay Grines). As he enters her bedroom it is clear that Mary Elizabeth does not recognise her father. Johnny senses the awkwardness of the situation and he rather coyly explains that he is a 'friend' of her mother. As he moves closer to the bed, Mary Elizabeth begins to recognise Johnny as her 'old daddy' from photographs shown to her by her mother. Despite this recognition, however, it is clear that Mary Elizabeth regards her absent father as a stranger and she initially refuses him a kiss because 'mummy said I mustn't kiss strangers'. She relents only when he convinces her that he cannot be a stranger because he has known her since she was very young. Feeling reassured, Mary Elizabeth is pleased to receive the attention of this friendly male figure, whom she asks to sing her a song. The song, 'Running Around in Circles', is given a child-like, nursery rhyme quality by its orchestration, and allegorises Johnny's situation. He's been 'running around in circles, getting nowhere … very fast' – and in these few brief moments in which he sings to his daughter, Johnny comes to recognise what he has lost through his prioritisation of his business interests over his family.

What makes this scene such a distinctive moment is the fact that it is focused so intensely on the relationship between father and child. In the context of a musical the narrative is primarily concerned with the romantic relationship between Johnny and Mary and the equilibrium is ultimately restored by reuniting them as a romantic couple. This scene signifies the moment when the increasing separation of the couple is halted and the process of bringing them back together begins. It is highly significant that this turning point in the narrative is focused not on the romance, but on the relationship between father and daughter. It is not Johnny's realisation of what he has lost through his separation from Mary that begins to reunite the couple, but his recognition of the pleasures he has missed as a father which initiates this process. This is evident in his facial expression, which captures his feelings of joy and pain while he embraces Mary Elizabeth and begins to realise the nature of this loss. Read in this way, the scene can be understood as an allegory of the pleasures of fatherhood. It offers a rare instance of the articulation in film of this nascent discourse, evident in Dr Spock's writing too, concerning the changing perception of the role of fathers within the family during the period immediately following the end of the war.

While *Notorious* and *Saratoga Trunk* are connected by discourses which attribute a rise in juvenile delinquency to the absence of paternal authority, *Margie* and *Blue Skies* are linked by a different discourse. It is one that attributes the cause of pater-nal absence to the separation of the social world into gendered spheres of activity.

In both films the fathers are absent from the family because of the priority they have given to their business activities and public life over family and the private sphere. The way these two pairs of films deploy the figure of the absent father suggests a retrospective orientation in the case of the former pair: they look back to the recent past, during the war, when fathers were physically distanced from family life. In the latter there is a prospective orientation, looking forward to the re-establishment of a civilian order in which a masculine public sphere provides the reason for paternal estrangement from the family. *Margie* is the more conservative of this latter pair, framing the separation of spheres as a return to equilibrium, a re-establishment of the 'way things ought to be'. Here the father remains remote from his family (as his posting to Nicaragua emphasises) and patriarchal order is reasserted by the inter-generational reproduction of the power dynamics of traditional, patriarchal structured family life. The husband substitutes for Margie's father as the source of paternal authority and becomes a father in his own turn. *Blue Skies*, however, offers a more progressive vision, in which the father comes to realise what he has lost by prioritising his business activities over family life. Johnny's return to the family is not framed in terms of the restoration of paternal authority, but indicates more strongly the acceptance of a more active nurturing role in relation to his daughter. It is a capacity to appreciate the pleasures of fatherhood which are central elements in emerging postwar discourses relating to childcare and which signal a movement towards the more domesticated masculinities which became ubiquitous during the 1950s.

As some of the recently published writing on masculinity indicates, for example, Susan Faludi's *Stiffed: The Betrayal of the Modern Man* (1999) and Anthony Clare's *On Men: Masculinity in Crisis* (2001) the phenomenon of absent fathers is not exclusively a feature of the years immediately following the Second World War. Nor is it even of the postwar period in general. Faludi does suggest, however, that there was a qualitative difference between the absence of fathers at other times and that which occurred after the war. Paternal absence stopped being seen primarily as a matter of individual failure and became instead a structural feature of a new familial order which developed in postwar America (1999: 375–6; see also Blenkenhorn 1995 on the enduring problem of absent fathers). The films discussed in this essay, therefore, register the emergence of a significant figure in postwar discourses about fatherhood and, therefore, about masculinity: a figure which is a key element in the discursive construction of the postwar 'crisis of masculinity'. To view the absent father simply in terms of crisis does not register the complexity of the construction of this figure. It does not address the often contradictory uses to which the figure is put in both Hollywood's narrative fiction and the wider discourses on fatherhood and parenting to which these representations both respond and contribute. While the idea of masculinity in crisis will undoubtedly maintain its appeal within journalistic discourse, its value in understanding the complexities of masculinities and, particularly, historically located representations of masculinities is extremely limited. It is only by giving detailed attention to particular empirical facets of these representations of masculinities that academic interest in the subject can progress beyond vague (albeit often impressive sounding) generalisations towards a real understanding of the role of representation in the historical, discursive construction of masculinities.

Notes

1   In 1954 *Life* magazine published a humorous article entitled *The New American Domesticated Male*. Much of the debate concerning a 'crisis of masculinity' during the 1950s is founded on the assumption that the increasing domesticity of men during that decade was accompanied by a concomitant decline in manliness. See Susan Faludi's (1999) account of the period for example. Bill Osgerby (2001) also provides a thorough account of the rise of domesticated masculinity during the 1950s.

Bibliography

Anon. (1946) 'Juvenile Delinquency', *Life*, 8 April, 83–93.

Anon. (1954) 'The New American Domesticated Male', *Life*, 4 January, 42–5.

Baber, R. E. (1943) 'Marriage and the Family After the War', in *Annals of the American Academy of Political and Social Science*, September, 164–75.

Beynon, J. (2002) *Masculinities and Culture*. Buckingham and Philadelphia: Open University Press.

Blenkenhorn, D. (1995) *Fatherless America: Confronting Our Most Urgent Social Problem*. New York: Basic Books.

Clare, A. (2001) *On Men: Masculinity in Crisis*. London: Arrow Books.

Danziger, J. (1944a) 'Life Without Father', *New York Times Magazine*, 7 May, 16 and 47.

_____ (1944b) 'Daddy Comes Home on Leave', *Parents*, October, 29, 70, 72 and 78.

Diggins, J. P. (1988) *The Proud Decades: America in War and Peace, 1941-1960*. New York: W. W. Norton.

Faludi, S. (1999) *Stiffed: The Betrayal of the Modern Man*. London: Chatto and Windus.

Harvey, S. (1998) 'Woman's Place: The Absent Family of Film Noir', in E. A. Kaplan (ed.) *Women in Film Noir*. London: British Film Institute, 35–46.

Osgerby, B. (2001) *Playboys in Paradise: Masculinity, Youth and Leisure-Style in Modern America*. Oxford: Berg.

Sobchak, V. (1998) 'Lounge Time: Postwar Crises and the Chronotope of Film Noir', in N. Browne (ed.) *Refiguring American Film Genres: Theory and History*. Berkeley: University of California Press, 129–70.

Spock, B. (1946) *The Pocket Book of Baby and Child Care*. New York: Pocket Books.

Waller, W. (1944) *The Veteran Comes Back*. New York: Dryden Press.

scenes
new technology and method

Introduction

Jacqueline Furby

With this section we introduce two approaches to the study of screen technology and industry. There is a shift of focus here. With the exception of Martin Lister's essay in the first section, all of the previous chapters have taken film as their primary object of study. This section broadens the field to embrace other screen-based technological forms such as the Internet, television and virtual reality. The focus also shifts from the various theoretical perspectives adopted in section two to demonstrate the practical use of audience research methods, and with the final essay we question what impact new technology might have on the future of film.

The most usual definition of the spectator within theoretical approaches is as 'an effect of discourse, a position, a hypothetical site of address of the filmic discourse' (Guilana Bruno, quoted in Stacey 1994: 22). Audience research studies, often referred to as an 'ethnographic approach', in contrast, comes out of the Cultural Studies discipline and is generally concerned with real film-goers, the audience that sit in the cinema, rather than a generalised spectator. As a very rough, thumbnail definition, then, spectatorship theory imagines the spectator as a passive entity constructed through and positioned by the text, and audience research methods examines empirical evidence that discloses, for example, how the consumer might make active choices about how to use the text.

Chapters twelve to fifteen employ various audience research methodologies.

Peter Krämer's work entails the analysis of box-office revenues, audience demographics and the identification of narrative themes that viewers have chosen as privileged texts. Krämer's essay seeks to identify a connection between Hollywood's major hits of the period between 1977 and 1997. These dates are chosen as significant because they mark the years of release of the two most economically successful movies of all time in the US box office: *Star Wars* (George Lucas, 1977) and *Titanic* (James Cameron, 1997). The essay asks why these films were particularly successful, and whether they can be said to represent a trend. Krämer reaches the conclusion that there is a connection between these two films in terms of 'epic scope' and 'an obsession with exciting physical action and awesome audiovisual spectacle', but goes beyond this in identifying a story structure common not only to these films, but to the majority of the most popular films during this period.

John Sedgwick is an economist and he applies his discipline to an analysis of the changing habits of cinemagoers in the postwar period. Like Peter Krämer, Sedgwick turns to the analysis of box-office revenues, in the latter's case in order to identify and track the changing patterns of consumption; not to identify connections, but to understand difference. Whereas Krämer identifies narrative themes that appeal to audiences during his period of investigation, Sedgwick looks at external historical factors such as changes in population distribution and the emergence of new technology such as television. Sedgwick argues, therefore, that the demise of the studio system of production in Hollywood was a consequence of the collapse in the market for films of a certain quality and that this was due to changes in the habits of cinemagoers, and that these changes were a direct consequence of certain social and cultural developments. The studios adapted to these changing conditions and Hollywood cinema continued to survive.

Deborah Jermyn's essay looks at one of the factors responsible for the changing face of Hollywood cinema, television. If Hollywood is the dream factory, then, as Jermyn argues, one of the pleasures of the British small screen is the factual television series. Reality TV, whatever the problems of definition of this term, has become increasingly popular in recent years with programmes such as *Big Brother*, *Wife Swap* and *I'm a Celebrity... Get Me Out of Here!* But the programme that Jermyn discusses here and cites as 'more popular than most entertainment shows', is *Crimewatch UK*, a 'serious information programme'. As Jermyn makes clear, there is 'an inherent dichotomy' between 'factual' programming and 'entertainment shows', particularly when the subject of the factual element is real-life crime reporting and investigation. This essay examines how *Crimewatch UK* might be seen to blur the boundaries between fact and fiction, how the critical discourse around the programme's boundary condition has been constructed, and what this suggests about attitudes towards television audiences and the sort of entertainment that the programme represents.

What this essay shares with the previous two, then, is an engagement with real audiences. Whereas Krämer and Sedgwick look at the economic trace left by the spending patterns of people who go to the cinema, or who buy or rent movies to view at home, Jermyn has recourse to reports of how people have responded to specific editions of the show and others like it. Her conclusion to the question of blurred boundaries between fact and fiction is that debates can usefully move beyond this preoccupation and consider instead how to 'negotiate the commonalities and spaces between them'.

With David Lusted's essay we remain with the consumer. His essay looks at attitudes to the new communications systems such as the Internet, connections between new technologies and old technologies, and how consumers use a variety of fantasy environments. Lusted examines the antecedents for contemporary fears about the potential criminal abuse of the Internet, and at 'points of continuity between contemporary communications and formative moments in the history of the entertainment media', and comes to the conclusion that new media offer a similar function to that offered by old media, which is a site of fantasy formation and as such represents a utopian solution, for example to societal shortfalls.

William Merrin also looks back in order to look forwards. His essay takes us through philosophical debates, and employs the interdisciplinary application of media theory and media history in order to understand the 'nature and implications of virtual reality, its relationship to the cinema, and their intertwining historical context'. Having survived the crisis period discussed by Sedgwick cinema may be heading for yet another evolutionary challenge. Merrin wonders if cinema will soon find itself in a technological cul-de-sac, where the only place to go forwards is into the world of virtual reality. Merrin argues, however, that virtual reality might not represent a future for cinema itself, but rather a return to an earlier pre-cinematic mode of entertainment, and therefore, perhaps an end to cinema as we understand it.

So, in this section, as well as refocusing our lens to regard the audience as consumers and how they might negotiate the text we also, to borrow and adapt Peter Kramer's phrase, look at the 'bigger picture' of the screen industry (large and small), and contemplate its past and its possible future.

Bibliography

Stacy, J. (1994) *Star Gazing*. London: Routledge.

CHAPTER TWELVE

Big Pictures: Studying Contemporary Hollywood Cinema through its Greatest Hits

Peter Krämer

Out of the darkness lights emerge, and moving through the water in a tiny submersible, treasure hunter Brock Lovett approaches the giant wreck of the Titanic (shown in documentary footage of the actual ship resting on the bottom of the ocean). Filming himself with a video camera, Lovett speaks an obviously rehearsed, disingenuous line: 'It still gets me every time to see the sad ruin of the great ship.' He disguises his search for a priceless diamond on the Titanic with false sentiment. Yet 101-year-old survivor Rose Calvert is genuinely and visibly shaken by her encounter with items recovered from the wreck, most notably a nude drawing of herself wearing the diamond Lovett is looking for. She is eager to tell him the story of the diamond, the drawing and the night the Titanic sank, because the memories of the fateful voyage she undertook on the ship 84 years before still haunt her. In particular, she cannot, and does not want to, let go of the memory of the young artist, Jack Dawson, whom she fell in love with on that voyage, who saved her life when the ship went down, and who slowly froze to death in the water while holding her hand. After Rose has told her story, it becomes clear that it is meant to pay homage to Jack: 'I've never spoken of him until now, not to anyone … But now you all know there was a man named Jack Dawson, and that he saved me … I don't even have a picture of him. He exists now only in my memory.' Of course, through Rose telling her story and the cinema screen bringing it to life in a long flashback, Jack also exists from then on in the memory of her audience: Brock Lovett and the others on the screen as well as the millions in the movie theatres. And while Rose does not have a picture of him, the cinema audience has: it is called *Titanic* (James Cameron, 1997). In response to Rose's enormous sense of loss, then, Jack has been resurrected, and the ship whose wreck we saw at the beginning has been resurrected too, albeit only temporarily and imaginarily, through the power of cinema.

By the end of the film's long run in American movie theatres, which started in December 1997, *Titanic*'s tale of loss and cinematic resurrection had taken over the top position in *Variety*'s list of all-time top grossing movies in the US with revenues of $601m (see appendix 1). Far behind in second place, with a $461m gross, came *Star Wars* (George Lucas, 1977) the very film that, upon its initial record-breaking

release, had first inspired *Titanic*'s writer-director James Cameron to commit himself to filmmaking as a career: 'I was really upset when I saw *Star Wars*. That was
the movie that I wanted to make. After seeing that movie I got very determined'
(quoted in Heard 1997: 9–10). The most direct source of inspiration for Cameron
appears to have been *Star Wars*' groundbreaking special effects, which increased
the power of filmmakers to translate their imagination into film: 'I saw that all
the things I had been seeing in my head all along could now be done' (quoted in
Shapiro 2000: 55). However, it is important to note that the *Star Wars* trilogy also
tells a story of loss and cinematic resurrection. Teenage orphan (or so it seems)
Luke Skywalker embarks on his big adventure after the original loss of his parents
is replayed through, and compounded by, the death of his aunt and uncle, who
had taken care of him. In the course of his adventure, his two mentors (Obi-Wan
and Yoda) die as well. Yet by gaining access to the mysterious power of the Force,
Luke is able not only to defeat the Evil Emperor, who is ultimately responsible for all
his losses, but also to redeem his own father who had gone over to the Dark Side.
At the very end of the trilogy, Anakin Skywalker as well as Obi-Wan and Yoda all
appear to Luke – and only to him – as spirits. In fact, they appear as superimposed
images on the screen, that is, as projections within the film which is being projected on the screen. Thus it is once again the power of cinema that, in response to
Luke's experience of loss, brings loved ones back to life.

   Going beyond the rather obvious fact that both *Star Wars* and *Titanic* have epic
scope and share an obsession with exciting physical action and awesome audiovisual spectacle, then, there are important narrative, thematic and personal connections between Hollywood's two biggest hits. To what extent do such connections
extend to the major hits Hollywood produced inbetween *Star Wars* and *Titanic*,
and indeed since *Titanic*? What might these connections tell us about the ways in
which the film industry and its audiences have operated since 1977? And how does
this recent period fit into longer-term developments in American cinema? More
fundamentally, what is the rationale for studying the films that made the most
money at the box office? And what do these films have to tell us about the power
of cinema?

The importance of hit

It is a truism that Hollywood is in the business of making money, and the trade press
as well as much reporting about cinema in newspapers and film magazines, on television and the Internet pays close attention to the amounts of money films earn
at the American box office as well as their chart rankings, and, to a lesser extent, to
the costs of movie production and marketing and the profits or losses generated by
a movie's release. Oddly enough, academic writing about contemporary American
cinema by and large keeps its distance from budgetary and box-office information
on individual films, from annual and all-time movie charts. A vast amount of film
academic writing is concerned with the critical interpretation (and mostly negative evaluation) of individual films or groups of films, and while much of this writing conceives of its object of study as 'popular cinema', it is rarely interested in the
question whether particular films did well or badly at the box office. Another dominant strand in the writing about contemporary American cinema deals with the

workings of the film industry, and while company profits and losses are central to such economic analysis, individual films or groups of films are only mentioned in passing, as examples for the general operations of these companies, rather than as important objects of study in their own right.

These are general tendencies in academic writing, and, of course, there are very important exceptions, most notably Scribner's authoritative *History of American Cinema* series (see Cook 2000, Prince 2000 and Monaco 2001; see also Garncarz 1994 and Sedgwick 2000). In fact, such exceptions have been multiplying in recent years. One of the reasons for the increasing academic interest in hit movies is the recognition that, whatever complexities there are in conceptualising 'the popular', commercial success surely is an important factor. Notwithstanding considerations of other media outlets for films (about which more below) and the fact that not all films are given the same chances in the marketplace, at a very basic level a film that grosses more money than another is, de facto, more popular, that is more people have bought tickets for it. What is more, despite all the complexities of the operations of today's multinational and multi-media conglomerates, it is widely acknowledged that they are basically hit-driven. A few of their products generate a substantial share of their revenues and profits (for an in-depth case study of Disney and *The Lion King* (Roger Allers and Rob Minkoff, 1994) see Krämer 2000).

Let us take a closer look at the audience reach and economic success of *Titanic*. The film grossed $601m at the domestic box office, $113m in 1997 and $488m in 1998 (*Variety* 1999: 62, 64). For simplicity's sake, the following calculations will assume that all $601m were generated in 1998. The total box-office revenues in North America in 1998 were $6.95 billion, which gives *Titanic* a market share of just under 9 per cent for the year (Moser 2000: 8). This means that of the more than 500 films which were released into American movie theatres in 1998, this one film generated almost every eleventh dollar spent on tickets in those theatres (Moser 2000: 11). At an average ticket price in the US of $4.69 (Moser 2000: 9), the number of tickets sold for *Titanic* is about 128m, which is the equivalent of almost half of the American population (an estimated 265m according to James Moser (1998: 16)). In fact, fewer people than this went to see *Titanic* because its most ardent fans bought several tickets, watching the film again and again. Nevertheless, it is an impressive figure indeed, especially in the light of the fact that in 1998 27 per cent of Americans aged 12 and over never went to the cinema at all, and another 12 per cent were infrequent moviegoers (about once a year) (Moser 2000: 10). It is reasonable to assume that *Titanic* could only achieve its enormous success because many infrequent moviegoers chose *Titanic* for their one cinema outing in 1998. We can therefore say that for up to 40 per cent of the population (over the age of 11) cinemagoing in 1998 meant *Titanic* or it meant nothing at all. Not only do Hollywood's megahits make enormous profits for the industry, they also pretty much constitute the cinematic experience for a substantial segment of the population.

However, it is well known that films generate most revenues and reach the majority of their audience outside American movie theatres – in foreign theatrical markets and on video and DVD as well as cable and broadcast television – and also that huge revenues are generated through tie-in products. How did *Titanic* fare in these respects? To begin with, *Titanic*'s revenues from foreign cinemas were more than twice as high as those in the US, a staggering $1.23 billion, $1.21 billion of which were earned in 1998 (Anon. 1999: 36). This made up 18 per cent of the foreign box-office receipts for films released by the major studios in 1998 (Woods 1999: 9). Furthermore, *Titanic* was the top-selling video in the US, and also, for example, in the UK in 1998, as well as one of the ten bestselling DVDs in the US in 1999 (*Variety* 1999: 362–3; *Variety* 2000: 381). Finally, the book about the making of the film, *James Cameron's Titanic*, was one of the biggest bestsellers of 1998 in the US, and the year's two top-selling albums were both related to the film: the *Titanic* soundtrack at number one followed by Celine Dion's *Let's Talk About Love* which featured the song 'My Heart Will Go On' from *Titanic* (*Variety* 1999: 324, 366).

In some respects (the immensity of its domestic and foreign theatrical income, for example), *Titanic's* level of success is unprecedented; in others, however, it is fairly typical of the commercial performance of the major hits since 1977: success at the North American box office is typically followed by success in foreign markets and on video and DVD, and by massive sales of various kinds of tie-in products (in most cases primarily toys and video games rather than making-of books and records). Yet the impact of Hollywood's biggest hits goes further than that: since the film industry (much like other culture industries) largely operates through a process of imitation and combination, and audiences tend to select films which promise familiar stories and attractions, megahits such as *Star Wars* and *Titanic* can have a huge impact on cinema culture as a whole.

Periods in Hollywood history

There is little doubt that *Star Wars* constitutes a turning point in American film history; it is a film which was expressive of, and in turn contributed to, a reorientation of executives, filmmakers and audiences, in particular in terms of their conception of what a big movie event is supposed to be like. Many of the top hits in the decade before *Star Wars* were, in one way or another, of a fairly adult nature due to their themes, their form and style, and/or their graphic depictions of sex and violence (see appendix 2; on the year 1967 as another historical turning point see Krämer 1998a: 297–9; see also Krämer 2005). In sharp contrast, the biggest hits of the two decades after *Star Wars* are, on the whole – like *Star Wars* – family-friendly. Among the top 25 of 1977–97 (see appendix 1) there are two *Star Wars* sequels and several spin-offs of key *Star Wars* elements: a revamped Han Solo figure inhabiting the world of archaeology, mythology and political intrigue in the *Indiana Jones* films; the opening shot of the huge starship entering at the top of the frame and the climactic attack on the Death Star restaged in *Independence Day* (Roland Emmerich, 1996); and an elaboration of the cantina scene into a movie in *Men in Black* (Barry Sonnenfeld, 1997). There are also numerous references to *Star Wars* in, for example, *E.T. The Extra-Terrestrial* (Steven Spielberg, 1982) and *Toy Story* (John Lasseter, 1995). Most of these films share fundamental narrative and thematic similarities. Indeed, following the example of *Star Wars*, almost all of them can be characterised as 'family-adventure movies', in terms of their central concern with the spectacular adventures of familial or quasi-familial groups, their multiple address of children and their parents as well as teenagers and young adults, and their release in the run-up to, or during, the summer or Christmas holidays (see Krämer 1998b).

Furthermore, it is worth pointing out that *Star Wars* also marks a change in terms of personnel. While it is true that both George Lucas and Steven Spielberg (the two top filmmakers of the period since 1977) had hits before 1977, none of the other top hitmakers from the earlier period could repeat their success after *Star Wars*. The two decades after *Star Wars* are dominated by Lucas (five films in the top 25, most of them as producer), *Star Wars* 'fan' James Cameron (two films), Lucas collaborator Spielberg (five films as director, another three as producer), the Spielberg protégés Robert Zemeckis (two films) and Chris Columbus (two films), Disney's animation division under the supervision of future Spielberg collaborator Jeffrey Katzenberg (two films), Pixar's animation division under former Disney and Lucasfilm employee John Lasseter, and, amongst writers of scripts and/or source novels, Spielberg collaborator Michael Crichton (three films). The Lucas-Spielberg-Disney nexus clearly dominates from 1977 to 1997.

Since 1997, this domination has by no means decreased, and the influence of *Star Wars* has arguably become more pronounced than ever. The top ten for the years 1997–2002 (see appendix 3) include two *Star Wars* sequels, two *Harry Potter* movies directed by Chris Columbus, and the Katzenberg production *Shrek* (Andrew Adamson and Vicky Jenson, 2002). The *Harry Potter* movies re-tell the *Star Wars* tale of an orphaned boy-wizard in training, and the two *Lord of the Rings* (Peter Jackson, 2001, 2002) films, which can also be found in the top ten, adapt one of the source texts of Lucas' science fiction saga.

The examination of Hollywood's breakaway hits, then, suggests that the twenty-five years since 1977 are a distinct and coherent (and not yet concluded) period in American film history. Further aspects of the period's distinctiveness are revealed when its biggest hits are compared to those of the decades before 1967 (Finler 2003: 356–9). Historical epics, biblical epics, musicals and animated films dominate, many of them vehicles for some of Hollywood's greatest female stars and most famous female characters: Julie Andrews and Elizabeth Taylor, Maria, Mary Poppins, Cleopatra, Scarlett O'Hara, Snow White and Lara. Most importantly, these films usually are love stories. In sharp contrast the megahits of the period since 1977 tend to be science fiction, fantasy, action and comedy, and none of them is a vehicle for a major female movie star. Furthermore, while several of these hits have a romantic component, it rarely serves as the main storyline (the rare exceptions include *Ghost* (Jerry Zucker, 1990) and *Aladdin* (Ron Clements and John Musker, 1992). Since the unprecedented success of *Titanic*, there does appear to be a minor revival of romance in Hollywood's megahits, most notably in *Shrek*, *Spider-Man* (Sam Raimi, 2002) and *Star Wars: Episode II – Attack of the Clones* (George Lucas, 2002). James Cameron explicitly stated that he partially modelled *Titanic* on the epic love stories of the pre-1967 period: 'I'd been looking for an opportunity to do an epic romance in the traditional vein of *Gone With the Wind* and *Doctor Zhivago*, where you're telling an intimate story on a very big canvas' (quoted in Anon. 1997: 16; see also Krämer 1998c). Similarly, in 1990 *Ghost* had been received by the press as an old-fashioned weepie of the kind that once was central to Hollywood's output, but was felt to be exceedingly rare in the 1980s and 1990s (Krämer 1999: 101–3). Thus, what marks the period since 1977 is not only the extraordinary success of numerous family-friendly films made primarily by Lucas, Spielberg and Disney, but also the rarity of highly successful love stories and vehicles for female stars.

What is more, since both love stories and female stars are often understood to appeal specifically to female moviegoers (and audience surveys tend to confirm this), the preferences of the female audience appear to be underrepresented (Krämer 1999). Indeed, women have gone more rarely to the cinema than men since the late 1960s. In the year before *Titanic*, for example, only 27 per cent of all females over 11 were frequent moviegoers (at least once a month) as compared to 30 per cent of the males, and 31 per cent were occasional moviegoers as compared to 33 per cent of the males. Conversely, 29 per cent of females never went to the cinema and 12 per cent went infrequently as compared to 27 per cent non-attenders and 10 per cent infrequent moviegoers amongst males (Moser 1998: 18). To put it differently: In 1996, out of every 100 American females over 11, 41 attended only once or not at all. Amongst males this figure was 37. Probably due to the impact of *Titanic*, the share of infrequent cinemagoers and non-attenders amongst women went down to 39 per cent in 1998 (while for men the figure went up to 39 per cent), yet this was only a temporary change: in 2001 the respective percentages for females and males were 43 and 39 (MPAA 2002: 13).

These may seem to be only minor differences, yet they must be seen in the light of the decades before 1967, when women did go to the cinema as often as men, and in some phases even more often, and when the general industry opinion was that the cinema's primary target audience were women (especially mothers who would bring their husbands and children along). Today, however, Hollywood assumes that women are more likely to go along with the choices of their children and husbands, rather than the other way round. These observations raise the question whether Hollywood could better serve the large sections of the American population which currently are somewhat reluctant to go to the cinema – including not only women, but also, for example, older people – and thus encourage them to attend more often. In this way, the study of box-office hits and audience statistics can have a critical dimension – although in this instance the criticism relates primarily to the industry's commercial operations and audience address, rather than to questions of filmic ideology (which is not to say that there is no connection between the two).

Conclusion

What, finally, are the values and worldview promoted in Hollywood's megahits? One answer to this question is provided by the playful way in which these films reflect on their own status as cinematic entertainment. Let us take another look at the films considered at the start of this essay. *Star Wars* ends, as we have already seen, with the projection of Luke's father and mentors making up for his previous loss. And Luke's story also starts that way: it is the projection of a brief scene in which Princess Leia asks for Obi-Wan Kenobi's help that inspires Luke to revive his dream of great adventures, and it is the stories Obi-Wan tells him later on that – together with the death of his aunt and uncle – convince him to translate that dream into reality. Similarly, *Titanic* starts with Brock Lovett acting both as an adventurer and as a cynical amateur videomaker, and proceeds to introduce a superior storyteller in Rose, whose heartfelt tale of love and loss has a tremendous impact on Lovett – to the point where he forgets the diamond he was looking for altogether. Lives are transformed, then, by stories and projections, and emotional resolutions are achieved this way both for the characters on the screen and, it is implied, for the people in the auditorium.

Star Wars, *Titanic* and most of the other superhits since 1977, then, tell a similar story, and in the process reflect on their own status as cinematic entertainment. Loved ones (family members or lovers) have been, or are being lost, and this loss influences the protagonists' outlook on the world; their wishes and anxieties gradually – or occasionally very abruptly – take shape in their reality, often magically so; they achieve an emotional resolution in the end, sometimes a spiritual reunion with those they have lost, yet rarely a reunion in the here and now; however, an alternative, closely-knit social network has been established, typically going beyond the sphere of family and romance. And always the power of cinema itself to bring fantastic scenes to life, to translate an individual's wishes and anxieties, dreams and nightmares into a shared reality, to make up – albeit only temporarily and imaginarily – for all our losses, to provide us with a stronger sense of communal bonds, is being foregrounded and celebrated. The films thus present a very optimistic vision of the impact of cinema on people's lives, which, it has to be said, is not shared by most critics of contemporary Hollywood. I do think, however, that this vision deserves serious consideration.

Appendix 1: Top Grossing Movies in North America, 1977–97

This list is based on *Variety* (1999: 64–6) and lists revenues from both the US and Canada. Figures were compiled at the end of 1998 and include revenues from *Titanic*'s extended run in that year. They also include revenues from re-releases (most notably for the *Star Wars* trilogy). The figures are not adjusted for inflation. (Figures not adjusted for inflation.)

1   *Titanic* (1997), $601m
2   *Star Wars* (1982), $461m
3   *E.T.* (1982), $400m
4   *Jurassic Park* (1993), $357m
5   *Forrest Gump* (1994), $330m
6   *The Lion King* (1994), $313m
7   *Return of the Jedi* (1983), $309m
8   *Independence Day* (1996), $306m
9   *The Empire Strikes Back* (1980), $290m
10 *Home Alone* (1990), $286m
11 *Batman* (1989), $251m
12 *Men in Black* (1997), $251m
13 *Raiders of the Lost Ark* (1981), $242m
14 *Twister* (1996), $242m
15 *Ghostbusters* (1984), $239m
16 *Beverly Hills Cop* (1984), $235m
17 *The Lost World* (1997), $229m
18 *Mrs Doubtfire* (1993), $219m
19 *Ghost* (1990), $217m
20 *Aladdin* (1992), $217m
21 *Back to the Future* (1985), $208m
22 *Terminator 2* (1991), $205m

23 *Indiana Jones and the Last Crusade* (1989), $197m
24 *Toy Story* (1995), $192m
25 *Dances with Wolves* (1990), $184m

Appendix 2: Top Grossing Movies in North America, 1967–76

This list is again based on *Variety* (1999: 64–6). *The Jungle Book* (1967, $142m) and *The Rocky Horror Picture Show* (1975, 139m) generated the bulk of their revenues in re-releases after 1976 and were therefore excluded from this list. (Figures not adjusted for inflation.)

1 *Jaws* (1975), $260m
2 *The Exorcist* (1973), $165m
3 *The Sting* (1973), $156m
4 *The Godfather* (1972), $135m
5 *Blazing Saddles* (1974), $120m
6 *Rocky* (1976), $117m
7 *The Towering Inferno* (1974), $116m
8 *American Graffiti* (1973), $115m
9 *One Flew Over the Cuckoo's Nest* (1975), $112m
10 *Love Story* (1970), $106m

Appendix 3: Top Grossing Movies in North America, 1998–2002

Based on 'The Top Grossing Movies of All Time at the USA Box Office', Internet Movie Database, http://www.imdb.com/charts/usatopmovies, accessed 23 September 2003. Figures include the revenues generated in 2003 for 2002 releases. (Figures not adjusted for inflation.)

1 *Star Wars: Episode 1 - The Phantom Menace* (1999), $431m
2 *Spider-Man* (2002), $404m
3 *The Lord of the Rings: The Two Towers* (2002), $340m
4 *Harry Potter and the Sorcerer's Stone* (2001), $318m
5 *The Lord of the Rings: The Fellowship of the Ring* (2001), $313m
6 *Star Wars: Episode 2 - Attack of the Clones* (2002), $311m
7 *The Sixth Sense* (1999), $294m
8 *Shrek* (2001), $268m
9 *Harry Potter and the Chamber of Secrets* (2002), $262m
10 *How the Grinch Stole Christmas* (2000), $260m

Bibliography

Anon. (1997) 'Captain of the Ship', *Preview*. November–December, 16–21.
_____ (1999) 'The Top 125 Worldwide', *Variety*, 25 January, 36.
Cook, D. A. (2000) *Lost Illusions: American Cinema in the Shadow of Watergate and Vietnam, 1970–1979. History of the American Cinema Volume 9*. New York: Scribner's.
Finler, J. W. (2003) *The Hollywood Story* (third edition). London: Wallflower Press.
Garncarz, J. (1994) 'Hollywood in Germany: The Role of American Films in Germany, 1925–1990', in D. W. Ellwood and R. Kroes (eds) *Hollywood in Europe: Experiences of a Cultural Hegemony*. Amsterdam: VU University Press, 122–35.
Heard, C. (1997) *Dreaming Aloud: The Life and Films of James Cameron*. Toronto: Doubleday

Canada.

Krämer, P. (1998a) 'Post-classical Hollywood', in J. Hill and P. Church Gibson (eds) *The Oxford Guide to Film Studies*. Oxford: Oxford University Press, 289–309.

_____ (1998b) 'Would You Take Your Child To See This Film? The Cultural and Social Work of the Family-Adventure Movie', in S. Neale and M. Smith (eds) *Contemporary Hollywood Cinema*. London: Routledge, 294–311.

_____ (1998c) 'Women First: *Titanic* (1997), Action-Adventure Films and Hollywood's Female Audience', *Historical Journal of Film, Radio and Television*, 18, 4, 599–618.

_____ (1999) 'A Powerful Cinema-going Force? Hollywood and Female Audiences since the 1960s', in M. Stokes and R. Maltby (eds) *Identifying Hollywood's Audiences: Cultural Identity and the Movies*. London: British Film Institute, 98–112.

_____ (2000) 'Entering the Magic Kingdom: The Walt Disney Company, *The Lion King* and the Limitations of Criticism', *Film Studies*, 2, 44–50.

_____ (2005) *The New Hollywood: From Bonnie and Clyde to Star Wars*. London: Wallflower Press.

Monaco, P. (2001) *The Sixties, 1960–1969. History of the American Cinema Volume 8*. New York: Scribner's.

Moser, J. D. (ed.) (1998) *International Motion Picture Almanac*. La Jolla: Quigley.

_____ (ed.) (2000) *International Motion Picture Almanac*. La Jolla: Quigley.

MPAA (2002) '2001 Motion Picture Attendance Study', published 13 March. Available online: http:/www.mpaa.org/useconomicreview/2001AttendanceStudy.

Prince, S. (2000) *A New Pot of Gold: Hollywood under the Electronic Rainbow, 1980–1989. History of the American Cinema Volume 10*. New York: Scribner's.

Sedgwick, J. (2000) *Popular Filmgoing in 1930s Britain: A Choice of Pleasures*. Exeter: University of Exeter Press.

Shapiro, M. (2000) *James Cameron: An Unauthorised Biography of the Filmmaker*. Los Angeles: Renaissance Books.

Variety (1999) *The Variety Insider*. New York: Perigee.

_____ (2000) *The Variety Alamanac 2000*. London: Boxtree.

Woods, M. (1999) 'That Championship Season', *Variety*, 9, 16, 127.

CHAPTER THIRTEEN

The Impact of Changes in Filmgoing Behaviour on the Structure and Practises of Hollywood between 1945 and 1946[1]

John Sedgwick

Audiences across the globe now consume films through a variety of media, but in the years immediately following the end of the Second World War consumption was confined to cinemas alone.[2] At that time US audiences, when counted by ticket admissions, were at an all-time high with an annual count of four and a half billion (33 visits per capita), dwarfing those attracted by other paid-for leisure activities.[3] After 1946 admissions fell continuously to a low point of 820 million in 1972, followed by a gentle recovery. During this period the mode of film consumption diversified from the cinema alone to home viewing on television sets, through the TV networks at first, and then video, cable and more recently satellite. Computer screens now constitute a third medium. Remarkably, during these changes, as before them, Hollywood has continued to dominate the global market for film.

The American market for film entertainment was, and remains, by far the most important source of theatrical revenue for film producers, contributing approximately half total worldwide sales in 1965. Unlike today, when approximately 70 per cent of film revenue is derived from non-theatrical sources, rental income from the box office was almost the sole source of revenue for production companies during the period under investigation (see Vogel 2001: 58–63). Indeed, rental agreements with the television networks did not start to make a significant contribution to the costs of film production until the widespread diffusion of colour television during the late 1960s and early 1970s (Izod 1988: 166–70). Before this Hollywood's earnings from television came not so much from its library of vintage films locked away in studio vaults as from its production of contemporary made-for-TV films and celebrity shows (Gomery 1996: 407–8).

However, this strategic response to declining audience numbers was not unproblematic for the major studios. Extending their product portfolio to made-for-TV programmes and films did not lessen the problem of how to compete effectively in the diminishing market for feature films and how, if possible, to arrest this decline. After all, making films and distributing and screening them had constituted the core business of Hollywood since the late 1910s (Balio 1993; Crafton 1997; Thompson 1985). In 1946 the principal studios dominated production and distribution, and five of them, Loew's/MGM, Paramount, RKO, Twentieth Century Fox and Warner Bros., controlled a significant share of the first-run exhibition market from which they were compelled to disengage themselves as a result the Supreme Court's Paramount Divorcement decree of 1948.[4] By 1965, most of the films released were made by production companies whose existence was short-lived, if not confined solely to the production of a single film output, and shown in divested cinemas.

The change in the organisational configuration of Hollywood is commonly explained as a consequence of the major studios no longer having a guaranteed retail outlet for their product (Izod 1988: 124–5; De Vany & Eckert 1991: 53–4). This essay proposes a different explanation based upon the changing pattern of demand: namely, that during the period 1946–65 not only did US box-office revenues fall dramatically, but they became increasingly unequally distributed, so that whilst the rental income of the annual top-ten films held up over the period, films ranked in lower classifications performed progressively poorly. These changes made untenable the portfolio approach to risk that had characterised studio production during the preceding two decades: middle- and low-budget films could no longer be relied upon to attenuate the risks associated with big-budget production (Sedgwick & Pokorny 1998). The outcome of this was that studio production became increasingly focused on the production of 'hit' films. To make their films more attractive to audiences, studios spent increasing amounts in order to enhance production values, including the introduction of an array of visual and audio innovations (see Belton 1992). Audiences for their part, given the physical and spatial constraints implicit in the postwar baby boom when coupled with the exodus of white Americans from the city to the suburbs, and after 1950 the rapid diffusion of television, were becoming increasingly occasional and selective filmgoers.

The context

In the immediate postwar period the United States experienced rapid social change occasioned by the growth in real disposable incomes, the build-up of wartime savings and the explosion in the birth rate. As David Halberstam has written, 'this was one of the great sellers' markets of all time. There was a desperate hunger for products after the long drought of fifteen years caused by the Depression and then World War Two' (1994: 118). The same author identifies the key symbolic products of the late 1940s and 1950s as cars, suburban (Levitt) homes – full of consumer durables, including televisions, bought at suburban (Korvettes) discount stores – fast foods (McDonald's) and advertising. To these should be added a whole range of outdoor recreation products including tourism, golf, gardening, participatory sports and fishing (Clawson & Knetch 1966; Oakley 1986).

Cinema was not on this list. Indeed audiences had stopped going to the cinema in large numbers. Referencing social survey evidence of 1948, Michael Conant identified the pressure on consumers' time as the most important factor in the decline of cinema attendances (1960: 12). Douglas Gomery writes:

SCREEN METHODS

When middle-class Americans moved to the suburbs in record numbers after the Second World War, they also abandoned propinquity to the matrix of downtown and neighbourhood movie theatres. In addition, these young adults, previously the most loyal fans, concentrated on raising families. (1992: 83)

Table 1 (below) reports the period as one of intensive urbanisation. The proportion of Americans living in urban areas, defined as cities with a population larger than 100,000, expanded from 46 per cent in 1950 to 58 per cent by 1970. More startling, however, is the growth in the number of Americans living in fringe areas of cities as opposed to city centres. Whilst the latter grew by 32 per cent over the period, the city fringe population grew by 161 per cent, a compound annual growth rate of over 5 per cent per year. Of course the record number of housing starts made this population movement to the suburbs possible, with the housing stock increasing by a quarter during both the 1940s and 1950s.[5] Alongside these changes was the increase in home ownership, rising dramatically from 44 per cent in 1940 to 55 per cent in 1950 and to 62 per cent in 1960.[6] The change in lifestyle that went with sub-urbanisation is of course a subject for numerous films during the period.

The baby boom is captured in columns 4–7 of Table 1. The number of under-fives increased by 57 per cent during the 14 years between 1946 and 1960, at a rate of 3.5 per cent per annum. Likewise the 5–14 age range also mushroomed – a 64 per cent growth between these same years at an annual rate of 3.9 per cent – whilst the next two age categories remained static. For men and women in their twenties and early thirties there were many more children of pre-school and schooling age to be looked after.

TABLE 1: SELECTED US POPULATION STATISTICS, 1946–70

year	US population (000s)	urbanised areas – central cities (000s)	urbanised areas-urban fringe (000s)	persons aged under 5 (000s)	ages 5–14 (000s)	ages 15–24 (000s)	ages 25–34 (000s)
	(1)	(2)	(3)	(4)	(5)	(6)	(7)
1946	–	–	–	12,974	21,844	23,382	22,954
1950	151,684	48,337	20,872	16,331	24,477	22,260	23,932
1960	180,671	57,975	37,873	20,341	35,735	24,576	22,919
1970	204,879	63,922	54,525	17,156	40,733	36,496	25,293

Source: Historical Statistics of the United States Chapter A, Series 29–42; Series 82–90; Series 288–319

Hence, whilst Americans had on average more leisure time at their disposal in the postwar period with the onset of institutional vacations and the decline in Saturday working, they found additional claims on their growing recreational budget through alternative recreational activities as well as family and house-owning responsibilities. Between 1946 and 1950 cinema audiences declined by a third, even though admission prices were falling in real terms (Conant 1960). From 1950 television became an additional attraction for Americans and the chief cause in the further decline of cinema numbers. The astonishing speed at which television services were diffused across the American population is captured in column 5 of Table 2 (below). In 1950 less than 9 per cent of American households possessed a television, yet five years later the proportion had risen to 64 per cent. A Stanford Research Institute report in which researchers showed that the diffusion of television accounted for more than 70 per cent of the drop in motion picture revenues in 1950 and 1951, falling to 60 per cent in 1952, 58 per cent in 1953 and 55.8 per cent in 1954 (Conant 1960: 14). Interestingly, the growth in television viewing brought with it a demand for vintage films (Conant 1960: 13–14).

In contrast to those exogenous factors responsible for the decline in audience numbers highlighted above, Robert Sklar (1975, 1999) has focused attention upon the contemporary reception of the product itself. Drawing upon scholarly work of the time he reports a series of conflicting arguments. Whilst all contemporary commentators accepted Leo Handel's (1950) findings – that younger people attended the cinema more regularly than older people, and that cinemagoers tended to have spent a longer period in education, and were of a higher socio-economic status but equally spread between the genders – they were interpreted in a variety of ways. Paul Lazarsfeld (1947) maintained that youth had become the chief arbiters of film success: they were its opinion leaders. The David and Evelyn Riesman (1952) concurred, arguing that the incipient orientation of filmmaking towards the taste of youth resulted in films that proved to be too fast and difficult to keep up with for older filmgoers. Gilbert Seldes (1950), however, believed that pandering to youth had resulted in a lowering of cinematic standards and that it was this that had turned audiences away. Eliot Friedson found that the cinema became a place where young people could be in a social setting of their own making, apart from the authority structures that normally governed their lives (1954).

TABLE 2: SELECTED PERSONAL CONSUMPTION STATISTICS, 1946–70
(All money values in U.S. $millions, 1958 prices)

Year	Total Personal Consumption Expenditure (1)	Recreational Expenditure (2)	Total US Box-Office (3)	Average Weekly Cinema Attendance (millions) (4)	Households with TV sets (000s) (5)
1946	203404	12112	2400	90	8
1950	230409	13446	1660	60	3,875
1955	274117	15170	1429	46	30,700
1960	316075	17779	924	40	45,750
1965	397830	24171	852	44	52,700

Source: *Historical Statistics of the United States*: Chapter G, Series 416 and 452; Chapter H, Series 874 and 884; Chapter R, Series 93–105. The price deflator used throughout the study is that given for Total Consumer Expenditure, Chapter E, Series 2.

With the decline in attendance the proportion of young people in the audience increased, so that by 1957 three-quarters of audiences were under thirty and half under twenty years of age.[7] A criticism levelled at Hollywood was that the major studios failed to respond vigorously to this market information. Indeed Sklar has argued that the logic of the situation demanded that Hollywood should have tried harder at attracting less educated and lower income groups. However, such strategies were anathema to the studio moguls who conceived their audience to be essentially homogeneous, characterised by a range of 'middle class' tastes that were known to, and intuitively understood by, them (Sklar 1975: 270–1). This opinion is no doubt overstated. One has only to examine the great mix of film-types categorised by genre from, say, the mid-1920s to realise that 'old' Hollywood also produced films for niche markets (Maltby 1999). Nevertheless, it would also be true to say that middle- and big-budget films were designed to achieve maximum penetration in the market place and this was achievable only if audiences had a common conception of film quality. To assess the studios' strategic response to the declining market it seems sensible to begin with the box office.

The data

In 1946 the weekly trade journal *Variety* published in either its first or second issue in January of each year an annual list of the most popular films released onto the American market, together with the rental incomes they generated for their distributors. The data set of 1820 films, with not less than 61 and not more than 130 top-ranking films recorded in each of the years of the study, provides a unique empirical source from which to study Hollywood during this time of declining theatrical audiences. The numbers of films reported each year – labelled by *Variety* 'Top Grossers' – are found in column 1 of Table 3 (overleaf) and were selected on the grounds that they generated a threshold number of dollars at the US and Canadian box office, net of the exhibitor's take.

On the surface the *Variety* returns might not appear to be a good basis for developing a thesis. They certainly were not produced from within an academy, or as the outcome of scientific method. The bases of the estimates were not recorded and hence are not transparent (Besas 1992: 281–3). Nevertheless, however imperfect they are, they are all that historians have to work on (Crafton 1997: 521). We can have some confidence because the trade treated the data with respect. It told a story about the relative and absolute popularity of films that accorded with the experience of those whose livelihood was bound up in the film business. This is most important, since without such verity it seems highly unlikely that *Variety* would have continued to serve as the principal trade publication.

From Table 3 it is clear that whilst the total box-office revenues of theatrical releases declined to about a third of their starting value over the period, the rental income accruing to the distributors of those films found in the *Variety* lists experienced a much smaller decline. One difficulty is the point in the supply chain at which the data have been collected: in the case of *Variety* the source is the rental incomes of the distribution companies, whilst the US Government data represent the box-office revenue captured by exhibitors. Joel Finler has suggested that the rental income constituted approximately half of the total box-office gross, with

TABLE 3: BOX-OFFICE REVENUES OF 'TOP-GROSSING FILMS', 1946–56
(All money values in US$millions, 1958 prices)

year	no. of films listed in *Variety* as 'Top Grossers' (1)	no. of 'Top Grossers' distributed by the major Hollywood studios* (2)	net rental income of films listed in *Variety* (3)	mean rental income of *Variety* listed films (4)	total US box office (5)
1946	61	61	303.55	4.98	2400.00
1947	75	75	329.27	4.39	2046.21
1948	92	90	278.61	3.03	1829.89
1949	89	86	246.14	2.77	1776.01
1950	95	92	263.67	2.78	1659.83
1951	130	130	277.40	2.13	1478.56
1952	118	115	294.10	2.49	1376.80
1953	131	129	329.67	2.52	1294.44
1954	112	109	301.89	2.70	1327.57
1955	107	103	341.97	3.20	1428.88
1956	106	101	272.42	2.57	1470.46
1957	95	92	293.27	3.09	1152.51
1958	76	70	249.17	3.28	992.00
1959	82	79	224.89	2.74	945.71
1960	74	65	244.55	3.30	924.20
1961	75	71	235.90	3.15	886.43
1962	72	67	238.90	3.32	860.82
1963	77	68	301.31	3.91	852.03
1964	70	67	229.54	3.28	850.09
1965	83	79	355.07	4.28	852.02

* Taken here to include Columbia, Disney, Loew's/MGM, Paramount, RKO, Twentieth Century Fox, United Artists, Universal and Warner Bros.

Note: The film rental data reported in *Variety* for any particular year included estimates for those films which were released during the year and were still on release. Occasionally, these films appeared as 'Top Grossers' during the following year with an updated figure. These films and their revenues have been attributed to the year of release. For the greater part of the period re-releases were relatively uncommon with the life cycle of films on theatrical release being completed within 15 months. Only five re-releases made the *Variety* charts: *Bridge on the River Kwai*, reissued in 1964: *Cinderella* reissued in 1965; *Gone With the Wind* reissued in 1961; *Hollywood Canteen* reissued in 1954; and *So Dear To My Heart* reissued in 1964.

SCREEN METHODS

the other half going to the exhibitor (2003: 276). As the figures stand in Table 3, it is apparent that the market share of *Variety* listed films increases dramatically over the period. Assuming that rental incomes were half the annual box-office revenue, the top films increased their share from 26 per cent in 1946 to 84 per cent by 1965.[8]

The period under investigation was notable for the increasing inequality of rental incomes. Table 4 (overleaf) shows the proportion of the rental income generated by the 60 top films for each year attributed to films ranked in sets of ten. A first observation is the growing importance of the top-ranking films as money earners. Column 4 shows that the top 10 films significantly increased their share of the rental incomes generated by the top 60 films. This rose from approximately a quarter during the immediate postwar years to above 30 per cent during much of the 1950s, climbing to over 40 per cent for most of the years from 1957 onwards and peaking at 51 per cent in 1965. Further, the actual revenues that accrued to these films also rose in real terms, trending upwards from postwar low levels of less than $50 million in 1949 and 1951, to aggregate rental incomes of above $100 million in 1957, 1958, 1960, 1963 and 1965. The peaks were generated by the extraordinary success of a small number of films – in the box-office year 1957, *The Ten Commandments* ($34.2 million) and *Around the World in 80 Days* ($22 million); in 1958, *South Pacific* ($17.5 million) and *Bridge on the River Kwai* ($17.2 million); in 1960, *Ben Hur* ($38 million); in 1962 *West Side Story* ($22 million); in 1963 *Cleopatra* ($23.5 million) and *How the West Was Won* ($23 million); and in 1965, *The Sound of Music* ($42.5 million), *Mary Poppins* ($31 million), *My Fair Lady* ($30 million) and *Goldfinger* ($22 million). However, this upward trend was highly volatile as is evident from the coefficient of variation statistic found in column 2, with marked falls in rental income being experienced in 1954, 1959, 1961 and 1964.

The growth in the market share of the annual top-ten films over the period of this investigation was of course at the expense of the shares taken by the other categories. Distinctive downward trends are noticeable in films grouped into ranks lower than 20, with their market share falling by approximately a third in the case of the films ranked 31 to 40 and by half in the bottom two categories. In 1946 the share of the top 10 films was a little over twice that of those ranked between 51st and 60th. By the 1960s the difference had increased to multiples of seven and above. This growing inequality of rental incomes causes annual Gini coefficients to trend upwards over the period.[9]

The impact on the industry

During the two decades prior to the Paramount decree, Hollywood's principal studios had pursued a portfolio approach to risk management through the production of a range of films in which the higher risks associated with big-budget production were offset by a greater number of middle- and low-budget films for which revenues were less variable and more evenly spread (see Sedgwick & Pokorny 1998). The increasing skew of rental income reported above, manifest in the dramatic decline in the real earnings of sub-top-twenty films, made portfolio production less tenable as the 1950s wore on, leading to the increase in independent production which David Bordwell, Janet Staiger and Kristen Thompson have termed the 'package-unit' system:

TABLE 4: PROPORTIONAL DISTRIBUTION OF RENTAL INCOME OF ANNUAL TOP 60 FILMS, 1946–65
(Column 1 in US$millions, 1958 prices)

year	top 60 rental income (1)	coefficient of variation (2)	Gini coefficient (3)	films ranked 1 to 10 (4)	films ranked 11 to 20 (5)	films ranked 21 to 30 (6)	films ranked 31 to 40 (7)	films ranked 41 to 50 (8)	films ranked 51 to 60 (9)
1946	300.35	0.29	0.11	0.25	0.19	0.17	0.14	0.13	0.11
1947	289.28	0.49	0.16	0.31	0.19	0.15	0.13	0.12	0.11
1948	211.42	0.24	0.10	0.24	0.19	0.16	0.14	0.14	0.13
1949	189.78	0.30	0.12	0.25	0.20	0.16	0.14	0.13	0.12
1950	201.63	0.53	0.15	0.31	0.17	0.15	0.14	0.12	0.11
1951	171.98	0.38	0.13	0.28	0.17	0.16	0.14	0.13	0.12
1952	210.06	0.79	0.21	0.37	0.16	0.14	0.12	0.11	0.09
1953	225.92	0.77	0.23	0.39	0.17	0.13	0.11	0.10	0.10
1954	226.54	0.51	0.18	0.31	0.20	0.16	0.13	0.11	0.10
1955	265.79	0.49	0.20	0.31	0.22	0.17	0.12	0.10	0.08
1956	211.02	0.52	0.21	0.33	0.22	0.16	0.11	0.10	0.09
1957	248.14	1.27	0.30	0.46	0.16	0.12	0.10	0.09	0.07
1958	231.07	0.87	0.29	0.43	0.18	0.13	0.11	0.08	0.07
1959	200.01	0.57	0.21	0.34	0.20	0.15	0.13	0.10	0.08
1960	228.08	1.26	0.29	0.44	0.17	0.13	0.11	0.08	0.07
1961	217.71	0.64	0.24	0.37	0.20	0.15	0.12	0.09	0.07
1962	225.82	0.88	0.27	0.41	0.19	0.15	0.11	0.08	0.06
1963	280.81	0.91	0.28	0.43	0.18	0.14	0.10	0.08	0.07
1964	219.09	0.75	0.24	0.37	0.20	0.16	0.12	0.09	0.07
1965	325.09	1.26	0.34	0.51	0.15	0.11	0.09	0.08	0.06

Source: *Variety*

Rather than an individual company containing the source of the labour and materials, the entire industry became the pool for these ... This system of production was intimately tied to the post-war industrial shift: instead of the mass production of many films by a few manufacturing firms, now there was the specialised production of a few films by many independents. The majors acted as financiers and distributors.'(Bordwell, Staiger & Thompson 1985: 330–1).

The trend in independent production, defined by John Izod as 'the work of companies that neither own nor are owned by a distribution company' (1988: 125), is shown in Table 5 (overleaf). From the copyright ownership records it is clear that for Loew's/MGM, Paramount, Twentieth Century Fox and Warner Bros., the scale and importance of wholly in-house production fell. The main change occurred between 1956 and 1960 with the completion of the divestiture process, and accelerated during the next five-year period as the major studios transformed themselves into distributor-financiers handling annual portfolios of films in which investment risk was shared to an increasing degree with independent producers.[10] The studio that bucked the trend was Disney with its distribution arm Buena Vista. However, as is evident from a comparison of columns 1 and 2 in Table 5, whilst the major studios cut back on production, their share of the top end of the market as distributors remained dominant and continued to be so, as Asu Aksoy and Kevin Robins (1992) have shown, for the remainder of the century. For these authors independent production was dependent on the major studios and should be seen as the consequence of their decision to produce, or co-finance, and distribute fewer but more costly films, a strategy designed to attract occasional filmgoers back to the cinema by offering superior attractions (1992: 8; see also Scott Berg 1989: 470).

Conclusion

Hollywood underwent dramatic change during the two decades following the Second World War as the supply side of the industry reacted to rapidly declining audiences. It can be argued in hindsight that the divestiture of cinemas, forced on Loew's/MGM, RKO, Paramount, Twentieth Century Fox and Warner Bros. through the Paramount decree of 1948, would have taken place anyway as audiences turned away from the cinema as a regular form of recreation. Evidence of the changing pattern of demand during the period emerges from the study of top-ranking film rental returns published annually by the trade journal *Variety*. The market was differentiated both horizontally (in terms of variety) and vertically (in terms of quality), with stars and genre serving as markers. Audiences became increasingly attracted to particular films, rather than films in general. Such films, in providing extraordinary levels of utility, transcended traditional patterns of genre loyalty and achieved very high levels of market penetration. On the supply side, the growing inequality of the rank distribution of film rentals led to a) the growth in independent production, b) the growth in the size of major studio film budgets dedicated to 'hit' production, and c) the transformation of these same studios into distributor-financier-producers. Abandoning in-house portfolio production, Hollywood's major studios adopted a new strategy to reduce their exposure to risk whilst maintaining their dominance of markets. Bordwell, Staiger and Thompson refer to this as the package-unit mode of production in which the studios as distributors organised production through market contract relations rather than in-house co-ordination. By changing in this way Hollywood was able to retain its dominant collective position in the film business.

TABLE 5: THE 'MAJOR' STUDIOS' CONTROL OF COPYRIGHT

'major' studios	period	no. of 'Top-Grossing' films distributed (1)	no. of 'Top-Grossing' films credited to the studio (2)	no. of 'Top-Grossing' films where copyright owned by studio (3)	ratio of column 3 to column 1 (4)
Columbia	1946–50	21	16	14	0.67
	1951–55	36	24	20	0.56
	1956–60	45	20	16	0.36
	1961–65	52	8	7	0.13
Disney/BV	1954–55	6	6	6	1.00
	1956–60	15	14	14	0.93[a]
	1961–65	25	25	25	1.00
Loew's/MGM	1946–50	87	85	86	0.99
	1951–55	97	96	96	0.99
	1956–60	65	38	31	0.48
	1961–65	63	13	18	0.29
Paramount	1946–50	63	59	51	0.81
	1951–55	85	62	67	0.79
	1956–60	56	20	23	0.41
	1961–65	44	6	6	0.14
RKO	1946–50	48	22	14	0.29
	1951–55	38	17	20	0.53
	1956–57	5	3	5	1.00
Twentieth Century Fox	1946–50	74	74	74	1.00
	1951–55	110	104	104	0.95
	1956–60	75	60	54	0.72
	1961–65	45	18	19	0.42
Universal	1946–50	33	27	24	0.73
	1951–55	88	88	88	1.00
	1956–60	44	38	40	0.91
	1961–65	44	10	13	0.30
Warners	1946–50	64	59	50	0.78
	1951–55	94	71	66	0.70
	1956–60	49	24	27	0.55
	1961–65	25	11	11	0.44
Total	1946–50	396	348	319	0.81
	1951–55	563	476	475	0.84
	1956–60	364	228	221	0.61
	1961–65	273	66	74	0.27

*The film that caused this proportion to fall below 1.0 was *The Big Fisherman* (1959). Source: *Library of Congress Catalog of Copyright Entries: Motion Pictures*

Notes

1   This essay is a shorter version of that published in the *Journal of Economic History*; see Sedg-wick (2002). I am grateful to the editors for giving me permission to reproduce aspectsof that article here. The research was made possible by a grant from the Leverhulme Trust, for whom I was a Research Fellow between 2000–01. Peter Armitage and Bernard Hrusa Marlow helped me shape the paper. Sam Cameron, John Curran, Mark Glancy, Manfred Holler, Ian Jarvie, James Obelkevich, Mike Pokorny and Guglielmo Volpe all made critical contributions. Comments from participants of seminars at Humbolt University, Berlin, and the Institute of Historical Research, London, and Southampton University, in the UK, also helped to form the final draft, as did the reviews of two anonymous referees.

2   For a general discussion of the characteristics of film as a commodity see Sedgwick (2000).

3   *Historical Statistics of the US*, Series H, 862–77, US Department of Commerce, Bureau of the Census.

4   Prior to divestiture the five majors owned 70 per cent of first run cinemas. See Conant (1960).

5   For an overview of the dramatic changes to the housing sector see Rome (2001).

6   US Census Bureau: *Historical Census of Housing*.

7   See Belton (1992: 81). With this came new generic conventions, in particular rock and roll, teenpics and sex. See Docherty (1995).

8   These shares are obtained by halving column 5 of Table 3 and expressing rental income as a percentage.

9   The Gini coefficient measures the degree of inequality of a statistical distribution, often represented by a Lorenz Curve. The coefficient ranges from 0 (complete equality) to 1 (extreme inequality). Perfect equality exists when a given percentage of films in a popula-tion generate the same percentage of revenues. Thus, while we know that 100 per cent of the films generate 100 per cent of the revenue, the fact that the Top 20 films might gener-ate 60 per cent of the revenues implies that the revenues are unequally distributed among films.

10   Information on the copyright ownership of films is found in the Library of Congress Catalog of Copyright Entries: Motion Pictures. Bernard Hrusa-Marlow brought this source to my attention.

Bibliography

Aksoy, A. and K. Robins (1992) 'Hollywood for the 21st Century: Global Competition for Critical Mass in Image Markets', *Cambridge Journal of Economics*, 16, 1–22.

Balio, T. (1993) *Grand Design: Hollywood as a Modern Business Enterprise*. Berkeley: University of California Press.

Belton, J. (1992) *Widescreen Cinema*. Cambridge, MA: Harvard University Press.

Besas, P. (2000) *Inside Variety: The Story of the Bible of Show Business, 1905–87*. New York: Ars Millenii.

Bordwell, D., J. Staiger and K. Thompson (1985) *The Classical Hollywood Cinema: Film Style and Mode of Production to 1960*. London: Routledge.

Clawson, M. and J. Knetch (1966) *The Economics of Outdoor Recreation*. Baltimore: Johns Hopkins University Press.

Conant, M. (1960) *Antitrust in the Motion Picture Industry*. Berkeley: University of California

Press.

Crafton, D. (1997) *The Talkies: American Cinema's Transition to Sound, 1926–1931*. Berkeley: University of California Press.

De Vany, A. and R. Eckert (1991) 'Motion Picture Antitrust: the Paramount Cases Revisited', *Research in Law and Economics*, 14, 51–112.

Docherty, T. (1995) 'Teenagers and Teenpics, 1955–1957: A Study in Exploitation Filmmaking', in J. Staiger (ed.) *The Studio System*. New Brunswick: Rutgers University Press, 298–316.

Finler, J. (2003) *The Hollywood Story* (third edition). London: Wallflower Press.

Friedson, E. (1954–5) 'Consumption of the Mass Media by Polish-American Children', *Quarterly Review of Film, Radio and Television*, 9, 92–101.

Gomery, D. (1992) *Shared Pleasures: a History of Movie Presentation in the United States*. London: British Film Institute.

_____ (1996) 'Towards a New Media Economics', in D. Bordwell and N. Carroll, *Post-Theory: Reconstructing Film Studies*. Madison: University of Wisconsin Press, 407–18.

Handel, L. (1950) *Hollywood Looks at its Audience*. Urbana: University of Illinois Press.

Halberstam, D. (1994) *The Fifties*. New York: Ballantine Books.

Izod, J. (1988) *Hollywood and the Box Office*. London: Macmillan.

Lazarsfeld, P. (1947) 'Audience Research in the Movie Field', *Annals of the American Academy of Political and Social Science*, 254, 160–8.

Library of Congress Catalog of Copyright Entries, Motion Pictures. vols. 1940–1949, 1950–1959, 1960–1969.

Maltby, R. (1999) 'Sticks, Hicks and Flaps: Classical Hollywood's Generic Conception of its Audiences', in M. Stokes and R. Maltby (eds) *Identifying Hollywood's Audiences: Cultural Identity and the Movies*. London: British Film Institute, 23–41.

Oakley, J. (1986) *God's Country: America in the Fifties*. New York: Dember.

Riesman, D. and E. Riesman (1952) 'Movies and Audiences', *American Quarterly*, 4, 195–202.

Rome, A. (2001) *The Bulldozer in the Countryside: Suburban Sprawl and the Rise of American Environmentalism*. Cambridge: Cambridge University Press.

Scott Berg, A. (1989) *Goldwyn*. London: Hamish Hamilton.

Sedgwick, J. (2000) *Filmgoing in 1930s Britain: A Choice of Pleasures*. Exeter: Exeter University Press.

_____ (2002) 'Product Differentiation at the Movies: Hollywood, 1946–65', *Journal of Economic History*, 62, 676–704.

Sedgwick, J. and M. Pokorny (1998) 'The Risk Environment of Film-Making: Warners in the Inter-War Period', *Explorations in Economic History*, 35, 196–220.

Seldes, G. (1950) *The Great Audience*. New York: Viking.

Sklar, R. (1975) *Movie-Made America: A Cultural History of American Movies*. New York: Random House.

_____ (1999) 'Lost Audience: 1950s Spectatorship and Historical Reception Studies', in M. Stokes and R. Maltby (eds) *Identifying Hollywood's Audiences: Cultural Identity and the Movies*. London: British Film Institute, 81–92.

Thompson, K. (1985) *Exporting Entertainment: America in the World Film Market, 1907–1934*, London: British Film Institute.

US Department of Commerce, Bureau of the Census (1975) *Historical Statistics of the US: Colonial Times to 1970*. Washington, DC.

Vogel, H. (2001) *Entertainment Industry Economics* (fifth edition). Cambridge: Cambridge University Press.

CHAPTER FOURTEEN

'Fact', 'Fiction' and Everything In Between: Negotiating Boundaries in *Crimewatch UK*

Deborah Jermyn   •

> *Crimewatch UK* is Britain's top-rated *factual TV series* with an audience of millions. Why has this *serious information programme* become more popular than most *entertainment* shows?
>
>   – Nick Ross and Sue Cook (1987; emphasis added)

As early as 1987 – some three years after the arrival of *Crimewatch UK* as Britain's leading television crime appeal programme – the inside cover blurb from the book of the series, quoted above, already seemed to grasp the concerns and critiques that have come to dominate the discourses surrounding the show. Equally, it revealed much about how the programme understood itself, as it wholeheartedly situated itself within the more sombre aspect of the BBC's public service broadcasting remit that requires it to 'inform, educate and entertain'. An inherent dichotomy is implicitly recognised and endorsed here; 'factual' programming, which is 'serious' in nature, is fundamentally distinguished from and opposed to 'entertainment shows'. At the same time the blurb is also at pains to emphasise *Crimewatch UK*'s massive popularity, where it has achieved audiences of up to 13 million, despite its 'serious' task of making national appeals to the public to help solve crimes and identify criminals. A number of latent oppositions emerge here, then. 'Serious information' shows lie in contrast with 'entertainment shows'; serious programming generally does not have the popularity of entertainment programming (which of course has particular implications for the BBC as a Public Service Broadcaster); and, implicitly, since 'serious information' programmes are 'factual', 'entertainment' shows, it would seem, are fictional.

In fact such distinctions are not always as evident as the writers above – the show's then presenters – seem to suggest; they were not clear in 1987, as the swift and enduring popularity of *Crimewatch UK* made clear, and they certainly are not so today in the contemporary televisual landscape. Since the late 1990s we have witnessed the explosion of 'reality TV' and 'real-crime' programming, dramatically shifting the ways in which we understand television culture, its formats, economics and audiences. We live in a television age which is visibly preoccupied with what it perceives as the increasing, and it is often implied somehow disingenuous, tendency of programming to 'blur the boundaries' between fact and fiction. These fears, however, precede the recent rise of reality TV. *Crimewatch UK* has been at the forefront of debates of this nature for almost two decades. Critics have been particularly eager to condemn *Crimewatch UK*, partly because of the higher standards demanded of the BBC in broadcasting generally, but also because of its subject matter; 'blurring' is all the more disquieting it would seem when it is representations – or more specifically *reconstructions* – of crime which are at stake. Bob Woffinden's concerns, expressed in *The Listener*, seem characteristic of this position: 'Clearly the public has a voracious appetite for true-life crime. And *Crimewatch* has enhanced entertainment value; quite simply it's better because it's real. A kind of blurring of distinctions thus occurs' (1989: 10). In this essay I reflect on just how useful and legitimate the concept of 'blurred boundaries' remains for contemporary screen studies.

Crimewatch UK, then, has been at the centre of numerous concerns and condemnations over the course of its history. With its use of photos, CCTV, interviews and reconstructions of serious unsolved crimes, the show was one of the earliest examples of the now commonplace zeal with which television has taken up the experiences and work of real detectives, victims and criminals, and made them the subject of prime-time. TV crime-appeal programming has stood accused of exploiting true-life crimes and victims in a distasteful and voyeuristic manner to boost audience figures, dressing lurid 'entertainment' of the basest kind in respectable, public service clothes (see Wolley 1984; Fairclough 1995: 174). Throughout the mid- to late 1980s in particular the genre was also lambasted for its role in heightening the public's 'fear of crime' as an impassioned debate about the moral responsibility of television's representation(s) of crime waged in Britain. It is no coincidence that in the same period the increasing deregulation of British television created a climate of nervousness where it was feared the genre 'could be laying the ground for a new breed of American-style shows in which the distinction between fact and fiction becomes increasingly blurred' (Minogue 1990: 23). Such sentiments are still common. More recently, for example, when learning that one of his cases was to be reconstructed on *Crimewatch UK*, the psychologist and criminal profiler Dr Julian Boon (2001) expressed distinct reservations:

> I don't want to denigrate *Crimewatch* or the people who watch it but the principle reason for watching it is not so they can say, 'Oh, right enough, on Tuesday now it comes back to me, I saw that bank robbery and I never thought anything about it. Gosh, someone got killed.' And it's just, no way. They're watching it because it's a series of little, titillating vignettes.

Inherent in many of the concerns expressed about *Crimewatch UK* and crime-appeal programming generally, then, is a sense that part of what makes them 'unethical' is their constructing of these crime 'stories' in ways more familiar from and appropriate to the modes of fiction. This apparent obfuscation evidently continues to perplex. Mark Fishman and Gray Cavender's useful analysis of crime and reality TV, for example, seems to feature an underlying but familiar hint of disapproval when they write, 'Television reality programmes are especially hard to categorise because they blur the line between news and entertainment: some even blur the line between fact and fiction' (1998: 3). Why is it that as cultural critics and academics we remain so reluctant to relinquish these evidently inadequate binaries when changes in television programming increasingly demand we must? This is not to say that these distinctions have absolutely no meaning in themselves at all any more; but that since much contemporary television does not adhere to them in any particularly rigid sense, our definitions and conceptualisations of the relationship between television and realism, between 'factual' and 'entertainment' shows, must also adapt.

In this essay I want to examine how this critical discourse on 'blurring' around *Crimewatch UK* has been constructed and the attitudes and assumptions it suggests about both television audiences and the representation of crime on television. Methodologically, in making this analysis I adopt a number of approaches that demonstrate the ways in which the television text and its audience(s) can be constructed from a range of intertextual 'evidence'. I draw on textual analysis of the programme itself; popular accounts of and responses to the programme in the British press; critical and academic analyses of the relationship between television and realism; the BBC's own audience research; and original interviews I have carried out with the producers of *Crimewatch UK*.[1] This work, then, incorporates a range of institutional, textual and theoretical perspectives that combine to form an analysis of 'realism' in *Crimewatch UK* informed by a variety of positions, indicating the diverse ways in which we can conceptualise the television text.

Focusing particularly on the use of reconstructions in a six-month sample of the programme from January–June 2000, I want to suggest that fears and criticisms of the crime-appeal format's 'blurring of boundaries' across fact/fiction are unfounded. Rather, through various signifiers and devices these stories' 'reconstruction' status – that is, not fact or fiction but not *neither* of them – is made entirely evident and it is well within audiences' grasp to understand this status. Rather than 'blurring boundaries', *Crimewatch UK*'s reconstructions evoke, construct and resituate 'realism' in complex and diverse ways in a kind of third space.[2] The distinction between crime 'fact' and 'fiction' as employing inherently different sets of conventions seems increasingly unstable. This is not to say that given aesthetics do not still carry associations with particular forms; for example the way in which the hand-held camera is enduringly linked with news or documentary actuality (see Hartley 1982). Rather, it is the case that within contemporary television we increasingly recognise that these aesthetics can be adopted and foregrounded to engage those associations across all kinds of programming. This essay does not examine issues of taste or quality or whether the programme's public-service rationale is disingenuous. Instead it focuses on arguing that the particular critical discourses surrounding the show's alleged unethical conflation of factual and fictional forms are unwarranted, since the programme quite explicitly highlights the hybrid nature of the reconstructions. These concerns about the programme arguably belong to the paternalistic, mass-society tradition of fears for/of the television audience and their alleged 'inability' to process contradictory or complex aesthetic forms.

Audiences, ambiguity and critical autonomy

How else, then, have fears about *Crimewatch UK* been manifested? Another recurrent concern about the show, crystallising many of the conflicts and issues at stake here, was the fear that it could be used as a 'textbook' for aspiring criminals in copy-cat crime. Like the 'fear-of-crime' debate this was/is an anxiety that again raises the spectre of the programme's 'effects' on the audience, with it resurrecting the 'hypodermic needle' tradition which conceptualises the audience as a vulnerable mass. One might equally argue though, that copycat crime actually demonstrates the audience as being active and discerning in the ways they 'use' the show (see Brooker & Jermyn 2002: 5–11). Nick Ross and Sue Cook reflected on the possibility of copycat crime in their book, where they concluded that the potential for this (mis)use is a risk that has to be taken:

> Might it tempt honest viewers into crime? Might *Crimewatch* give new ideas to already dishonest people by revealing the techniques of other criminals? … The straight answer was yes … Of course detailed reconstructions, how-ever sensitively done, would always introduce corrupt methods to innocent minds. Yet any reporting of crime (or of open courts and open justice) shoul-ders all those dangers. (1987: 155)

And in July 2000, criminologist Martin Gill's study of 341 robbers and raiders in prison appeared to bear out Ross and Cook's fears:

> Jailed bandits say the crime-fighting television show gave them ideas for raids and showed them how easy it was. They said bank staff on the pro-gramme rarely resist and the quality of security film was so poor suspects were difficult to identify. (Quoted in Burrell 2000: 9)

Crucially though, Gill's findings do not just demonstrate the legitimacy of the 'media effects' debate. They also demonstrate how access to the 'realism' of genu-ine robberies via CCTV footage can actually be appropriated in different ways by audiences. In fact CCTV is appropriated here in a manner counter-productive to *Crimewatch UK*'s intentions, undermining the programme's aims of criminal deter-rence and identification, as it is used instead to confirm the dubious quality of some video footage and the relative ease and anonymity with which some robberies occur. CCTV here is not perceived, by the criminal audience at least, as an imposing deterrent. Rather these respondents reflect on the use of CCTV footage as expos-ing its inadequacies. In addition, the fact that some criminals actually felt *reassured* by the quality of indistinct CCTV footage – to the extent that they claim to have been prompted to commit robberies by it – would seem to indicate that this audi-ence at least is not in any doubt about which elements of *Crimewatch UK* show 'the real thing'.

Nevertheless, in its first decade particularly, *Crimewatch UK* was dogged by intermittent and alarmist reports of viewer confusion. In 1993 the programme was reprimanded following the arrest and trial of a mentally-ill man for murder, after a viewer volunteered his name due to his resemblance to the actor playing the mur-derer in a reconstruction (see Campbell 1993: 26). On another occasion in 1984 a reconstruction included a car shown in half-light. It was explained that police only had scant information about it and viewers who knew more about it were invited to phone in. As a result,

One woman rang to say she thought it's colour was red and white. When the detective answering the phone asked how she knew, she replied she had seen the colours by looking very closely at the screen. Clearly she, *and many others, thought the film showed the real events*, and her job was to spot any clues it contained. (Wooley 1984: 10; emphasis added)

Though one should not underestimate the potential gravity of such misunderstandings, the extent of the concerns expressed on this theme does not seem proportionate to the confusion experienced by what actually appears to have amounted to a very limited number of viewers. Given that *Crimewatch UK*'s viewing figures amount to millions and the reports of such cases have been isolated incidents, where is the evidence of the confusion among 'many others' casually referred to by Benjamin Wooley above? Is it the case that such stories become virtually mythologised since they offer the rest of the audience a gratifying endorsement of their own superior cultural capital, and perhaps a degree of amusement? And should we conclude that viewers are confused about what they are watching when they phone in after a reconstruction with a name based, quite rationally, on a description that both suspect and actor *share*? Perhaps it was inevitable to a degree that following the show's introduction a small minority of viewers would undergo uncertainty as they went through a transitional period of adapting to what was, after all, an unfamiliar format. But in contrast, the BBC's special project audience research in 1988 found that 'there was widespread awareness that the purpose of reconstructions is to jog people's memories' (BBC 1988: 13) and the issue of confusion about whether they 'showed the real events' or not did not emerge at all.

Annette Hill has compared three examples of emergency services-based reality TV in Britain, namely *999*, *Blues and Twos* and *Coppers*. She found that their relationships with, and invoking of, reality all held different nuances but that these were made manifest to the viewer. *999*, which reconstructs and holds interviews with public and personnel involved in serious emergency services incidents, was evidently 'borrowing certain conventions from *Crimewatch UK*' (2000: 222). Hill concludes, just as I am arguing in relation to *Crimewatch UK*, that *999*'s similar mix of studio interviews, filmed footage, logos and voiceovers means that 'When the reconstruction begins we are in no doubt that this is an account of a crisis, not real footage of the crisis itself … *999* is very careful to give the viewer as much information as they need to ensure that they know what is real and what is reconstructed' (2000: 224). To claim in the current climate then, where different forms of reality TV co-exist and are emerging all the time, that contemporary audiences find it difficult to determine a text's relationship to reality would be to suggest that television audiences are in a permanent state of confusion. In fact, to look at it another way, one could argue that this multiplicity of television forms, their modes of address and invoking of 'reality' indicate the growing sophistication of television audiences.

Generally, these fears about audience competence echo a paternalistic tradition which questions whether mass audiences are perceptive enough to 'cope' with ambiguities of any kind in the media, a pessimistic outlook which owes much to the Frankfurt School. For example, the same kinds of fears and a distinction between the educated viewer and vulnerable or 'other' viewer have also run through drama documentary debates, another television form that has similarly been accused of blurring fact and fiction. As writer David Edgar noted,

> Through all the criticisms of drama-documentary runs a single thread of assumption: that while clever educated people are able to recognise and judge a thesis when they see one, ordinary television viewers can somehow be duped into accepting an argument as objective fact. (1982: 28)

Furthermore, the presumptuous but enduring attitude nicely summarised by Edgar here sidesteps a crucial point; that arguably, if anything, regular viewing by the 'ordinary television viewer' is *more* likely to equip them with the particular cultural capital necessary to distinguish between television forms than the intermittent (read: 'discerning') viewer.

Textual tension

These accusations of 'blurring the boundaries' demand that we look not just at how the audience is constructed, but at the texts. The suggestion that reconstructions present themselves unproblematically as 'real life' accounts assumes that reconstructions adhere to a consistent, coherent, realist aesthetic. Definitions of 'realism' are of course both copious and notoriously thorny. But some critics underestimate this when they imply that reconstructions are presented as undemanding, straightforward accounts. Benjamin Wooley, for example, has argued that 'The problem with reconstructions is that *they are presented as being indistinguishable from real events* and this confuses at least a few members of the audience' (1984: 10; emphasis added). Such a description rather simplifies the complex processes of dénouement that occur in many reconstructions. As Norman Fairclough concluded in his analysis of the variety of discourses and generic influences brought to bear in the programme, these films are frequently 'internally complex' (1995: 154). He points to how the programme is characterised by 'generic diversity' with reconstructions 'draw[ing] upon a number of genres *narrative, biography* and *public appeal*' (1994: 155). Furthermore, I want to argue that though a 'realist' aesthetic is typically sought and does indeed predominate, there is a tension present in the reconstructions since they do not all sit easily within this aesthetic and their form can vary significantly both between and within reconstructions. The creative agency with which reconstructions are approached is partly about necessity, filling in the gaps of incomplete and irresolute 'stories'. But it is also about aesthetic autonomy and even experimentation, since as *Crimewatch UK* Series Producer Katie Thomson confirmed, there is no designated 'house style' constricting the numerous directors who work on the show (personal interview, 2002).

Clearly, as narratives appearing on prime-time television for a mass audience with the serious purpose of endeavouring to solve crime, the programme-makers do seek to impose order and sense on these stories. The challenge for the programme is that though there is a desire for authenticity and coherency, these stories are by their very nature riddled with ellipses and irresolution. These gaps are elements which the programme must struggle to contend with and which on occasion are addressed in ways which highlight a tension between the traditions of a classical, contained narrative and the problem of restricted knowledge. The ellipses necessitate the programme having to feed the audience with questions, provisos and guarded speculation and result in a style which cannot unfailingly maintain a conventional realist aesthetic. What we see in many of the reconstructions is a negotiation or slippage between different traditions and conventions, from real forensic evidence to surreal and abstract imagery and digression. It is this movement which underlines the reconstructions' hybridity and the fact that these are not in themselves 'the real event'.

Consider for example the use of a lengthy distorted point-of-view shot in the April 2000 reconstruction of a rape where the victim believes she was drugged in a bar. Though of course this is intended to show her perspective 'realistically' the eerie, chaotic series of images of blinding lights and looming bodies which make up this point-of-view shot as the victim stumbles through London's Leicester Square and into a busy nightclub arguably incorporate a disruptive element of surrealism or anti-realism into the film. It draws attention to the fact that this is by no means an 'objective' news report or 'at-the-scene' account of some kind. In fact, presenter Fiona Bruce's introduction to this story compares it directly to a dream and indicates that what follows will be fragmented and disorderly:

> We all know that feeling after a nightmare, you wake up in the morning and you think, thank goodness for that, that was just a dream. But what if it wasn't? One woman realised the images in her nightmare were real. We've pieced together what happened from her flashbacks.

The structure here then, 'pieced together' from the jigsaw of the victims' disjointed memories, does not lend itself easily to a coherent narrative although it is constructed in a manner which seeks to give it as logical a structure as is possible. So though it opens with an identifiable and everyday scene of a group of friends enjoying a night out on the town ('Nothing out of the ordinary') later there are gaps in cause and effect (the victim says of her suspected drugging 'I've thought and thought and thought how it could have happened or where it was done … It doesn't make any sense at all'); setting (she is unsure where she was raped) as well as irresolution (her attackers remain unidentified).

In some cases it is the choice of graphics that momentarily ruptures any move towards a realist aesthetic, highlights the restricted knowledge and reminds us that these are evidently not 'the real event'. For example, in March 2000 the Stephen Lawrence murder appeal featured a videofit without a face, in effect amounting to a hairstyle on an otherwise blank head; in April 2000 in the Jill Dando murder reconstruction, a large, disembodied, animated question mark floats on to the screen over the image of the mysterious man seen lurking on her road whom police want to find. Another case of profound narrative ambiguity and a conspicuous narrative device is to be found in the account of the suspicious death of a young art student, Jessie Earl, featured in February 2000. Nick Ross introduces her parents in the studio and says 'Tonight we're praying someone watching *Crimewatch* will help end twenty years of agony for them'. A video begins, opening with a close-up photograph of a smiling young woman. We are told that this was the Earls' daughter and as Ross explains that she disappeared in 1980 we see an image of a seagull, flying and reeling through a clear blue sky. This image becomes an abstraction, not in any useful way related to the crime, but rather the means adopted by the programme to cope with representing the ellipsis.

We see footage of the exterior of Jessie's old home and a black-and-white photo of her bedroom the way it was left, as Ross explains that a week before her art college finals in Eastbourne she was meant to visit her parents but never turned up. This is a classic mystery in the vein of the 'Marie Celeste'; when her mother arrived at Jessie's home 'it was as if she'd just popped out for a minute – the window was open, her purse was on the side'. Police 'searched the walks she loved to take and read her diary for clues in hope of an explanation but found only that Jessie seemed bright, happy and well-balanced'. We then cut to an image of the hand-written pages of her diary complete with doodles in the margins, the authentic artefact. Gradually scenes of a remote clifftop are superimposed over these pages as a young woman reads extracts from the diary, Jessie's own vivid description of how she had visited there and been overwhelmed by the scenery:

> I walked up the cliffs and climbed to the top. It was so beautiful. I ran up most of the way and down over the clifftops, my arms spread out like sails. It was like flying.

Not only is this a strikingly personal insight into this woman's imagination and private thoughts, it is an elegiac and poetic digression from the pragmatic business of clues and evidence which for a few moments disrupts the narrative drive towards answers and explanations. Though this is clearly a sequence intended to win audience empathy, it is a moment in the account of a real criminal enquiry that does not sit easily with expectations of a conventional realist aesthetic. Such moments are admittedly intermittent rather than representative of a predominant approach. From this ethereal poeticism we switch mood quite abruptly to cold facts and the business of crime appeal, when we hear that nine years later her decomposed body was found at Beachy Head and see forensic photos of her knotted bra found there. But this jarring shift in tone and style demonstrates a struggle between a classical narrative reaching for cause and effect and the inventiveness called on to fill in the gaps that confound it. Regular audiences will be well aware that very often despite the programme-maker's best efforts, not all reconstructions follow the path of conventional, linear narratives.

By necessity there is always fluidity between fact and (informed) speculation in the reconstructions. But there is no satisfactory or substantial evidence to suggest that audiences do not ascertain this is the case. In fact the BBC's audience research on the programme found that viewers made astute distinctions between the kinds of crime they saw on television: 'they certainly claim that they do not watch [*Crimewatch UK*] as if it were light entertainment or police fiction' (BBC 1988: 2). When given a list of programme titles (including *L.A. Law*, *Inspector Morse*, *Watchdog*, *The Cook Report* and *Horizon*, as well as *Crimewatch UK*) and asked to group them, the researchers found that *Crimewatch UK* was 'never associated with police fiction programmes'. Though *Crimewatch UK* was loosely grouped with programmes such as *The Cook Report* and *Panorama* as 'information' or 'real-life' programmes, the respondents broke this group down further separating *Crimewatch*

UK into a sub-set of its own on the grounds that it was the only programme solely 'about crime' and the only one where 'the public is asked for help' (BBC 1988: 6–7). Though of course, as always, one needs to be conscious here of the kind of agenda which may lay behind this source – the BBC clearly had a vested interest in demonstrating audiences are competent in distinguishing the different kinds of crime seen on television – these results merely point to a level of cultural competence that any relatively regular British television viewer could be expected to obtain.

Beyond these research findings and the individual reconstructions described here, one can point to other consistent motifs in the programme which routinely reinforce our awareness of the fact that we are watching reconstructions. They are unfailingly framed at the beginning and end by photographs or video footage of the actual victim and the early scenes carry a logo on-screen proclaiming '*Crimewatch* reconstruction'. This is a matter of standard good practice at the BBC since the internal 'Producers' Guidelines' stipulate that 'all reconstructions must be clearly signalled' throughout crime programming (BBC n.d.: 151). Performance style is another factor; though clearly one could counter-argue that *Crimewatch UK*'s generally unpolished performances in reconstructions could be deemed 'naturalistic' and thus construed as authentic, arguably the rather self-conscious and mannered style of most acting, and scripting, within the reconstructions marks them as being just that. Rather than performance ability, Series Producer Katie Thomson explained that the programme-makers were far more concerned with getting actors who physically resembled the people they were 'playing' where needed, and with producing scripts that were as close as possible to verbatim transcripts of actual witness statements (personal interview, 2002). Interestingly, then, scripts are another way in which the programme aligns itself with the authentic and protects itself from accusations of sensationalism, but audiences would not necessarily be aware of this loyalty to original 'source' material here. The scripts' efforts to include verbatim material make them feel abrupt, not polished drama but also not news-like; they lie somewhere between fact and fiction and thus again underline the hybrid nature of the reconstructions.

The reconstructions also go to some lengths to offer personal insights into and testimonies about the victims, 'back-story' if you like, using photos, home videos and interviews.[3] These processes of characterisation clearly point to how these films are just as much about appealing to audience pleasure via classic-realist modes of address, dramatic structuring and identification, as they are about appealing for help in solving crime. Thomson was frank about this, since without audiences the programme's raison d'être would of course be redundant: 'We need people to watch to be witnesses. It's a constant concern. You have to make it interesting enough for people to watch' (personal interview, 2002). This style, mixing re-enactment with contemplative personal and familial testimony, the momentum of action with the introspection of characterisation, again underlines both how the reconstructions seek in many ways to incorporate the conventions of classical drama and equally, how audiences would be most unlikely to think they were watching *actual* crime footage unfolding. In Fairclough's words, 'This focus upon character and personality which shapes so much of the re-enactment is central to its character as *fictionalised entertainment*' (1995: 160; emphasis added). Rather than rendering them pure fiction, the reconstructions' bolstering of characterisation suggests again the generic permeability between the construction of real-life and fictional crime.

Finally one should also remember here that the fluidity of form which has made some commentators so nervous about reconstructions might equally be said to be evident elsewhere in *news* coverage. What *Crimewatch UK* ultimately points to perhaps is the operation of a mutual exchange, where representations of crime across the media in both fictional and real-life accounts recycle many of the same sets of generic motifs. Bill Nichols has gone as far as to point out 'the proximity of news to circus' arguing, as numerous other commentators have, that the entertainment function of news is very much evident in the way it 'borrows' from the modes of 'fiction'. For example,

> network news makes heavy use of melodramatic codings in its representations of reality. It recounts events as tales between forces of good and evil, between 'our' family and 'theirs' in foreign news, and as a tale of conflict, rivalry, sacrifice or betrayal among members of our own family in domestic news. (1994: 49–50)

One cannot help but conclude that such 'blurring' is less a cause for media concern when it occurs in news, since the audience for news is constructed as/assumed to be educated and rational and thus able to cope with generic blurring. By contrast, the less distinct, less 'known' and therefore more perturbing audience for crime reconstruction programmes, needs parochial 'protection' from the confusion and even harm that such ambiguity might apparently lead to. These fears become all the more potent and loaded since, if *Crimewatch UK*'s audience is representative of the crime-appeal audience as a whole, it would appear that these programmes have a predominantly female and working-/lower-middle-class audience, something the disapproving critiques of the programme have very often seemed to suspect. Katie Thomson confirmed that *Crimewatch UK*'s own audience research had indicated they have 'quite a low demograph in that it's more C/D than A/B' (personal interview, 2002). Meanwhile in the US, inspired by the format and success of *Crimewatch UK*, Rupert Murdoch's Fox network consciously developed *America's Most Wanted* to target the low-income audience neglected by the three major networks, apparently with some success (Fishman 1998: 66). To what extent then might fears of the crime-appeal programme's generic 'blurring' really amount to fears of its audience?

Reimagining 'reality'

My analysis underlines how real-crime and crime fiction in the media might be more fully understood as drawing on a reciprocal, dynamic and fluid set of aesthetics, a movement encapsulated in the hybridity of the crime-appeal format. It is the notion of 'blurring' that seems to be the term most pointedly at stake throughout the debates that *Crimewatch UK* has figured in. Be it the blurring of fact and fiction, the blurring of entertainment with information, the blurring of police/public/journalistic roles or the blurring of public service television's 'responsibilities' with commercial interests, the interest in the 'collapse' of such distinctions is testimony both to the power they hold in our imaginations and to the fears they suggest about the future and quality of British television. I would argue that Television Studies, and analysis of crime appeals, real-crime programming and reality TV in particular, now needs to move beyond this preoccupation with 'blurring the boundaries' and ask how much currency this conceptualisation continues to hold. *Crimewatch UK*, like so much contemporary television, does not so much 'blur the boundaries' of fact and fiction as invite us to negotiate the commonalities and spaces between them.

Notes

1   On 22 January 2002 I interviewed Katie Thomson, Series Producer of *Crimewatch UK* and on 19 February 2002 I interviewed Belinda Phillips, Assistant Producer of *Crimewatch UK*, both at BBC TV offices, Wood Lane, London.
2   The programme's use of CCTV and video is also intriguing in this respect. See Jermyn 2003b.
3   For a detailed discussion of photography in *Crimewatch UK*, and particularly the use of 'family albums', see Jermyn 2003a.

Bibliography

BBC (1998) Broadcasting Research Department, Special Projects Report, *Crimewatch UK*, October.
____ (n.d.) *Producers' Guidelines: The BBC's Values and Standards* (fourth edition).
Boon, J. (2001) *The Real Cracker*, video-recording, tx Channel 4, 11 March.
Brooker, W. and D. Jermyn (2002) 'Paradigm shifts: From "effects" to "uses and gratifications"', *The Audience Studies Reader*. London: Routledge, 5–11.
Burrell, I. (2000) '*Crimewatch*? It's enough to make you go out and rob a bank', *The Independent*, 1 July, 9.
Campbell, D. (1993) 'Murder suspect goes free at the 11th hour', *The Guardian*, 12 November, 26.
Edgar, D. (1982) 'On Drama Documentary', in F. Pike (ed.) *Ah! Mischief: The Writer and Television*. London: Faber and Faber.
Fairclough, N. (1995) *Media Discourse*. London: Arnold
Fishman, M. (1998) 'Ratings and Reality: The Persistence of the Reality Crime Genre', in M. Fishman and G. Cavender (eds) *Entertaining Crime: Television Reality Programs*. New York: Aldine De Gruyter, 59–75.
Fishman, M. and G. Cavender (eds) (1998) *Entertaining Crime: Television Reality Programs*. New York: Aldine De Gruyter.
Hartley, J. (1982) *Understanding News*. London: Routledge
Hill, A. (2000) 'Crime and Crisis: British Reality TV in Action', *British Television: A Reader*. Ed Buscombe (ed.) Oxford: Oxford University Press, 218–34.
Jermyn, D. (2003a) 'Photo Stories and Family Albums: Imaging Criminals and Victims on *Crimewatch UK*', in P. Mason (ed.) *Criminal Visions: Media Representations of Crime and Justice*. Cullumpton: Willan Publishing, 175–91.
____ (2003b) '"This *is* about real people!" Video technologies, actuality and affect in the television crime appeal', in Su Holmes and Deborah Jermyn (eds) *Understanding Reality TV*. London: Routledge, 71–90.

Minogue, T. (1990) 'Putting real crime on prime-time', *Guardian*, 3 September, 23.

Nichols, Bill (1994) *Blurred Boundaries: Questions of Meaning in Contemporary Culture*. Bloomington: Indiana University Press.

Ross, N. and S. Cook (1987) *Crimewatch UK*. London: Hodder and Stoughton.

Woffinden, B. (1989) 'Crime Time Viewing', *The Listener*, 122, 3139, 9 November, 10–11.

Wooley, B. (1984) 'An arresting programme', *The Listener*, 112, 2072, 23 August, 11.

CHAPTER FIFTEEN

Fantasy Disguise: Where New Communications Meet Old Entertainments

David Lusted

I know a person who spends hours of his day as a fantasy character who resembles 'a cross between Thorin Oakenshield and the Little Prince', and is an architect and educator and bit of a magician aboard an imaginary space colony. By day, David is an energy economist in Boulder, Colorado, father of three; at night, he's Spark of Cyberion City – a place where I'm known only as Pollenator.

> – Howard Rheingold (1994: 147)

People need to know that there are some very scary people out there in chat rooms.

> – Michelle Elliott, director of Kidscape (quoted in Carter 2003: 3)

If the 'very scary people' building fantasy worlds during the early days of the Internet were ever once objects of amusement among academic observers, they are now public objects of fear and suspicion. The two quotations above are from sources about ten years apart, yet they suggest significant changes in attitude to the possibilities for identity swapping afforded by new communications technologies. Where Howard Rheingold's colourful account represents the early days of Internet use for what could be termed fantasy disguise, the more recent report by Helen Carter represents widespread contemporary fears of criminal and paedophile exploitation of chat rooms. There is, however, some continuity in the historical shift; a binary and temporal continuity in which initial derision is located mainly within the academic community before fear and suspicion breaks out in the public sphere.

The process through which an awareness of the potential uses of any new technological medium gradually emerges from elite circles to enter the public sphere is a general and historical one. Media-driven moral panics over the cultural use of new media technologies have a history as long as the mass media itself and, before those, earlier forms of popular entertainment. Contemporary fears about the potential for criminal abuse of the Internet have many antecedents. Just to take one example, moral panics over the effects of cinema films on child psychology and anti-social behaviour in 1930s Britain also coded less explicit fears of child molestation in the darkened environments of cinemas (Breakwell & Hammond 1990: 32), especially during matinees (Staples 1997: 29–41). Comic or sinister, the possibilities afforded by new media forms for users to escape into fantasy identities – and new material possibilities – have been the subject of a long-standing history of suspicion. What sustains the process is another continuity, the history of elite fears of the working class as 'mass' (Lusted 1985: 11–18).

Connections between this collection of uses of and attitudes to the new communications systems and earlier entertainment forms become clear when they are thought through historically, when the contemporary is locked into a series of comparable moments in British cultural history. In so doing, it may help to see how we have been here before, often, and even often in our own lifetimes. What is at stake is a cultural struggle over the conceptualisation of the entry into the imaginary, a process whereby consumers of popular cultures (whether conceptualised as readers, audiences or spectators) construct a virtual space within the physical space of relationship with a new cultural medium in order to transform the imagination of the self. The wider historical context is inevitably the power of elite groups to determine the agenda of understanding of new popular forms.

This essay is about some points of continuity between contemporary communications and formative moments in the history of the entertainment media, specifically within the current British television institution, the history of the fairground and the classical period of the melodrama stage as exemplary moments of a longer cultural tradition of popular imagining. It draws on textual studies of a prime-time British television series and scenes from two Hollywood films in order to explore instances of how these entertainment media have historically thought fantasy identity, less with derision or fear and rather more as romance.

The critical context

Amongst contemporary critical opinion, there are two extreme reactions to the new cultural phenomenon of media communications-assisted fantasy disguise. One is a postmodern despair over the 'train spotting' practices associated with the Internet and the tragic social isolates whose virtual reality displaces a real one. This is a realm where seeming 'inadequates' mainline in a hyperspace of the unreal, escaping daily routines far from the mundane social marginality of an otherwise depressed Dave or a frustrated Howard to assume a control missing from the social world among the fantasy identities of a Spark or Pollenator. This is the view of academics like Kevin Robins (1996) and, in the most apocalyptic vision, of dystopian postmodernists like Jean Baudrillard. It is a view shared also by more popular sceptics like humourist Douglas Adams (of *Hitchhiker's Guide to the Galaxy* fame) and broadcaster Janet Street-Porter, who famously raged against computer nerds and 'anoraks in cyberspace' (see Jeffries 1996).

At the other extreme of critical reaction, there is the view that this kind of fantasising is part of the democratising possibilities of the new media. The key word here is not 'escape' but 'interaction', indicating a fundamental shift in the historic media system of point-to-point, one-way communication from a powerful centre to recipient peripheries. Typified by historical patterns of broadcasting, this is a system undermined once and forever by the new technological ability to respond generally and instantly to any communication from anywhere and thereby changing if not the world, then certainly everyday experience of it. As the telephone model of interaction replaces the broadcast model of transmission, there is the promise of a revolutionary new consciousness for the new millennium and beyond – provided, of course, you can afford the technology or have ready access to it. Such a view as this is promoted most obviously by the inventors and commercial providers of the new communications technologies popularised by Bill Gates and Microsoft. It is made academically respectable by writers like Barrie Sherman and Phil Judkin (1992).

In contrast to these elite agendas, it is valuable to invoke Raymond Williams' key insight (1974: 9–31) that cultures are as responsible for the production of new technologies as inventors and investors, that it is a more general aspiration for changes in social exchange and leisure pursuit that impels the production of new technologies better able to provide them. The spectacle that results – such as the facility to destroy the military might of an alien empire on a video game, to find out about cosmetic surgery on the latest wannabe celebrity's website, or to invent an imaginary identity for either innocent or criminal purpose – is subject to negotiation between the technical potential and commercialisation of the new technologies on the one hand and the desires of their users on the other. Williams' notion of cultural technologies draws attention to the forms new technologies take and how these can then be seen in a continuum of change rather than as a series of radical breaks. This alternative stress on the cultures rather than the technologies allows for an understanding that their interaction with new entertainment media is a common, regular and historical one. The Internet may well be revolutionary but only insofar as its antecedents once were in broadcasting, cinema, the melodrama stage, the fairground and even the box-camera and magic lantern in their own moments of full cultural engagement.

Indeed, although technology is often associated with cultural change, it is really the cultural change itself that is most revealing about historical shifts in any media economy. Take the most dramatic landmarks in British broadcasting as example: the moment of the formation of the BBC in the 1920s, then of ITV and the commercial challenge to public service broadcasting in the 1950s, then of Channel 4 and broadcast publishing in the 1980s and, most recently, of the deregulation that enabled the proliferation of satellite and cable channels. The significance of these moments lies in their association with new cultural forms that led to changes in perception of personal and social imagining; that made it possible to rethink personal identity, enabled people to understand themselves anew. Today, developments in communication and information define the commercial value of the Internet. But, as with instances in broadcast history, the social meaning of these developments lies in the range of practices, actual and potential, associated with it, not least with the 'new' time it promises to release. These are all cultural matters and their determinants are to be found beyond the technology that produced the ideas and practices associated with the technology in the first place.

In *Visible Fictions* (1985), John Ellis examines the contention that cultural change results from technological invention. He calls the idea 'technological determinism' and sees its cultural currency as too simple an explanation for the changes that lie in a more complex set of political, economic and social causes. As an example, Anthony Smith's major work on the origins of broadcasting, *The Shadow in the Cave* (1975), examines how and why the state organised broadcasting in the way it did at the time it did. After all, broadcast technology preceded the formation of the BBC by some twenty years. Smith's answer lies in the state's complex negotiation of cultural fears of social agitation, arising political desires to maintain social control, and emerging discourses about psychology and citizenship. The consequence was the state rendering the new technology in the shape of a public service institution like the BBC rather than in any commercial model such as that favoured and adopted in the USA.

Cultural theory

The historical drive to promote new technological media for economic and commercial reasons, then, has also been bound up in debates over controls of its cultural associations. Moral panics emerge in the public sphere where modes of control through political regulation are found by governing elites to be insufficient. More recent cultural theory has sought to shift attention from the dynamics of governance to the politics of consumption; from producers to consumers, from an audience thought of as a monolithic, passive 'mass' to a more heterogeneous aggregation of differences negotiating meaning not out of a liberal 'consumer choice' but from a complex of negotiated positions and identities. It makes another sense of fantasy imagining on the Internet when the work is invoked of critics like Henry Jenkins (1992) who has theorised the phenomenon of fandom. From his interviews with Trekkies, the hard-core fans of the *Star Trek* series, Jenkins argues that what appears as a comical and singular obsession to observers provides both social extension (bonding with the fan community) and personal extension (through entering into imaginary worlds of shared narratives, characters and meanings) for its participants, imagining new identities through a range of fantasy disguises. There is a broader principle here, that cultural forms invite identity extension through fantasy disguise.

Cultural fantasy

The issue, then, is not technology, old or new, but culture; it is not what the technology does but what people do with the technology. What, then, of prevailing attitudes to the cultures associated with these new communications technologies? The history of elite and media reaction to cultural technologies in Britain is a history of disregard and objection reaching way back to at least the Industrial Revolution. In particular, it is a history associated with social distance from cultures of modernity and their new forms of consumerism and entertainment. In opposing this dominant mode of understanding, what is always required is the forging of syntactic connections between the cultural forms any new technologies take and earlier moments of comparable technology-driven cultural change.

In this context, what is particularly odd (and worthy of more serious academic study) about the phenomenon of fantasising on the Internet is the communication form it takes. Communication is centrally a social, oral exchange. Failing the means for that, print exchange has proved a more than adequate replacement, with its own dynamics and possibilities for personalisation and the private sphere. Yet so much of modern communication insists on visualising that exchange, creating (by typing or texting) words and perhaps even images emphatically within the frame of even the tiniest screens. Is this merely adapting the found properties of the technology, or does it express a desire – personal, cultural – to visualise through language? And how does this process relate to the phenomenon of assuming fantasy identities, of masquerade and disguise?

The connected desire to visualise and fictionalise seems everywhere in contemporary media cultures. As an example, the case of the natural history documentary is revealing. This documentary form has been central to broadcasting and a significant part of earlier media histories like film and photography. In the current age of celebrity television, reality shows and make-over programmes, it remains the one documentary form maintaining a prominent profile in prime-time programming. The forebears of the globetrotting David Attenborough and the BBC's Natural History Unit based in Bristol are in the 1950s undersea world of Hans and Lotte Haas, and the Africa of Armand and Michaela Dennis. They, in turn, drew on a history of colonial photography and colour magazines like *National Geographic*. All these natural historians would likely be in awe of the access to and construction of the natural world now made available by new camera technology and computerised digital image-making.

The BBC's *Alien World* series demonstrates some of these visualisation and fictionalising processes, as well as some of their important ramifications. One of the extraordinary sights of this series is the use of micro-cameras attached to birds to create the experience of flight from the point of view of their aerial state. Elsewhere, scenes such as rabbits scurrying into burrows to escape predators or insects exploring the concealed pollen in flowers equally draw on this first-person experience to explore quite novel perceptions of the natural world. Such new practices offer an original visualisation but also the equivalent of an 'out of body experience' from the point of view of an impossible Other. Like Internet exchange, the experience is made physical through a virtual made visual.

Furthermore, in the first moment of *Alien World*, there is another example of a general process of fantasy visualisation. In a pre-credit sequence, infra-red lighting and new camera technology construct a night-time human world at risk from a giant preying mantis. Two-track imaging combines scenic backgrounds to quite separate foreground details realised by digital slow-motion and micro-camera processes. These processes explore a world otherwise invisible to the eye in previously unrecognised detail. But this world is, more obviously, nonetheless dramatised, a world as much of the imagination as of natural history. In other words, it is a kind of fiction, a fiction in visual disguise.

However, the fictional forms through which this new media world is experienced are otherwise quite traditional. Planet Earth, satellite, city landscape – images underpinned by a music track that together evoke the authority of news and the futurism of science fiction. This is the context for the home that we see in the pre-credit sequence as the site for 'a battle fought for hundreds of millions of years'. The home is suburban, ordinary, typical. But there is a joke here; it is notionally on

Elm Street, the film fictional site of the worst nightmare. The joke takes aesthetic form; some would say postmodern play or parody, but for me a convention-bound tongue-in-cheek rendering of everyday insect survival as a modern horror film. Insects do not really threaten the human world as this scene suggests but there is human pleasure and insight from imagining that they could.

In a final example from *Alien World*, the predominant mode is again melodrama (that is, dramatising everyday conflict through music-stimulated emotional modes of action and image). A voiceover that accompanies images of insect predators successfully attacking and consuming their prey talks of a 'deadly air-raid, performed like an aerial ballet', poetically calling up a combination of images of war and dance to produce a hallucinatory, mesmerising experience. Nothing in everyday life makes us as close to such matters – physically and affectively – as the formal strategies of *Alien World*. Such new technological processes do indeed produce new realisms. But the cultural forms they rely upon are appropriations of long-standing, familiar and therefore conventional modes of imagining, even when parodied or, others may say, clichéd. By these means, modernising media constructs like *Alien World* represent a development of – rather than a break with – earlier cultural forms; they offer continuities in new formations.

Fantasy experiences like these, expressed through contemporary advances in surveillance camera and digital technology, are everywhere evident in contemporary film and television genres. But the consequent identity-shifting in new entertainment media is not an entirely new phenomenon.

Mechanical pleasures

In the mid- to late nineteenth century, another moment linking technological and cultural change suggests an earlier form of connection between new entertainment and the process of fantasy disguise. The new entertainment form is the fairground. A scene from a postwar Hollywood film exemplifies certain of its ramifications. In *Letter from an Unknown Woman* (Max Ophüls, 1948), the heroine is an ordinary youth romanced by an older man who is unaware of her long admiration for him from afar since childhood. He is a celebrity but unworthy of her and his dissolute life ultimately comes to destroy her. The film is set in Hollywood's version of a middle-European city, and the scene is set on a cold winter's evening at a fairground. The hero, a man of some means, pays for our heroine to dance to the music of a band whose members would long ago have left for home were it not for our hero's purchasing power. He buys toffee apples, not just a new sweet delicacy of its time but also a symbol of a new consumerism, a foodstuff only fancifully related to its natural origins. Finally, they sit opposite each other, in front of a train carriage window, romance inspired by spectacular scenes of European tourist spots implausibly passing by. Implausible, because impossible. For this is a fairground train, a defunct carriage in front of cyclorama scenes that pass by thanks only to the pedal power of a labouring owner on his fixed bicycle. The romantic pair are taken on a virtual journey, experiencing the sites and sights of European romance without moving an inch. And when they have exhausted all the countries available on the cyclorama, they pay yet again for more, to revisit 'the scenes of our youth'.

Letter from an Unknown Woman was directed by a Frenchman, Max Ophüls, working in what was to him an alien empire, America. Everything about the film attests to that sense of alienation. It is concerned to reveal both the construction and lure of artifice, overtly faking its time, place and character (from the synthetic snow of the studio-bound scene to the false intentions of our unworthy hero), in order to make a point about romance: that romance is insubstantial, transitory, untrustworthy, illusory, a manipulative masculine device to get women into bed. Yet romance is also pleasurable, compulsive and supremely desired. The scene is a detailed exploration of the centrality of romance as a powerful mode of imagining the most intimate of personal relations, and it achieves its haunting effect on an audience through an awareness of these sophisticated levels of fantasy disguise.

Crucially, and more generally, the scene explores quite modern ideas about the romance of life inspired by new entertainment technologies. The mechanical fairground was a nineteenth-century urban development from traditional country fairs. It applied new mechanical technologies to devise extraordinarily new cultural experiences in time and space. For instance, a trip on the big wheel (momentarily seen in the fairground scene) physically shocks the body in ways that are nonetheless contained and controlled, and hence pleasurable. To feel the power to control risk contrasts aggressively with the everyday feelings of powerlessness over the forces that command ordinary working lives. The waxwork museum (embodiment of the celebrity culture of the day), seen just as briefly, replaced the freak circus as the mark of civilised entertainment about the experience of difference – and the voyeuristic shift from the disabled to the famous has to be cultural progress of some kind. The film scene is rich with such connotations, and as suggestive of the meaning of the pleasures offered by the contemporary equivalents to the fairground: the theme parks of the likes of Disneyland and Thorpe Park.

The key arena in the scene, though, is the cyclorama train. The cyclorama was one of several related technologies (others included the panorama and diorama) that composed many exhibitions in Victorian England. These briefly took their 'travellers' out of their own world and into a world of other places and peoples. They recreated cheaply, widely and accessibly the experience of sailing on ships and flying in balloons to see places barely heard of and never possible to visit in person. The modern city that gradually soaked up migrant populations from the rural areas of Victorian England shaped new communities taken out of themselves and into new social relationships with the popular entertainment of the period.

The nineteenth-century fairground made a remote world seem smaller, less unknown and fearful. It was part of the process of Empire-building of course, bringing home sights beyond Europe as items of possession and curiosity, but it was also part of another process that expanded the common interaction of otherwise hostile peoples. Modern European refugee migration begins in this period, with Jews, Irish, Poles, Greeks and Italians in particular, in a pattern of diasporas later to be made just as familiar by the later twentieth-century movement of Asian and Afro-Caribbean peoples. If the idea of cultural integration is taken for granted now, something of its origins can be seen in the period in which the film is set and popularised through such entertainment as the fairground. Whatever social and political changes industrialisation wrought on the ordinary people of Europe and America – in relations both of constraint and liberation – popular cultural forms of the period were at the heart of making personal a changing social experience.

One final point arising from the film scene: what it also does is to expose something of the labour that must always go into the operation of technologies and also into the production of romance. The labourer whose feats of cycling and whistling go into the creation of travels to romantic places on the mock-up of the then modern communication system of the railway operates in a different relation to the fantasy of escape than those who consume it. For sure, it is all part of the film's romance that this labour is fondly revealed, but nonetheless it suggests that access to the means of fantasy production depends on social class position, every bit as much as it does in the more contemporary story of Spark, The Pollenator and the Internet.

The general point, however, is that the new entertainment technologies of the newly industrialised late nineteenth century provided new lived experiences, recognised and romanticised in scenes like this from a twentieth-century Hollywood film. That they were largely limited to those – like our profligate hero – with sufficient disposable incomes who were also freed of the routines of industrial labour to enter into consumer relations of the times in the first place differs little from issues of access to the new technologies today.

Spectacular pleasures

A final example, from a time when new entertainment technologies were socially more inclusive and incorporative, is suggested by an exceptional scene from a further Hollywood film, *Heller in Pink Tights* (George Cukor, 1960). It concerns a travelling troupe of theatre melodrama players, 'loosely based on the career of Adah Isaac Menken who brought culture and the footlights to the (American Western) frontier in the 1860s' (Hardy 1991: 276). In the scene, we are about to witness with a rowdy on-screen theatre audience of Westerners the climax to a performance of 'Mazzepa', a classical story about a prince whose banishment into the wilderness takes on positively religious overtones. What starts out as, even then, a rather creaky rendition of an outworn cultural form of popular melodrama theatre is suddenly made dramatic through the spectacle of Mazzepa's staged escape, an illusion constructed whilst also exposing the new stage mechanics of the day that produce it. The leading woman of the troupe plays Mazzepa. Roughly manhandled into the wings in chains, she returns in body stocking, the implied male nakedness strikingly reformed by the voluptuous female form of film star Sophia Loren. S/he is tied to the back of a horse that dangerously strides round the auditorium and then off backstage. The on-screen audience is now roused from its indifference to a howl of climactic approval as the horse, suddenly revealed again on the stage, appears to gallop full pelt against a cyclorama prairie behind a black frame. The effect is produced by a concealed travellator beneath the horse's hoofs, staging an illusion of movement that yet moves nowhere.

The spectacle that develops here is typical of turn-of-the-century theatre (see Grimsted 1971). On the Drury Lane stage in the same period as the film is set, audiences could see teams of horses in the chariot race from *Ben Hur* (although incidentally it took sixty stage-hands and horse-handlers to set the scene and dismantle it behind closed curtains in two twenty-minute intermissions!). On another occasion, the Valkyries rode across concealed scaffolding at the Opera House in a coup-de-théâtre (see Booth 1981), nowadays only matched on stages in musicals, like a descending helicopter in *Miss Saigon* and an elevating house interior in *Sunset Boulevard*.

That the theatrical experience looks forward to the coming of cinema is evident in the screen-like framing of Mazeppa's ride that concludes the entertainment (see Vardac 1987). Theatre mechanics could only go so far in creating a spectacular experience of space and time. The late melodrama stage predicted new combinations of realism and melodrama that cinema could create much more economically and reliably with its camera movement and shot editing (see Fell 1987). The scene from *Heller in Pink Tights* brilliantly encapsulates that formative moment of cultural change.

Furthermore, it demonstrates a new form of interactive relation to the performance on the stage/screen. The horse bearing Mazeppa breaks the frame of the proscenium arch to join the audience, in a mode of interaction common to popular forms like music hall, cabaret and pantomime, though today most commonly met only in stand-up comedy. The structures of looking that developed in the Hollywood film during its classic period also invited audience participation through the system of narrative point-of-view. Interactive technology may now appear new, postmodern even, but the cultural conditions for it are older, at least a hundred years old if you bow to the recent centenary celebrations of cinema. When we see shots of the audience in *Heller in Pink Tights*, a newly enfranchised working class with purchasing power, we may be reminded of the legacy of fantasy production in socially interactive cultural forms.

Conclusion

Much is made of the possibilities of, and anxieties over, new media communications technology. In Film Studies, the central metaphor of the screen as an ideological rather than a transparent window on the world has influenced a generation of scholars. In Cultural Studies, Rachel Bowlby's founding book on consumer cultures, *Just Looking* (1985), gave rise to reciprocations such as Anne Friedberg's *Window Shopping* (1993). Where Bowlby argues that the screen is the twentieth-century metaphor for the politically conservative nature of consumerism, Friedberg sees nineteenth-century visual experiences anticipating those of contemporary media like cinema and video, and cultural practices associated with shopping malls and virtual reality technologies. New confirmations of the liberating possibilities of modern entertainment media like these exceed the obsessive hedonism argued by some of the less miserabilist critics of postmodernity.

The condition of staring into the space of that screen, window or proscenium arch, for information or amusement, can be understood as troubling in many ways. But it would be wrong to concern ourselves only with the consumerist potential and criminal abuse of the act. The visual frame has also long been associated with fantasies of power among socially marginalised peoples. In the face of myriad uses of new technologies, I would only want to hold out for possibilities – not unproblematic and not merely nostalgic – and the cultural opportunities they may afford to a marginal social experience realised in the essential need to desire and imagine, through fantasy, always something better.

Bibliography

Breakwell, I. and P. Hammond (eds) (1990) *Seeing in the Dark: A Compendium of Cinemagoing*. London: Serpent's Tail.

Booth, M. R. (1981) *Victorian Spectacular Theatre 1850–1910*. London: Routledge and Kegan Paul.

Bowlby, R. (1985) *Just Looking: Consumer Desire in Dreiser, Gissing and Zola*. London: MacMillan.

Carter, H. (2003) 'Switching off … chatrooms proving too hot for children to handle', *Guardian*, 24 September: 3.

Ellis, J. (1985) *Visible Fictions*. London: Routledge and Kegan Paul.

Jeffries, S. (1996) 'Street of Shame', *Guardian*, 20 March, 19.

Fell, J. L. (1974) *Film and the Narrative Tradition*. Oklahoma: University of Ohio Press.

Friedberg, A. (1993) *Window Shopping: Cinema and the Postmodern*. Berkeley: University of California Press.

Grimsted, D. (1971) 'Melodrama as Echo of the Historically Voiceless', in T. K. Hareven (ed.) *Anonymous Americans*. Englewood Cliffs: Prentice Hall, 80–98.

Hardy, P. (ed.) (1991) *The Aurum Film Encyclopaedia: The Western*. London: Aurum Press.

Jenkins, H. (1992) *Textual Poachers: Television Fans and Participatory Culture*. London and New York: Columbia University Press.

Lusted, D. (1985) 'A History of Suspicion: Educational Attitudes to Television', in D. Lusted and P. Drummond (eds) *TV and Schooling*. London: British Film Institute, 11–18.

Rheingold, H. (1994) *The Virtual Community: Finding Connections in a Computerised World*. London: Secker and Warburg.

Robins, K. (1996) 'Cyberspace and the World We Live In', in J. Dovey (ed.) *Fractal Dreams: New Media in Social Context*. London: Lawrence and Wishart, 1–30.

Sherman, B. and P. Judkin (1992) *Glimpses of Heaven, Visions of Hell: Virtual Reality and its Implications*. London: Hodder & Stoughton.

Smith, A. (1975) *The Shadow in the Cave*. London: Quartet.

Staples, T. (1997) *All Pals Together: The Story of Children's Cinema*. Edinburgh: Edinburgh University Press.

Williams, R. (1974) *Television, Technology and Cultural Form*. London: Collins.

Vardac, A. N. (1987) *Stage to Screen: Theatrical Origins of Early Film*. New York: Da Capo Press.

CHAPTER SIXTEEN

Buckle Your Seat-belt Dorothy … 'Cause Cinema is Going Bye-byes

William Merrin

In the Wachowskis' film *The Matrix* (1999), Keanu Reeves' 'Neo' is introduced to Lawrence Fishburne's 'Morpheus' who offers him the chance to learn the secrets of the 'Matrix'. As he offers Neo the tracer pill, Morpheus' colleague, Cypher, quips, 'Buckle your seat-belt Dorothy, 'cause Kansas is going bye-byes'. Jacked out of the entire enveloping, life-long virtual reality system of his prior existence into the annihilated reality of the future, Neo's everyday life goes bye-byes, much as Dorothy's did in *The Wizard of Oz* (Victor Fleming, 1939), except here this is no dream from which to later wake, but a one-way trip *into* reality. The film itself, however, offers more than a fantastic, theme-park ride of special effects tracing this journey, visualising, in its depiction of a perfected visual reality system, a possible path of development of electronic media and considering its implications for experiential reality itself. As such the film's most important contribution may be, not to cinema, but to the medium that may replace it, in providing a canonical vision of an environmental electronic form that, whatever its impact upon reality may be, has the potential to radically transform the cinematic medium and experience.

It is this possibility that I want to explore, using *The Matrix* as a case study enabling us to consider the question, not of the future of Film Studies, but of film itself. My method is the inter-disciplinary application of contemporary media theory, media history and philosophy to help understand the nature and implications of virtual reality, its relationship to cinema, and their intertwining historical context. I want to use these disciplines to argue that virtual reality has a longer history preceding cinema, and that its development represents a rediscovery of pre-cinematic modes of experience and entertainment. I want to begin, therefore, with the question of virtual reality and its depiction in *The Matrix*.

Virtual reality has found its definitive expression in its literary and cinematic representations, especially in Vernor Vinge's *True Names* (2001), William Gibson's *Neuromancer* (995) and later 'cyberpunk' novels, and in films such as *Tron* (Steven Lisberger, 1982), *The Lawnmower Man* (Brett Leonard, 1992), *eXistenZ* (David Cronenberg, 1999) and, of course, *The Matrix*, leaving us, ironically, with a situation in which *actual* virtual reality lags behind *virtual* virtual reality. This state is complicated further by the impossibility of determining how far virtual reality *has* advanced, given the inaccessibility of military, space programme and scientific and corporate research, by the changing complex of technologies that constitute its possible form, by the lack of agreement as to its eventual form, functions and use, and the lack of infrastructures for its exploitation or application. Even if one thing is agreed upon – that virtual reality stands for 'an *experience* – the experience of being in a virtual world or a remote location' (Rheingold 1991: 46) – this could range from everyday electronic mediation, to more advanced, remote-sensor tele-presence, to the experience and exploration of a complete, simulated environment. All of these, in turn, have a potentially long history in their electronic form, being realisable in different ways by different technologies, and may aim at differing levels of virtuality, further complicating discussions of virtual reality.

Thanks to its fictional success in the popular imagination, however, virtual reality has attained that coherence and finality it lacks in actuality, with literature and cinema retrospectively defining its completed form from its anticipated future. Interestingly, its virtual representation has followed its real advances in simulating the human sensorium, leaving behind the crude, block graphics and garish, neon, videogame aesthetics of *Tron*, *The Lawnmower Man* and *Neuromancer*, to see the most radical potential of virtual reality, as *The Matrix* makes clear, as the recreation of the banal corporeality of everyday life. Unreality gives way, therefore, to reality, or rather to a hyperrealisation of the real in which the most exciting – and disturbing – use of virtual reality is to produce the vertiginous experience of simulacral exactitude; of a hyper-fidelity that opens out into *the uncanny*, a moment in which, as Heidegger says, 'everyday familiarity collapses' (1962: 233). It collapses here, however, in the perfected resemblance of everyday familiarity; in that 'hyperrealism' whose effect Jean Baudrillard describes as 'the hallucination of the real … down to disquietingly strange details' (1994: 124). A cognisant virtual reality, therefore, gives us a simultaneous grounding, in the hyperrealism of the everyday, and an ungrounding in the realisation of its resemblant production.

This is precisely Neo's dual experience as he grasps a chair in the virtual reality training program, ostensibly to ask if it is 'real', but metaphorically as a support for a world pulled from underneath him. As Morpheus replies to his query:

> What is real? How do you define real? If you are talking about what you can feel; what you can smell; what you can taste and see, then 'real' is simply electrical signals interpreted by your brain.

If our sensory experience is only an electrical signal which we interpret then if this signal could be perfectly reproduced then it would not be a *false* signal, but precisely a *real* signal indistinguishable from that produced by the object. If, as *The Matrix* postulates, the standard, clumsy, prosthetic, exo-technologies of visual reality – the head-mounted display, data-suits and gloves – could be bypassed to feed the signal directly into our central nervous system to perfectly simulate every sensory input, then, from within, it is no longer virtual reality but *the* reality. The simulacrum, as is its wont, becomes the real: the virtual chair Neo holds is identical to the actual chair. Hence, in the 1996 script, Neo's response to Morpheus' question about virtual reality, as he describes it as a hardware system using prosthetic devices 'to make you feel that you are in a computer program'. If, Morpheus asks, this apparatus 'was wired to all of your senses and controlled them completely, would you be able to tell the difference between the virtual world and the real world?' 'You might not, no', Neo replies. 'No, you wouldn't', Morpheus corrects (Andy & Larry Wachowski 1996). Trapped within it and lacking the consciousness of its existence that would provide the ungrounding vertigo of resemblance, all that is left is grounded reality.

These issues are not new, recurring throughout Western epistemological debates, but they appeared with a new urgency in the seventeenth and eighteenth centuries in particular, reflecting new doubts concerning the limits of human knowledge and of the certainty and stability of our mental representations and physical sensations; doubts themselves expressing a fear of deception and of the misattribution of reality to the apparent. Hence, René Descartes' *cogito*, unable to trust images of the world potentially sent by a *mal genie* – that 'evil demon' assailing it with forms whose representation and even external reference is uncertain – finds a guarantee only in God that the mind's images do indeed have an exact physical counterpart and reality. At the end of his meditations he contents himself with the assurance of this realm's fidelity to the real but *res extensa* remains ever denied *res cogitans* and so he remains trapped in an imagic virtuality that, for all its divine guarantees, remains experientially identical to that diabolic virtuality that all others happily and ignorantly assent to. David Hume, in contrast, saw no such guarantee for experience, marooning us in a virtual world of sensory images whose external reference and physical reality, resemblance to our impressions, and continuity and subjection to determinant laws are all unknowable, being assumed by the operations of the mind and memory from familiar and repeated 'impressions'. But again this virtual reality is sufficient for, as he himself admits, all sceptical 'chimeras' are easily banished simply by relaxing and dining with friends; from immersing ourselves and sinking back into the seductive reality of familiar, comfortable sensations: the imagic realm defeats all scepticism, not with reason, but with its own efficacy.

All of Immanuel Kant's subsequent attempts to define the limits of reason and to open out from there the possibilities of a universal knowledge in pure, aesthetic and practical reason – in *a priori* categories of thought; in the experience of the beautiful and the sublime, and in moral consciousness – represent an explicit response to this Humean dilemma of the power of an experiential totality to ground itself as the limit of knowledge and the only reality. *The Matrix* reintroduces the same problematic, conceived as the inevitable consequence of the developmental path of electronic simulation technologies, deriving its effect from eschewing the traditional narrative journey into the unreal in favour of the philosopher's shocking revelation that *we may already inhabit the virtual not the real world*; thereby instantly ungrounding all everyday experience and reality.

It is appropriate, therefore, that when these epistemological debates and the question of sensation and its overwhelming, sublime form reach their height in the late eighteenth century, these experiences find themselves reproduced in a popular form in commercial entertainments. New entertainments such as the panorama and phantasmagoria emerged at precisely this time to offer immersive, environmental, multi-media realities replicating and reflecting this duality of the overriding reality of empirical experience and its vertiginous ungrounding both in its overwhelming sensation and in the knowledge of its artificiality. Their profitability derived from their proto-theme-park play with the self and its stable reality, turning these philosophical problematics into safe, synasthetic pleasures.

The effect of Robert Barker's 'panorama' – invented in 1787 and comprising an entire technical ensemble to display a giant 360-degree scenic painting viewed from a realistic viewing platform with false terrain and roof obscuring all cognisance of its boundaries – was of a hyperrealistic, immersive environment. Its three-dimensional simulation abolished the frame of traditional art and its detached, single-point perspective, spectatorial position in favour of the envelopment of the viewer, replacing the aesthetic aim of *representation* with the aim of pure *presentation*: of providing not an image of the world but its actual, physical, sensory experience, to replace the real with its exact simulacrum (Comment 1999: 84–103; 129–33). Testimony to its success in this was common, from Princess Charlotte's sea-sickness at the sight of the British Fleet at Spithead (Oettermann 1997: 105) to the apocryphal stories of the Newfoundland dog trying to leap into the painted waters to rescue struggling sailors; of the royal lady asking for a branch from a tree to take home with her, or the Chinese servant driven insensible by the sight of his homeland in a panorama (Herbert 2000: 60–1). With hindsight, such tales clearly express the experience and confusions not of their – too convenient – targets, but of those recounting them, and contemporary reviewers were certainly eager to declare the panorama's reality 'complete' and sufficient to negate the necessity of foreign travel, transporting the sites to us 'on the wings of the wind' (Oettermann 1997: 113; 170). Later developments in the platform, such as Charles Langlois' use of a real frigate from the naval battle shown, or in 'moving panoramas', such as the astonishing mareorama and Trans-Siberian railway of 1900, brought gains to its immersive realism but at the cost of reducing the participant to a spectatorial role (see Comment 1999: 62–5; 73–6).

Developing almost contemporaneously, the phantasmagoria shared this immersive form and the use of proto-virtual reality technologies to create an effective reality. Though predecessors are traceable, the show was perfected and demonstrated by Paul Philidor in Paris from 1792–3, and successfully revived by Etienne Gaspard Robertson from 1798 (see Mannoni 2000: 136–75). This *gathering of ghosts* employed the mobile, back-projection of eerily lifelike, moving apparitions from a magic lantern, all within the enclosed environment of a funereally decorated room plunged into darkness. Tolling bells, thunder and rain, ghostly music and the spectral messages of the dead from the opening mouths of the spirits all added to the realism, as did real actors in masks, the Megascopic projection of solid objects, and, as the climax of one early show (emphasising their environmental incorporation), the electrocution of the audience by under-floor wiring.

If to modern minds the show's content sounds unconvincing, contemporary engravings show the audience cowering from the apparitions, raising swords or sticks to ward off the advancing spirits (see Robinson 1993: 49; 55; 64). In a description encompassing the central elements of virtual reality – environmental immersion, control of the senses and the transportation into another effective reality – Grimod de la Reyniere declared of Robertson's show, 'it is certain that the illusion is complete … everything serves to strike your imagination and to seize exclusively all your observational senses … your weakened brain can only believe what it is made to see, and we believe ourselves to be transported into another world and into other centuries' (quoted in Mannoni 2000: 162). Replicating these effects nearly two centuries later, Thomas Weynants describes them as producing a fully-developed 'virtual reality experience' superior to that of cinema (quoted in Crompton, Franklin and Herbert 1997: 64).

This immersive form emerging in the late eighteenth century was systematically reduced, domesticated and reversed by the major developments in media entertainments in the nineteenth century. Though the panorama and phantasmagoria are often discussed as contributory forms for the evolution of cinema, we can see that the latter depended precisely upon the abolition of their immersive hyperrealism and the giddy pleasures of simulation and of the vacillating, simultaneous experience of both its artifice and reality, in favour of an opposing mode of realism based upon the detached spectator's certain knowledge and experience of the screen image and its mode of production. Thus a synchronic reading of these media, emphasising their contemporary affinities, reveals that they were more closely related to each other than either were individually with the diorama and dissolving views shows that replaced them and that were responsible for the destruction of their specific experiential effects.

Thus, by the 1830s, phantasmagoria shows had ceded their place to diorama-like shows of dissolving views whose popularity laid the basis for the later development of the magic lantern entertainment industry but which, as Mervyn Heard argues, 'expunged, watered down or downgraded some of the wilder, more theatrical techniques' that had marked its earlier incarnation (quoted in Williams 1996: 25). Importantly these shows broke the immersive reality of the phantasmagoria, moving the lantern in front of the audience to allow them to constitute themselves as the detached, entertained, knowing spectator, on-side, *in*-on, and appreciative of the illusions, rather than as the confused and frightened victims of a spectral assault. For Charles Musser it is this tradition of 'screen practice' and the creation of that historical subject the 'spectator' that defines cinema (1990: 18), and its reintroduction here was part of a deliberate domestication of a more dangerous and thrilling mode of experience. Mid-century Victorian society was also a different world and the advance of practical science and its stable certainties had succeeded in banishing those epistemological phantoms that had troubled earlier philosophers and in exorcising the experiential phantoms of popular entertainments. Purged of its simulacral, diabolical effects the lantern became a central instrument in the enlightenment and instruction of the public, though its phantoms, expelled from its halls, were to find refuge in the new commodity culture of the streets, in those arcades and departments stores into which their phantasmagorical forms fled to bewitch the public anew (Marx 1954: 76–7), accelerating a process of the simulacral usurpation of the real that theorists from Lukacs to Benjamin, Adorno, Debord and Baudrillard would later trace through the following century.

Whilst the diorama, which replaced the panorama for a while in the public's affection, achieved its own remarkable realism, it also did so by abolishing immersion to reposition the participant as a spectator of a screen show, thereby confirming not confusing their empirical certainty. Invented by L. J. M. Daguerre, creator of stage illusions and 'a celebrity in the theatrical world' (Gernsheim & Gernsheim

1968: 11), the diorama's reintroduction of the detached, spectatorial, perspectival point made its theatrical lineage and debt to related entertainments, such as the 'spectacles de décoration', 'Eidophusikon' and 'Diaphanorama', explicit. If Daguerre's diorama was instrumental in the passage from the absorbed, uncertain participant to the stable, self-constituted spectator and a certain empirical experience his contribution of a successful photographic method reinforced this process. Now, with the daguerreotype, the living image of the camera obscura – and, with it, the final immersive elements of this medium – were captured and fixed to be appropriated, possessed and displayed as a framed and contained image, returning them to faces they knew or to other places, to fix unstable memory or guarantee images of scenes unseen.

Thus photographic realism reinforced spectatorial detachment, control and certainty and, although popular misunderstandings of its mechanisms and results persisted (see Mayhew 1985: 335–46), amateur knowledge of its processes developed alongside improved technical equipment until anyone could at least 'press the button'. Photography's merit was its objectivity – it was a sun-writing; nature's own 'pencil', or means of self-reproduction (Trachtenberg 1980: 5; 28; 13), 'something directly stencilled off the real' (Sontag 1977: 154), capturing, in the objectif, the light of the object itself. This is an image that will abolish itself before us, to leave the direct contemplation of the real (Barthes 1993: 4–7), though its transformation is a controlled and framed one that we can ourselves produce or observe. It was this photographic realism that, with its temporal dimension restored, would provide the basis for cinema's own realism.

The invention of cinema was, therefore, the culmination of a simultaneous movement through the nineteenth century towards a mode of realism and away from a mode of hyperrealism, a process involving the detachment and establishment of the screen spectator and the achievement of visual, representational fidelity. The competing modes of realism were forgotten in the success of this, and cinematic realism arrived, as convincingly and surely as the train into the station in the Lumières' 1896 film, Arrivée d'un train en gâre de la Ciotat, whose effect upon the audience, who fled its path, has become the founding myth of the medium. In some ways, however, it is an unconvincing myth, not only because preceding realisms render any evolutionary view problematic, but also because cinema itself quickly seized upon the story to mythologise itself, in films such as R. W. Paul's The Countryman and the Cinematograph (1901), and Thomas Edison's Uncle Josh at the Moving Picture Show (1902).

Here, within only a few years of its birth, cinema celebrated its own startling power of illusion but did so in a way that distanced its own contemporary, urban – and urbane – audience from the 'rube's' outdated and unsophisticated confusion. The knowing spectator it employed could enter into the game of illusion whilst retaining cognisance of a limited and bounded virtuality that never threatened, as earlier forms had, to overwhelm experience: actualities reinforced actuality.

Of course cinema occasionally dreamed of a more complete realism, in forms such as Charles A. Chase's 1894 'stereopticon-cyclorama', Raoul Grimoin-Sanson's 1900 'Cineorama' and the simulated journey's of 'Hale's Tours', only achieving a commercially successful sensory immersion in giant, wide-screen systems which retained the privileged position of both spectator and screen (see Oettermann

1997: 83–90; Fell 1983: 116–30; Hayward & Wollen 1993: 10–30; Williams 1996; 217–27. If today technical, economic and imaginative limitations limit contemporary hyperrealistic forms to the theme park it should be remembered that early cinema systems once enjoyed a similar billing. Just as the stuttering cards of the hand-cranked viewer are far removed from contemporary multiplexes and effects-fests such as *The Matrix*, so we should expect future developments in virtual reality to consign these clumsy rides, and cinema too, to an uncertain past.

The future forms of virtual reality and their social and cultural impact remain, however, difficult to predict. One argument sees virtual reality developing specifically as an entertainment medium – Morton Heilig said in 1955, 'open your eyes, listen, smell and feel – sense the world in all its magnificent colours, depth, sounds, odours and textures – this is the cinema of the future' (quoted in Rheingold 1991: 56) – and digital prophet Nicholas Negroponte agrees, describing virtual reality's potential 'as a consumer entertainment medium' as 'nothing short of awesome' (1995: 118–19). Others argue, however, that a virtual reality revolution would constitute a revolution not in media but in reality, transforming our entire mode of experience and knowledge. Contemporary critics already warn of this, from Baudrillard's unease at the on-going virtualisation of everyday life (1996), to Paul Virilio's fears of an emerging 'stereo-reality' and the reduction of humanity to an immobile, plugged-in 'terminal citizen' (1997), through to the extropians and transhumanists who dream of downloading consciousness into a virtual form to leave the physical world behind (Moravec 1988). Here virtual reality does not constitute an 'entertainment' within reality, or even offer, as *The Matrix* suggests, another – *one other* – reality, but holds instead the possibility of a programmed, multi-reality existence, each as real as any other; of the fractal disintegration of the shared, empirical reality central to Western epistemology; of the dispersal of the subject among shifting, endless realities whose form, relationship and even interaction can barely be conceived, or even of the end of single subjectivities in the development of a sentient, cosmic consciousness, as Hans Moravec suggests (1988: 115–16).

The latter is, of course, only science fiction – as, indeed, is *The Matrix*. But returning now to this film we can see that its prognosis is ultimately conservative in siding with its own medium, defending even a devastated reality against an endless virtuality and setting Neo the task of its destruction to protect the '100 per cent pure, old-fashioned, home-grown human'. Thus the film repeats the historical Western response to the simulacral threat of the image and its destabilisation of certain knowledge, in trying to demonise, repress and domesticate the virtual. But this virtuality represents part of a longer history of simulation; one retrieving, extending and radicalising earlier technological forms since eclipsed by a cinema that may itself soon prove to be a technological cul-de-sac; one returning us to the pleasure and vertigo of forms whose future possibilities we have yet to even conceive of but which carry the potential to unground and transform not just cinema and entertainment, but our entire cultural epistemology. We should think about this whilst we can, for when the gap between *virtual* virtual reality and the *actual* virtual reality has closed it will be too late.

So buckle your seat-belt Dorothy … 'cause Kansas, *The Wizard of Oz*, *The Matrix*, cinema, and reality itself, are going bye-byes.

Bibliography

Barthes, R. (1993) *Camera Lucida*. London: Vintage.

Baudrillard, J (1994) *Simulacra and Simulation*. Michigan: University of Michigan Press.

___ (1996) *The Perfect Crime*. London: Verso.

Comment, B. (1999) *The Panorama*. London: Reaktion.

Crompton, D., R. Franklin and S. Herbert (eds) (1997) *Servants of Light. The Book of the Lantern*. London: The Magic Lantern Society.

Fell, J. L. (ed.) (1983) *Film Before Griffith*. London: University of California Press.

Gernsheim, H. and A. Gernsheim (1968) *L. J. M. Daguerre: The History of the Diorama and the Daguerreotype*. New York: Dover Publications.

Gibson, W. (1995) *Neuromancer*. London: HarperCollins.

Hayward, P. and T. Wollen (eds) (1993) *Future Visions. New Technologies of the Screen*. London: British Film Institute.

Heidegger, M. (1962) *Being and Time*. Oxford: Basil Blackwell.

Herbert, S. (ed.) (2000) *A History of Pre-Cinema, volume 2*. London: Routledge.

Mayhew, H. (1985) *London Labour and the London Poor*. London: Penguin.

Mannoni, L. (2000) *The Great Art of Light and Shadow*. Exeter: University of Exeter Press.

Marx, K. (1954 [1876]) *Capital, volume 1*. London: Lawrence and Wishart.

Moravec, H. (1988) *Mind Children*. London: Harvard University Press.

Musser, C. (1990) *History of American Cinema, vol. 1: The Emergence of Cinema – The American Screen to 1907*. Berkeley: University of California Press.

Negroponte, N. (1995) *Being Digital*. London: Coronet.

Oettermann, S. (1997) *The Panorama*. New York: Zone Books.

Rheingold, H. (1991) *Virtual Reality*. London: Mandarin.

Robinson, D. (ed.) (1993) *The Lantern Image: Iconography of the Magic Lantern 1420–1880*. London: The Magic Lantern Society.

Sontag, S. (1977) *On Photography*. London: Penguin.

Trachtenberg, A. (ed.) (1980) *Classic Essays on Photography*. New Haven: Leete's Island Books.

Vinge, V. (2001) *True Names and the Opening of the Cyberspace Frontier*. New York: Tom Doherty Associates.

Virilio, P. (1997) *Open Sky*. London: Verso.

Wachowski, A. and L. Wachowski (1996) *The Matrix*. 8 April, http://members.xoom.com/_XOOM/moviescript/scripts/matrixthe.txt.

Williams, C. (ed.) (1996) *Cinema: The Beginnings and the Future*. London: University of Westminster Press.

Afterword

Jacqueline Furby and Karen Randell

So where is Film Studies in the twenty-first century? It is clear from this collection that it is a field full of possibility. In the past two decades, the debates concerning textual analysis and reception studies appeared to place the two approaches into competing camps; this made deciding on a way into the text difficult for many students – one had to make a choice. The essays in this collection have explored the many ways in which a more nuanced approach is actually in play. Formal textual analysis is still very much a core constituent, as Jacqueline Furby has shown in her discussion on *American Beauty*, but flavour this with phenomenology and it becomes a philosophical debate converning the very notion of time and space. Peter Krämer's essay concerns audience figures and shows that the reception of a text should be a prime concern of the film scholar; however, place this methodology within the context of gender and one is able to read the findings as indicative of not only changing audience habits but of filmmaking itself.

Film history scholarship will be familiar to many film students but this does not only concern early film history and practices. David Lusted's essay shows that by keeping past histories in mind we can make sense of current media practices and cultural fears: there is much to be learnt from the past that can place relevant readings on contemporary texts. Michael Williams and Monica Pearl teach us that key readings can be made when we consider the discourse around issues of sexuality: both of their essays focus on a single film text in great detail, however the incorporation of contemporary debates via newspaper articles, reviews and features provides a cross-fertilisation approach so that one text enlightens another.

So how will you judge which approach is the most suitable for you? Film scholarship is one of the most exciting fields to be working in because of its potential for following your own investigative heart. Where will you start your investigation? With the text; with the social and cultural context; with the investigation of technological advances? Wherever you wish to begin we hope that this volume has given you an insight and clarity into the possibilities for your study – methodology need not be madness.

Index